Education, Liberal Democracy and Populism

Education, Liberal Democracy and Populism: Arguments from Plato, Locke, Rousseau and Mill provides a lucid and critical guide shedding light on the continuing relevance of earlier thinkers to the debates between populists and liberals about the nature of education in democratic societies.

The book discusses the relationship Rousseau and Plato posited between education and society, and contrasts their work with the development of liberal thinking about education from John Locke, and John Stuart Mill's arguments for the importance of education to representative democracy. It explores some of the roots of populism and offer a broader perspective from which to assess the questions which populists pose and the answers which liberals offer. The book makes a substantial contribution to the current debate about democracy, by emphasising the central importance of education to political thought and practice, and suggests that only an education system based on liberal democratic principles can offer the possibility of a genuinely free society.

This book is ideal reading for researchers and post-graduate students in education, politics, philosophy and history. It will also be of great interest to Educational practitioners and policy makers.

David Sullivan, prior to his retirement, was Head of the School of Lifelong Learning and Senior Lecturer in the School of Philosophy and Religion at Bangor University, Wales, United Kingdom. He has written widely on political philosophy, philosophy of education and international politics and the second edition of his *Francis Fukuyama and the End of History* (jointly authored with Howard Williams and Gwynn Mathews) was published in 2016.

Routledge Research in Education Policy and Politics

The Routledge Research in Education Policy and Politics series aims to enhance our understanding of key challenges and facilitate on-going academic debate within the influential and growing field of Education Policy and Politics.
Books in the series include:

Academies and Free Schools in England
A History and Philosophy of The Gove Act
Adrian Hilton

Risk Society and School Educational Policy
Grant Rodwell

Neoliberalism and Market Forces in Education
Lessons from Sweden
Magnus Dahlstedt and Andreas Fejes

Reforming Principal Preparation at the State Level
Perspectives on Policy Reform from Illinois
Edited by Erika Hunt, Alicia Haller, Lisa Hood, and Maureen Kincaid

Theresa May, The Hostile Environment and Public Pedagogies of Hate and Threat
The Case for a Future Without Borders
Mike Cole

Teaching History in a Neoliberal Age
Policy, Agency and Teacher Voice
Mary Woolley

Education, Liberal Democracy and Populism
Arguments from Plato, Locke, Rousseau and Mill
David Sullivan

For more information about this series, please visit: www.routledge.com/Routledge-Research-in-Education-Policy-and-Politics/book-series/RREPP

Education, Liberal Democracy and Populism
Arguments from Plato, Locke, Rousseau and Mill

David Sullivan

LONDON AND NEW YORK

First published 2020
by Routledge
2 Park Square, Milton Park, Abingdon, Oxon OX14 4RN

and by Routledge
52 Vanderbilt Avenue, New York, NY 10017

Routledge is an imprint of the Taylor & Francis Group, an informa business

© 2020 David Sullivan

The right of David Sullivan to be identified as author of this work has been asserted by him in accordance with sections 77 and 78 of the Copyright, Designs and Patents Act 1988.

All rights reserved. No part of this book may be reprinted or reproduced or utilised in any form or by any electronic, mechanical, or other means, now known or hereafter invented, including photocopying and recording, or in any information storage or retrieval system, without permission in writing from the publishers.

Trademark notice: Product or corporate names may be trademarks or registered trademarks, and are used only for identification and explanation without intent to infringe.

British Library Cataloguing-in-Publication Data
A catalogue record for this book is available from the British Library

Library of Congress Cataloging-in-Publication Data
A catalog record has been requested for this book

ISBN: 978-1-138-56929-4 (hbk)
ISBN: 978-0-203-70433-2 (ebk)

Typeset in Galliard
by Wearset Ltd, Boldon, Tyne and Wear

In memory of my parents, Frederick and Irene Sullivan

Contents

Acknowledgements		viii
Introduction		1
1	Populism, education and challenges to liberal order: the crisis of democracy	8
2	Plato: two philosophies of education?	31
3	John Locke: a liberal philosophy of education	44
4	Jean-Jacques Rousseau: education, Emile and remaking society	70
5	John Stuart Mill: education and liberty	103
6	Education in democratic societies	123
Bibliography		149
Index		157

Acknowledgements

I have benefited greatly from conversations about philosophy, politics and education with colleagues and students over many years. I would particularly like to thank Sheila Hughes, Dr Neil Evans, Professor Howard Williams, Gwynn Mathews, Dr Anne-Marie Smith, Dr Jean Ware, Tony Elliott, Tim Jepson, Dr Shirley Egley and Ian McGreggor-Brown.

I am very grateful to the editorial team at Routledge for their friendly advice and proficiency. Chloe Barnes steered the book through its initial development while Emilie Coin and Swapnil Joshi have provided much guidance and support in the later stages. I also wish to express my gratitude to Rebecca White for her skilful copy-editing.

Very special thanks to Dr Lucy Huskinson, Eleanor Huskinson-Smith and Ludo.

Introduction

On the 3rd December 2018, the Rector of the Central European University (CEU) held a press conference to announce the decision to move the majority of the University's teaching and research from Budapest to Vienna.[1] The reason given was, to many in the Western media and academic community, dramatic and shocking, though not unexpected. The CEU, an English language graduate school with an international reputation for the excellence of its teaching and research in the Social Sciences has a strongly liberal and cosmopolitan ethos. The Rector, Michael Ignatieff, claimed that the populist Hungarian government led by Prime Minister Viktor Orbán had sought to undermine academic freedom in Hungary and had particularly targeted the CEU because its liberal values were perceived as a threat to the government's populist policies.

Many commentators believe this dispute is of great importance because it epitomises the conflict between the established liberal principles which have dominated discussion of European and North American politics and education policy since the end of the Cold War and the rapidly growing challenge to these principles by populists. '… [F]or much of the past two years,' Franklin Foer writes, in the June 2019 edition of *The Atlantic* (Foer 2019),

> CEU has been the barricades of a civilizational struggle, where liberalism would mount a defense against right-wing populism. The fate of the university was a test of whether liberalism had the tactical savvy and emotional fortitude to beat back its new ideological foe.

Any suggestion that the clash between the CEU and the Hungarian government is merely a disagreement over local educational arrangements misrepresents the manner in which politics and education are deeply intertwined.

In modern societies of any sophistication and complexity a certain level of education is required for society and the economy to function and to help develop and sustain social cohesion and stability. This is well understood in democratic societies, whose governments regularly stress their commitment to the ideals of an education system which encourages a shared social identity. What differentiates liberal democratic societies, such as the United States and the United Kingdom, from illiberal societies such as China, which has invested particularly heavily in developing a sophisticated higher education system, is the emphasis which liberal education places on encouraging critical thinking and freedom of expression.

Despite a broad consensus on the importance of education, there is much disagreement about the precise way in which education should function in a democratic society; a disagreement which reflects a more general debate about the nature of democracy and about the kind of cohesion democratic governments should promote. This is not to suggest that political attitudes and policies come first and educational policies are merely derived from them. The process of education, as one generation of children grows to maturity learning about, and learning to question, the values and beliefs of their society, alters the culture of that society, often modifying the expectations of how government should function, and even which specific policies it should promote.[2] Because education and political life are as intimately linked in democratic societies as in any other, the conflict between the CEU and the democratically elected but self-proclaimed illiberal government of Hungary highlights this dispute in a particularly dramatic way. The two protagonists represent the contrast between liberal and populist philosophies of education and politics in strikingly clear ways.

I will discuss the dispute between the CEU and the government of Viktor Orbán in more detail in Chapter 1 but it is important to step back from current issues and to emphasise that the essential elements in these arguments are not new: they draw on ideas that are much older and which resurface frequently, though often in different guises, in Western culture. The importance of these ideas – of all ideas – is sometimes disparaged in politics but the language and concepts which people use to talk about, and act within, political society invariably embody political ideas, even if that is not always realised. Politicians, particularly those who want to change society and remake it into something better, do often realise this very well, as do their opponents who are fearful of the changes proposed, which explains why both the Hungarian government and their critics see the issue of the CEU as so important.

The significance of ideas, and of how they shape society through education, is very evident in some of the debates around the presidential campaign and subsequent inauguration and presidency of Donald Trump. Presidential election campaigns in the United States invariably attract sophisticated commentaries in the American media, but the election of 2016 elicited an unusually large number of discussions of philosophy and of the work of particular philosophers, despite such apparently abstract and rarefied debates being at variance with the rhetoric and attitudes of Donald Trump and his advisers.

One of the more remarkable features of this public discussion of philosophy was an interest in the ideas of Jean-Jacques Rousseau and their alleged influence on the populist attitudes and policies of the Trump campaign. Articles critical of Rousseau's alleged influence, such as Pankaj Mishra's 'The Anti-Elite, Post Fact Worlds of Trump and Rousseau' (Mishra 2016) in *The New Yorker* and Michael Gerson's nationally syndicated opinion piece 'Trump's Funeral Oration at the Death of Reaganism' (Gerson 2017) led to a robust debate, including a particularly trenchant response to Gerson by the Rousseau scholar David Lay Williams in the *Washington Post* (Williams 2017).

Nor was Rousseau the only philosopher to be brought into the debate. Concerned by the attacks by Trump and his supporters on experts, which included, along with politicians and Wall Street financiers, liberal intellectuals in universities and the media, the journalist Andrew Sullivan argued that Plato offers valuable insights into the importance of skilled and knowledgeable leaders and the dangers of demagogues misleading the masses (Sullivan 2016).

Liberal critics of Trump, and of populist politicians more generally, might argue that these ideas are treated as being irrelevant by populists who are anti-intellectual and dismissive of ideas. One of the most penetrating commentaries on Trump's campaign and election is that of James Kloppenberg, the distinguished Harvard professor of American intellectual history, a term which itself would, no doubt, seem suspicious to Trump and many of his supporters. In an opinion piece for the *Washington Post*, 'Trump's Inaugural Address was a Radical Break with American Tradition', Kloppenberg (2017) argues that Trump offers a negative picture of the United States and, unlike previous presidents, has failed to offer the hope of reconciliation and of working together. The implication, shared by many, is that Trump, a man with no interest in ideas, lacks any intellectual foundation upon which to build an optimistic vision of America's future.

The op-ed is of necessity a short piece but Kloppenberg has written extensively about the way in which President Obama has consciously drawn on the American intellectual tradition of Pragmatism in developing a highly articulate and sophisticated view of American politics and of how to govern.[3] Obama, in Kloppenberg's opinion, is the most intellectually sophisticated President since Woodrow Wilson and the contrast with Trump could hardly be greater.

And yet at least some of Trump's advisers, such as Steve Bannon who is credited with writing most of the inaugural address which Kloppenberg so much deplores (Wolff 2018: 42–3, 148), have stressed the importance of ideas, and have consciously sought to challenge the liberal, cosmopolitan, pragmatic progressivism attributed to Obama. The clash of ideas is reflected in the attacks by Trump and many of his followers on what they see as a liberal bias in education, including elite universities such as Harvard, as well as in publicly-funded schools. The appointment of Betsy DeVos as Education Secretary in Trump's first Cabinet has been widely seen, not least by supporters of DeVos, as an attempt to change the ethos of educational institutions in the United States. The appointment of Associate Justices of the Supreme Court who are believed to be sympathetic to attempts to reverse liberal policies on affirmative action in recruitment of students to American universities reinforces this perception that the importance of educational issues in current politics is intimately connected to broader political issues.

Rousseau and Plato would both agree with this understanding that educational reform is an essential part of any far-reaching political change. Whether Rousseau, let alone Plato, would agree with the values and attitudes of the current wave of populism is something to be discussed later. Neither of these thinkers are liberal – a claim that is undeniably true of Plato, more controversially so of Rousseau – but liberal thinkers also stress the importance of education and two of the most historically significant of these, John Locke and John Stuart Mill, do so in ways that offer both challenges to Rousseau and Plato and powerful defences of education in a liberal society.

Four thinkers

The central chapters of the book are given over to an analysis of these four thinkers. They are chosen because of the philosophical depth and power of their arguments concerning the relationship between education and politics, something which is reflected in their enormous historical significance in modern Western thought. What gives the juxtaposition of discussions of their ideas a particular cohesiveness is the manner in which Rousseau and Mill comment extensively on Plato, Rousseau, particularly in *Emile*, engages frequently and critically with Locke's *Some Thoughts Concerning Education* and Mill develops many of Locke's liberal ideas in new and more democratic ways.

This is a book about political philosophy and the philosophy of education and as such is principally concerned with the analysis of ideas. It is important to try and reconstruct the arguments in order to properly engage with them and to help understand of how they relate to each other and how in turn they have influenced contemporary thought. It is impossible, though, to read texts, especially such rich and complex ones as the *Republic, Emile, Some Thoughts Concerning Education* or *On Liberty*, without bringing our own assumptions and it would be foolish to ignore commentaries on them. Consequently, I have discussed competing interpretations where it seems particularly appropriate to do so, but I have endeavoured to keep the arguments of the philosophers themselves, and the texts they wrote, at the centre of the discussion.

Four themes

In order to focus on ideas within these writers' works which are most relevant to the current debate between liberals and populists I have identified four themes that will act as threads when discussing their ideas. These are: the role of education in promoting a stable society, the place of expertise in education and political life, the significance of critical thinking and the promotion of autonomy.

The significance of these ideas, and the different ways in which they are understood by the four thinkers, will emerge in the course of the discussion and will be analysed in depth in the final chapter but I give a brief overview here.

Education and a stable society

All societies require a measure of stability and consensus in order to function. In some societies, stability and consensus are enforced by fear or through the imposition of religious or ideological beliefs, a process in which control of the education system frequently plays a vital part. Liberal democratic societies claim to be different in that the stability is based on a consensus which is both voluntary and open to internal revision. Locke and Mill both discuss the implications of this for education in considerable depth.

One criticism of this liberal approach, which is found in Plato, Rousseau and contemporary populism, is that this process of constant revision, and the critical spirit which it encourages, is likely to lead to instability. If children and young adults are constantly taught to question and challenge prevailing values and opinions this may well lead to a polarised and adversarial society. An important liberal response is to argue that a key element in securing stability is through the encouragement of civility, an idea much discussed in contemporary politics, particularly in the context of conflicts between liberals and populists. Civility, in this account, stresses the importance of tolerance for the views of others and the need to be respectful in debate. To be most effective, the teaching of civility should be a significant part of education, an idea developed at length by John Locke, as we will discuss in Chapter 3.

Contemporary populists are often accused of incivility, at least towards those they regard as members of the liberal elite, whom they consider to be detached from their own culture. This is linked to the populist wish to promote national identity as a means of ensuring stability and their argument that education should teach the importance of patriotism and encourage acceptance of one's own community. In this they reflect Rousseau, who emphasises the importance of belonging to a specific community and who argues that only patriotically-minded citizens should be allowed to be teachers.

Following the end of the Second World War, fought in part to resist the horrors perpetrated by proponents of a virulently violent and exclusionary form of nationalism, liberals have been very critical of nationalism. This in part fuels the antagonism of many liberals towards contemporary populism but many theories of nationalism in the nineteenth century were based on liberal values. Mill's defence of nationality, particularly in *Considerations on Representative Government*, coupled with his concerns about the dangers of an illiberal state-run education system, offers an area for potentially fruitful debate between liberals and populists.

Expertise in education and politics

One difficulty with the argument about the need for stability in society is how to ensure that rulers can be trusted to promote order. How is it possible to ensure a political stability that is both just and effective? One answer, expressed powerfully by Plato in the *Republic*, is to allow only people who are highly educated experts to rule.

This hierarchical view of education and society is rejected by liberals such as Locke and by liberal democrats such as Mill. Populists argue, though, that liberals embrace a belief in expertise that, while not wholly rejecting democracy, effectively restricts the ability of the people at large to properly participate. This argument has some plausibility when the ideas of Locke and Mill are examined in detail, and the ambiguity of their position can be seen in contemporary liberalism. But populists, particularly when they exercise political power, as in

Hungary, are not immune to this criticism, either. All forms of education, particularly higher education, are problematic in this view because the knowledge and skills acquired often create a gap between a highly educated elite and those who have not received the same level of education.

Education, politics and critical thinking

Modern liberals, taking their cue in part from Mill, respond to criticisms about elitism by arguing for the provision of universal education and for this education to provide a large measure of training in critical thinking. Populists also support universal provision of education but argue that an education which encourages too much critical thinking, or critical thinking of the wrong sort, may undermine attempts to teach children the norms of behaviour appropriate to their society and in doing so may undermine national stability and cohesion.

Liberals such as Mill acknowledge that there is considerable potential for conflict between critical thinking and social stability but argue that this is inevitable in a free society. Such conflict may even, Mill claims, be a necessary condition of a society being free. Populists who follow arguments set out by Rousseau contend that duties to the community (often explicitly identified with a national community) take precedence over individual freedom. Indeed, they argue, again in keeping with Rousseau, that freedom is only possible when individuals acknowledge the primacy of the community in moulding and shaping their values and beliefs. This implies a view of education very different from that held by liberals like Mill and is in many respects at the heart of the intellectual disagreement between the CEU and the Hungarian government.

There is another, closely related, issue over the relationship between critical thinking and education. Illiberal rulers claim to offer stability through order, and they view education as a means of reproducing the values and beliefs which sustain that order. Liberals maintain that this amounts to using education as a form of propaganda and are vociferous in their criticism, but populists argue that liberals do the same things, merely more obliquely. Teaching the importance of civility, and closely linked concepts such as toleration, as part of preparing people to enter society as responsible citizens, carries the danger, from a populist perspective, of smuggling a substantive liberal world view into the curriculum while appearing to be neutral.

Autonomy in education and politics

'Autonomy' and related terms such as 'liberty' and 'freedom' are often treated as synonyms, though differences will become apparent in the course of the book. I favour the term 'autonomy' because the concept of autonomy has been widely discussed in contemporary political philosophy and philosophy of education.

Autonomy has often been associated particularly with liberalism, and understandably so, as liberal political theorists, including Locke and Mill, have developed versions of the concept into a central theme in liberal thought. For both of these thinkers, autonomy is to be understood primarily in terms of the freedom of the individual, arrestingly expressed by Locke when he writes in the *Two Treatises of Government* that, 'every Man has a *Property* in his own *Person*. This no Body has any Right to but himself' (1988, Second Treatise Chapter V, Section 27: 287) and by Mill when he argues in *On Liberty* that 'the sole end for which mankind are warranted, individually or collectively, in interfering with the liberty of action of any of their number, is self-protection' (Mill CW, XVIII: 223).[4]

Yet liberals do not have exclusive claims on the concept. If we define autonomy as 'self-rule' or 'self-direction', populists may also be understood as advocating autonomy. Indeed, much of their political discourse is couched in terms of the need to free people from various types of oppressive rule, whether from the tyranny of expert guidance, from the rule of unresponsive internal elites such as politicians and bankers or by external powers such as the European Union, international organisations such as the United Nations and international agreements such as the Paris Climate Treaty.

This suggests that the meaning of the term 'autonomy' is highly contested, and that there are competing and sometimes overlapping uses of the term in liberal and populist thought. This also has implications for the relationship between autonomy and democracy. This relationship is a complex one, and illustrates some of the places where liberal democracy and populism may intersect, as well as places where their divergence is particularly strong. The role of education in promoting autonomy is, from the perspective of the present argument, of great importance and particularly revealing of these complex intersections.

Notes

1 A video of the press conference is available online. See Central European University (2018) 'CEU – Press Conference, December 3, 2018', www.youtube.com/watch?v=c3fObmmlkEk.
2 Beyond education in schools, the work which is carried out in universities as part of their function as research institutions often has a significant impact both on government policies and on the ways in which people in general come to understand the nature of society.
3 Kloppenberg has written a book length study of Obama's thought, *Reading Obama: Dreams, Hope, and the American Political Tradition*, first published in 2010, and republished with a new preface in 2012 (Kloppenberg 2012) and a number of later shorter pieces on the same topic (Kloppenberg 2014; 2016b).
4 Most references to Mill are to his *Collected Works* and are given in the format CW, volume number: page number. See Chapter 5, note 1 for further details.

1 Populism, education and challenges to liberal order

The crisis of democracy

In the early 1990s, when leaders and opinion makers in liberal democratic societies were euphoric at the end of the Cold War and the collapse of Communism in the old Soviet Union, fears about the future of liberal democracy might have seemed absurd (Fukuyama 1989; 1992). At that point in time, its intellectual pre-eminence seemed unassailable and the educational institutions of the advanced democracies of the West were confidently expected to reflect and promote those values, not only internally but also as part of a process of creating a cosmopolitan, global society. In the closing years of the second decade of the twenty-first century things seem very different. Liberal democracy is being challenged geopolitically by the rise of illiberal states such as China and internally by the growth of populism.

President Trump's election, the vote in the United Kingdom to leave the European Union and the rise of governments in Eastern European countries such as Hungary and Poland which are seen as increasingly illiberal have led many commentators to argue that liberal democracy is under threat. Some, like Paul Ginsborg, have argued that it is in crisis (Ginsborg 2008). The title of Ginsborg's book, *Democracy: Crisis and Renewal*, offers hope as well as warning, but the road to renewal is not clear and may well involve painful self-reflection and a willingness to make significant readjustments.

Populism is sometimes linked in the minds of its critics with authoritarianism, and following the election of President Trump a number of commentators have raised the spectre of the emergence of an authoritarian regime in the United States. Some, including the Yale philosopher Jason Stanley and former American Secretary of State Madeline Albright, have even gone as far as arguing that the Trump administration is paving the way for the emergence of fascism in the United States (Stanley 2018; Albright 2018), and have expressed their fears in very strong terms. In response to the rhetorical question of why she thinks it relevant to discuss fascism so long after the defeat of the Fascist regimes in 1945, Albright writes that '[o]ne reason, frankly, is Donald Trump. If we think of fascism as a wound from the past that had almost healed, putting Trump in the White House was like ripping off the bandage and picking at the scab' (Albright 2018: 4–5). That a distinguished figure like Albright would make such a claim in language as colourful as this is an indication of the heightened rhetoric that accompanies much of the debate. Seeing the underlying arguments as part of a very long intellectual tradition helps to put such claims in a broader perspective.

It is sometimes argued that the rise of authoritarianism as a serious challenge to liberal democracy is apparent in the economic growth of China and the increasingly successful alternative model it appears to offer to liberal democratic societies (Runciman 2013: 318–23). The enthusiasm in many Western Universities for collaboration with institutions in China, based in part on a belief in the role of higher education in building a more cosmopolitan world (as well as more pragmatic economic considerations), has increasingly had to come to terms with confident Chinese academics and politicians whose blend of Confucianism and Marxism reflects a very different view of the nature of education and of its role in society (Yang 2010; Liu 2012). But this is an alternative to liberal democracy which does not present the same kind of threat as populism, not least because the philosophical foundations of the Chinese education system are so different to those of the West. Consequently, I will not discuss this aspect of authoritarianism in the book.

There is, though, a quite different problem posed by increasing authoritarianism in countries such as Russia and Turkey. Both these countries have experienced a measure of democracy since the end of the Cold War and both share some Western values. Turkey has many links with Western society and still has ambitions to join the European Union. Turkish and Russian institutions and individual academics participate widely in educational projects with European partners, including schemes such as Erasmus. Russia, since the fall of Communism, has discarded Marxist-Leninism and increasingly argued that, unlike what it sees as a decadent, secularised West, it is defending Christian values and Christian civilisation. With their emphasis on the people, on the need for moral regeneration and strong, charismatic leaders, the governments of these countries share much in common with populism and are frequently seen as part of the same broad phenomenon.

One of the most striking aspects of the growth of populism is the way it has become particularly influential in some of the states of Eastern Europe which were once part of the Soviet Empire, particularly in Hungary and Poland. These two countries are by no means identical in their political systems or in the policies of their governments, but, as we have already seen, one of them, Hungary, provides a particularly striking example of populist opposition to liberal views of education through its antagonistic relationship with the CEU.

Historical scepticism about democracy

Challenges to democracy, whether internal or external, serve as a reminder that until recently democracy was viewed with scepticism even in what are now its strongholds of Western Europe and North America. The threats to democracy in much of the twentieth century from the challenges of fascism and communism are a potent recent reminder of these challenges, as in this context are the rise of non-democratic states such as China. In all these non-democratic regimes, the state has sought to control education and use it as a tool of social and political coercion.

If we consider that one aspect of democracy is that of empowering the mass of the people, an idea that is central to populist thought but also an important part of liberal democratic theory (although liberals may offer a somewhat different definition of 'empowering' and 'the people'), the reluctance by liberal writers such as Locke to embrace democracy is not altogether surprising, even from the perspective of well-established democracies such as the contemporary United Kingdom or United States. Referring in particular to the horrors of the sixteenth century wars of religion, the savagery of the English Civil Wars and the barbarism of the Thirty Years War, James Kloppenberg stresses a factor which has implications still for how democracy is viewed by conservative and authoritarian critics.

> Such abominations left a legacy of fear, suspicion and hatred; not only were people willing to die for their beliefs, they were willing to kill for them. Apprehensions provoked by democratic revolutions in Europe and North America ... must be understood in the context of profound cultural anxieties concerning the balance between the desirability of empowering the people and the very real dangers of zealotry.
> (Kloppenberg 2016a: 11–12)

The idea that education might be a means of overcoming this savagery is a powerful response to such fears, and helps to explain why democrats like John Stuart Mill argue that providing a well-balanced education for all children is essential to the development of a healthy democratic society. In different ways, all four of the thinkers discussed in this book believe that a properly functioning education system can help to create a society where people can live in a measure of harmony rather than a condition akin either to Hobbes' state of nature or to the rule of his absolutist sovereign (Hobbes 1996). But their contrasting views of what education would be best, to whom it might directly apply and how it might fit into a broader understanding of society, is itself illuminating.

In order to conduct a fruitful discussion of the relationships between liberal democracy and populism and their relationship to education, it would seem reasonable to begin by trying to clarify the meaning of the terms 'liberal' and 'populist'. This is not entirely straight forward, and a clear sense of the terms used is not always apparent either in academic literature or in more popular writings. Given the ways in which the concepts change over time, including, particularly in the current incarnation of populism, a very short space of a few years, this is not altogether surprising.

Robert Dahl, in his seminal *A Preface to Democratic Theory*, acknowledges that '[o]ne of the difficulties one must face at the outset is that there is no democratic theory – there are only democratic theories' (2006: 1). The same may be said of liberalism. But at least advocates of democracy and liberalism have developed theories to be discussed. Populism is more problematic because there is no comparable body of theories which are explicitly populist, even though Rousseau's writings offer searching discussions of some themes that have become central to much later populist thinking. In suggesting working definitions of the two terms in this chapter I will pick out some of the main ideas in each approach, but a danger is that this runs the risk of offering definitions that are either too broad or too one-sided. It is in part to address this last problem that Chapters 2 to 5 examine the work of each of the four thinkers in sufficient detail to allow a proper examination of how each understands the key ideas, or earlier precursors, and their relationship to education. Doing so is intended not only to provide detailed concrete examples of some of the most powerful versions of these theories but also to show how the use of these concepts in current debate draws on much older concepts in Western political thought. I will argue that only by examining these concepts in the context of the work of the four major thinkers is it possible to properly draw out both the ambiguity and some connecting strands in the underlying concepts.

Liberalism

Two uses of 'liberalism'

The term 'liberalism' often has different connotations depending on whether it is used in Britain or America. In political debate in the United States, the term is usually used to describe people who believe in the need for a strong state to provide welfare and other benefits to the population. It refers broadly to ideas associated with the Progressive Movement in the United States in the first part of the twentieth century, identified particularly with the presidencies of Theodore Roosevelt, William Howard Taft and Woodrow Wilson, and the writings of Pragmatists such as John Dewey – the ideas which Kloppenberg, as we noted earlier (p. 3), believed had such a profound influence on the thinking of President Obama – and which in turn influenced the New Deal policies of Franklin D. Roosevelt.

In the classical British liberalism of Locke and Mill, by contrast, there is greater fear of the dangers posed by the state, a concern also apparent in earlier American liberals such as Thomas Jefferson and James Madison. This earlier version of liberalism does not necessarily preclude state intervention in some aspects of welfare. Mill was highly critical of the economic inequalities of his own day and thought that government had a duty to correct some of them, but concern about an overbearing state is a constant theme in Mill's work as it is in classical liberalism generally. In what follows, I will begin by sketching out some of the key themes in liberalism as defended by Locke and Mill, though during the course of the book it will become clearer that there are differences between them and that liberalism itself is far from a homogeneous body of thought. In a theory which prizes debate and critical analysis so highly it would be surprising if it were otherwise.

The moral primacy of the individual

The most fundamental principle of liberalism is that of the moral primacy of the individual. In Locke's case, as in much twentieth and twenty-first century liberalism, this is partly expressed through a theory of human (or, in Locke's phrase 'natural') rights. These are rights which are not granted by the state but are part of human nature – in Locke's version they are given by God (Locke 1988: Second Treatise, Chapter II, Sections 4–6, 269–71). This is not to deny that there are significant differences between Locke's concept of natural rights and twenty-first century concepts of human rights, including disagreement over what count as rights and differing accounts of how rights might be justified.[1] What they do have in common is the belief that people have a moral right to be respected as individuals and that states have an obligation to treat them accordingly.

Because liberals stress the freedom of the individual they seek limits on the power of the state. In Locke's version this is justified in terms of a social contract. Under the terms of the contract, people living in a state of nature give up some freedoms in return for the security which a government can provide, but the scope of government power is limited by its obligation to respect and uphold the rights of its citizens (Locke 1988: Second Treatise, Chapter VII, Sections 89–93, 325–8). Many more recent liberal writers also use variations of social contract theory, from Kant to John Rawls (though both refer to a hypothetical, rather than a historical, contract) and it remains an influential strand in liberal theory. Mill does not base his liberalism on social contract theory but also argues that there should be strict limits on the way in which the state may legitimately restrict the freedom of the individual.

The rule of law

Liberalism is thereby opposed both to absolutism and to arbitrary government. One of the most important ways of restricting the power of government is through the impartial rule of law. In a law-governed society, attempts at arbitrary government can be resisted by appeals to the law and an independent judiciary. But both Locke and Mill are aware of the dangers of extra-legal activities on the part of the government. Locke, writing in the midst of the political upheavals of late Restoration England, argues that if a government becomes tyrannical, to use his term, those who are oppressed have a right to rebel and overthrow the tyrant, by force of arms if necessary (Locke 1988: Second Treatise, Chapter XVIII, Section 209, 404–5). Mill, living in the more settled political society of Victorian England, is more concerned with a different kind of tyranny – the threat to individual liberty posed by an intolerant majority of the population (Mill CW, XVIII: 218–23).

One consequence of the liberal desire to restrict the power of government is that both Locke and Mill are opposed to a state funded education system with the power to determine what education all children should receive. The problem is particularly acute for Mill because of his belief in the importance of universal education, as will be discussed in Chapter 5. His concern is that such a system could very easily become a means of indoctrination and would create a society in which everyone would be taught to think in the same way and critical thinking would be discouraged.

The development of liberal ideas

Another important element in liberalism is a belief in the progressive elaboration and unfolding of liberal values. Two examples may be used to illustrate this: the development of liberalism to the point where it comes to reject ideas of racial inferiority and its gradual recognition – strongly supported by Mill – of the equality of women and men. This does not necessarily mean that liberals believe that there are no universal moral truths. Locke is very clear that there are – an argument which he bases on his belief that there is a moral law given by God (Locke 1988: Second Treatise, Chapter II, Section 6, 270–1). Mill's position also seems to imply that there are universal principles such as the principle of liberty, though Isaiah Berlin argues in 'John Stuart Mill and the Ends of Life' that, at least implicitly, Mill is committed to the view that there is no single set of moral principles to which we can unproblematically apply (Berlin 1969b).

Liberals recognise the importance of education in helping to explore and articulate the new insights and draw practical implications for education policy. Two of these are particularly relevant to our discussion. The first is that students of all ages should be provided with the critical skills to judge the emerging values and play a part in discussing, criticising, defending and, where appropriate, applying them. The second is the liberal belief in the particular role of universities as places where there are the resources, in terms of such assets as teachers, libraries and seminar rooms, to creatively focus on these ideas. Alfred North Whitehead once remarked that universities might have a role analogous to monasteries in the Middle Ages, of preserving Western culture in a dark and hostile world[2] and there may be at least some echoes of that need in the concerns some liberals have over populist disdain for experts of all kinds. Some populists might reply that universities are exactly the kind of out of touch elite institutions which they so dislike, and much of whose work goes against the grain of the straight-forward thinking of sensible people. We will take this point up again later but, to return to Whitehead's metaphor, monasteries were indeed an important element in the preservation of Western culture, but they were not impartial in their assessment of what was important and valuable and nor are universities. It is a long time since Fellows of Oxbridge colleges were required to take holy orders (Locke struggled for many years to avoid doing so in Restoration England) but the debate both about the nature and limits of academic freedom and genuinely open debate is far from over.

The idea of liberal values as constantly developing raises a problem about what is to be taught in a liberal society. It might be argued that a liberal education ought to focus on developing critical skills and enhancing the autonomy of the student. But while these are important elements in a liberal theory of education, they are not sufficient in and of themselves. Locke and Mill both argue that it is important that students learn some basic principles of morality, the observance of which by its citizens enables the society to function peacefully and with a measure of harmony. If these values change rapidly, and especially if a large number of people within the society feel alienated by the displacement of one set of values by another, social harmony will be in danger of breaking down. This danger of disruption and alienation in liberal societies is one of the features that is criticised by populists, and the fear and uncertainty caused by attacks on traditional values and practices is perceived to be a major reason for the growth of support for populism.[3]

This idea of development is also linked to a view which came to prominence in liberal thought during and after the Second World War. Liberal philosophers such as Karl Popper and Isaiah Berlin were concerned with the dangers posed by anti-liberal regimes which based themselves on the belief that they had, in Popper's phrase, a blueprint for social change which if adhered to would bring about a just society. Popper and Berlin both referred to this view as 'utopian' and Popper argued in the first volume of *The Open Society and Its Enemies* (Popper 1945) that Plato's philosophy was at the root of this flawed, dangerous and profoundly illiberal view of society. Berlin proposed a similar argument but developed it in a different way in his influential essay 'Two Concepts of Liberty'. For Berlin, such utopian schemes are bound to fail because basic values most revered in a liberal society, such as liberty and equality, are often in conflict with each other. There simply is no way of reconciling the conflicting effects of these values.[4] Although Berlin claims that this understanding, which is the basis of the view he ascribes to Mill in 'John Stuart Mill and the Ends of Life' (Berlin 1969b), does not amount to moral relativism, such arguments are seen by populists as implying precisely that. This relativism, they argue, means that liberal education policies, with their emphasis on critical thinking and individual autonomy, leave students confused and uncertain, lacking the intellectual and moral strengths needed to contribute positively to a stable and cohesive society.

It is possible, of course, to argue that a liberal society ought to encourage children to acknowledge these conflicts and to think critically about how to deal with them while accepting that, for example, both liberty and equality are inherently good values. But if this view is expressed at a time of rapid social change, when long-held views are being called into question or even quickly repudiated, it can be very difficult to maintain a sense of social cohesion, especially when large numbers of people think that 'their' traditional values are being discarded by an out of touch elite.

Cosmopolitanism

This leads to a further element in contemporary liberalism which has an important place in the debate between liberals and populists and has a particular significance in their accounts of education. This is the idea, already mentioned in passing, of cosmopolitanism, an idea which in its modern form developed during the eighteenth century Enlightenment and was given powerful expression in Kant's *Essay on Perpetual Peace* (Kant 1991: 93–130). Cosmopolitanism is the view that there are universal moral values which should be recognised and honoured in all societies and that while we have on-going duties to our own families and local communities we also have strong, and sometimes overriding, obligations to all other members of humanity as well. Contemporary cosmopolitans such as David Held, who draws upon Kant's work, regard nationalism with suspicion, support transnational organisations such as the United Nations and the European Union and favour open borders and cross-border migration (Held 2006: Chapter 11).

With regard to education, cosmopolitans argue that children and young people should be taught to regard themselves as citizens of the world, rather than as exclusively citizens of particular countries. So education from a cosmopolitan perspective is not seen as a means of defending and reinforcing the values, or even identity, of a particular community but as developing a sense of belonging to a global community: an education for global citizenship. Held argues that the idea of a citizenship of the European Union which sits alongside (and may one day replace) citizenship of particular member countries, and which may in turn prepare the way for citizenship of a global community is one example of this (Held 2006: 304–8). It may well be that the nation state will be the focus of primary loyalty and provider of primary needs, including education, for some time to come (Held 2004: 58) but the long-term hope for humankind is the gradual emergence of a global identity and global community.

Populism

Defining populism

In a new Preface to his influential book *The Populist Persuasion*, first published in 1995, Michael Kazin points out the awkwardness of applying the term populism during the 2016 United States Presidential primaries to both Donald Trump and Bernie Sanders, whose views on politics, society and economic are radically different. In a similar fashion he notes the oddness in applying the term to European politicians as diverse as Viktor Orbán and Jeremy Corbyn, the leader of the British Labour Party (Kazin 2017).

The problem in usage, particularly in an American context, arises in part from the history of populism and the changing perceptions of historians and political theorists. The People's Party which emerged in the United States in the late nineteenth century was initially characterised by liberal historians as a populist left-wing party committed to the defence and expansion of workers' rights; in European terms as a social democratic, rather than revolutionary socialist, party. This interpretation of the Peoples' Party as progressive was challenged by the liberal historian Richard Hofstadter (Hofstadter 1955) in the mid-twentieth century who, while acknowledging the grievances of those the Peoples' Party claimed to represent, read back into the party all the dangers which had been apparent in the right-wing mass movements in Europe and the United States in the 1930s. In the words of Nils Gilman: 'For mid-century liberals like Hofstadter, populism meant the street level of mobilizations of Italian fascism, the torch-lit rallies of Nazi Germany, and the malevolent crowds of the anti-New Deal America First movement' (Gilman 2018: 39). Hofstadter's perception of populism was also coloured by the fact

16 *Populism, education and liberal order*

that he was writing at the time of Senator Joe McCarthy's rabble-rousing reactionary demagoguery, which many of McCarthy's critics saw as an expression of populism.

Hofstadter's view was challenged at the time by C. Vann Woodward (Vann Woodward 1960: Chapter 7) and gradually an understanding of the social democratic nature of the populism of The Peoples' Party was re-established through the work of historians such as Lawrence Goodwyn's *The Populist Moment* (1978), Kazin's *The Populist Persuasion* (2017) and Charles Postel's *The Populist Vision* (2007) (see Gilman 2018: 39). This longer historical perspective from which Hofstadter's criticism is now seen, and the help it provides in the seeing more clearly the way in which his ideas were influenced by the times in which he lived, ought to encourage contemporary writers on populism in their efforts to be self-reflective. A recent example of how hard this is to do can be seen in the use of term 'populism' in Jeffrey Rosen's discussion of the contrasting attitudes to the American Presidency by Theodore Roosevelt and William Howard Taft in *William Howard Taft* (Rosen 2018). Rosen characterises Taft, the only person to serve as both President of the United States and as Chief Justice of the United States Supreme Court, as a constitutionalist who believes that the rule of law under the United States Constitution ought to form the basis of good government and who is opposed to the direct, unreflective expression of public opinion. As Rosen says, he was certainly not opposed to democracy as such but, like the authors of *The Federalist Papers* (Madison, Hamilton and Jay 1987), he believed that the will of the people should be filtered through institutions which would allow time for measured and considerate judgment about issues (see for example Rosen 2018: 131). Rosen contrasts this with the 'populism' of Theodore Roosevelt, citing his argument for 'pure democracy' in a speech, 'A Character for Democracy', delivered as he was preparing to stand against Taft for nomination as the Republican Party candidate in 1912:

> Roosevelt endorsed a series of populist reforms, including elected state judiciaries, presidential primaries based on 'direct nominations by the people' and direct election of U.S. Senators, adding 'I believe in the initiative and the referendum, which should be used not to destroy representative government, but to correct it when it ever becomes more misrepresentative'.
>
> (Rosen 2018: 94–5)

Rosen's characterisation of Roosevelt as a populist is unusual and this, along with his sympathetic defence of Taft's Constitutionalism, is strongly influenced, as he acknowledges, by recent events such as the Brexit referendum in the United Kingdom and the populist presidency of Donald Trump (Rosen 2018: 133, 136–7). This example, like that of Hofstadter, illustrates the difficulty in avoiding contemporary categories when viewing the past. It also highlights the difficulties in using 'populism' as a term in analysing contemporary movements and individuals.

Unsurprisingly, the meaning of the term 'populism' is the subject of much debate both in academic writing such as the excellent overviews by Jan-Werner Müller *What is Populism?* (2016) and Cas Mudde and Cristóbal Rovira Kaltwasser's *Populism* (2017) as well as more general discussions of populism in relation to the current crisis of democracy, including Paul Ginsborg's *Democracy: Crisis and Renewal* (2008), David Runciman's *The Confidence Trap: A History of Democracy in Crisis from World War I to the Present* (2013) and Francis Fukuyama's *Identity: Contemporary Identity Politics and the Struggle for Recognition* (2018b) and in the high quality journalism that overlaps it such as Fareed Zakaria's 'Populism on the March: Why the West is in Trouble' (2016) and *The Future of Freedom: Illiberal Democracy at Home and Abroad* (2007) and John B. Judis' *The Populist Explosion: How the Great Recession Transformed American and European Politics* (2016). To this list of works largely critical of populism may be added the last book by one of the late twentieth century's most significant political thinkers, Samuel Huntington's *Who Are We: America's Great Debate* (2004). This book, which was much criticised on its publication, is unusual in that it offers a serious, sustained defence of some of the central ideas associated with contemporary populism. I will refer to it a number of times in the following chapters.

I will take as a starting point of a working definition the characterisation of populism by Mudde and Kaltwasser as

> a thin-centred ideology that considers society to be ultimately separated into two homogeneous and antagonistic groups, 'the pure people' and 'the corrupt elite,' and which argues that politics should be an expression of the *volonté générale* (general will) of the people.
>
> (Mudde and Kaltwasser 2017: 6;
> Mudde and Kaltwasser 2013: 498; cf. Mudde 2004: 543)

This definition has the benefit of emphasising what many take to be the primarily negative nature of populism, as a critical attack on the political, economic and educational status quo. The inclusion of the phrase 'thin-centred ideology' (which was absent from Mudde's earlier version of the definition, see Mudde 2004: 543) captures a feature arising from this negativity; that populists often disagree strongly among themselves on what they are aiming to replace the current order with. It also, very importantly, highlights the importance of a concept drawn from the writings of Rousseau, that of the general will, which will be discussed in detail in Chapter 4. To this initial definition of populism may be added Müller's claim that while versions of contemporary populism in Europe and North America are not anti-democratic as such, many are seen by their critics as anti-pluralist and illiberal (Müller 2016: 6).

Much of the current debate in Europe and the United States centres on what is usually referred to as right-wing populism and that will be the focus of the book. Although there are left-wing versions of populism (notably the self-identifying work of Laclau 2005, 2006; Mouffe and Errejon 2016) these do not currently present the most forceful challenges to liberal democracy. Nor is a defence of nationalism an important part of the argument of left-wing populism, whereas it is extremely significant in what are most often regarded as right-wing populism, such as that of Trump's slogan Make America Great Again (MAGA) and the Fidesz government in Hungary.[5] If we take Kazin's two examples of left-wing populists, Sanders and Corbyn, both are internationalists who are strongly opposed to the kind of nationalism advocated by Donald Trump or Viktor Orbán.

With this in mind we can outline some of the important strands of this populism: the general will, the people, the criticism of elites, the need for the purification of society and the importance of the nation.

The general will

Discussion of the general will is sometimes conflated with another idea often appealed to by populists, that of the will of the majority. Rousseau certainly did not equate the general will with the will of the majority, but contemporary populism sometimes does seek to identify the will of the majority with the general will, or 'the will of the people', particularly when expressed as the result of a general election or a referendum. The result of the British referendum in 2016 has been seen in these terms by those in the United Kingdom who advocate leaving the European Union. Following Robert Dahl this may be characterised as 'the attempt to identify democracy with the unlimited power of majorities' which he regards as a defining characteristic of what he refers to as 'populistic democracy' (Dahl 2006: 35).

The distinction between the general will and the will of the majority has significant implications for education. If, as in the case of the United Kingdom, for example, referenda are a last resort, a means of resolving major constitutional issues where the citizens of the country, including members of the government and opposition are deeply divided, it might be argued that the most appropriate education system is one based on liberal principles such as critical analysis, toleration and civility. The last two are particularly important because the decision arrived at in the referendum is not the will of the people as a single body but of the majority of the people, sometimes, as in the case of the referendum on Britain's membership of the European Union, a slim one. It is important to stress this because of the need to recognise that while the divide within a country on a particular issue may be deep, on many other issues there may be little disagreement, or, frequently, either no clear majority or a majority composed of different people.[6]

A society governed by the general will, by contrast, is one in which the exercise of independent critical analysis is subordinated to the deeper insight of the people. As a consequence, civility need not be extended to those who persistently oppose these insights. Such an approach requires a very different education system, one in which the need to reinforce the values of a stable society take precedence over the encouragement of critical thinking or individual autonomy. A (rather more subtle) version of this view of the relationship between education and the general will is advocated by Rousseau and will be discussed at length in Chapter 4.

The people

Mudde and Kaltwasser draw attention to the importance of 'the people' in their definition of populism, and the previous paragraphs (p. 18) provide examples of its use. Populists use this term a great deal to refer to those who they believe express the genuine values of the community and, who, because they give expression to the general will are, therefore, the source of legitimate authority in the state. Liberals often either avoid the term altogether, other than to criticise the populist use of it as divisive, or use it in a very general, and often cosmopolitan way. This is problematic because the term 'the people' is used in many of the founding works of liberalism, among them the document so often appealed to against the alleged threat to American democracy by populist appeals to the people, the Constitution of the United States with its opening phrase, 'We the people'. Liberals, just as much as populists, have a concept of 'the people'. Part of the reason for this reverence liberals and populists share for the importance of the people, however differently they understand the term, is that, as David Polansky writes, '[i]n a sense, popular sovereignty—the idea that the people are the ultimate source of political authority—is the locus of modern politics'. He also makes a crucial point when he argues that the concept of the people 'grounds the nation-state, which remains the dominant political form in our world' (Polansky 2018).

Elites

One of the reasons why populists appeal to the idea of the people is to differentiate them from members of elites who are allegedly out of touch with the true values of society and consequently cannot reflect the general will. Populists criticise groups such as professional politicians, intelligence agencies and senior military personnel over actions like the Vietnam War and the Second Gulf War and professional politicians and bankers over the financial crisis of 2008.

Such criticisms might be seen as part of the healthy scepticism which a democracy requires of its citizens.[7] However, a closely related populist claim goes beyond scepticism about particular policies and actions and claims that 'the people' have been coerced into accepting the economically and politically unjust system under which they live. This, it is argued, has been accomplished through a variety of methods, including a media, owned and controlled by members of elite, which constantly provides a misleading view of reality: not just individual items of 'fake news' but a systematically false world view. Most important for our present purposes is the argument that the media is underpinned by an education system designed to perpetuate the power of the elite, which it does in two ways. The first involves providing a superior education for the children of the elite, equipping them with high level knowledge and skills, and often encouraging them to think of themselves as primarily citizens of the world. The second element in this hierarchical education system involves a lower tier of education which indoctrinates the great majority of children with a false understanding of the world, designed to keep them in subordination. In this way education plays an extremely important role in perpetuating inequality in society.

The purification of society

Commentators on populism often argue that it is a phenomenon which has emerged within democratic societies as a reaction to some of the perceived problems of liberal democracy, such as the power of unrepresentative and uncaring elites. Müller makes this point forcefully:

> The danger to democracies today is not some comprehensive ideology that systematically denies democratic ideals. The danger is populism – a degraded form of democracy that promises to make good on democracy's highest ideals ('Let the people rule!'). The danger comes, in other words, from within the democratic world – the political actors posing the danger speak the language of democratic values. That the end result is a form of politics that is blatantly antidemocratic should trouble us all….
>
> (Müller 2016: 6)

There is a good deal of truth in what Müller says here, but the contrast he draws is too broad because there may be situations where differences between liberals and populists are a legitimate part of democratic debate. His argument that 'the end result' of populist promises 'to make good on democracy's highest ideals' is 'a form of politics that is blatantly anti-democratic' certainly has some plausibility but it is too strong to claim that this is an inevitable part of populism. It is really an aspect of a particular strand in populist thought which may indeed be dangerous: the belief that in order to make society just it has to be purified.

At its strongest, the idea of the need to purify society seeks to transform it into something not simply more just, but just by a different order of magnitude – a society cleansed of those elements which corrupt and debase its people, and which prevent them living harmonious and contended lives. Populists who make this claim not only wish to criticise the allegedly corrupt elites which govern their societies but also foreigners whose presence as settled inhabitants threatens to undermine the integrity of the community. There are echoes of this idea in the Trump administration's policy on migrants from some Moslem countries and from Central America and the policies of the governments of Hungary and Poland towards non-Christian immigrants.

This idea of the purification of society has many echoes in Western civilisation, but it is evident in Rousseau's work and has its roots in Plato. It is a potent factor in the attempt in the early modern period by both Protestant and Roman Catholic churchmen to use the power of the state to suppress heresy, but it can also be seen in secular forms such as the attempt to impose virtue during the French Revolution or in the zeal of Fascist and Communist regimes to purge society of its critics and remake its citizens as new men and women. What they all have in common is a rejection of liberal values, particularly the value of pluralism. And for all their differences in religious and ideological views, they share a belief that the control of education is a vital tool in imposing their will on society. As will be argued in Chapters 2 and 4, Plato and Rousseau both think that education is a key to the purification of society.

Nationalism

These ideas have clear connections in the modern world with certain forms of nationalism and part of the concern liberals have expressed over the success of populism over the past few years has been the use by populist politicians of rhetoric that incorporates the language of nationalism. Putting 'nationalism' and 'purification' in the same sentence immediately, and rightly, rings very serious alarm bells. Nazism carried to its most hideous extreme the belief that preservation of national identity required the purification of society and I referred earlier to the claims of writers such as Stanley (2018) and Albright (2018) that the nationalism of populist movements such as that associated with MAGA risks creating something similar today.

For a long period after the end of the Second World War it was believed, particularly in Western Europe and North America, that as democracy and material well-being spread nationalist sentiment would disappear. The hope that nationalism would lose its hold on the imagination of the people of the various European states was very understandable in the post-war world and inspired men such as Jean Monet to create the institutions which would later develop into the European Union as a bulwark against the re-emergence of national assertion and aggression. The European Union's emphasis on education exchanges and partnerships between individuals and institutions in the member states as a means of fostering trans-European values is an important element in this.

The belief in the permanent demise of nationalism has become increasingly difficult to sustain as an account of how the world is, as opposed to cosmopolitan desires of how it should be, and we seem to have reached what Ghia Nodia has recently called 'The end of the postnational illusion' (2017). Nodia argues that the contemporary wave of populism has encouraged what he refers to as the third wave of nationalism (Nodia 2017: 11). The links between nationalism and populism are apparent particularly in populist objections to the large-scale immigration of people who do not share the same culture. The theoretical underpinning for this lies in the idea of 'the people', who make up the true or original inhabitants of society or the nation. In both cases, the concept of the general will as expressing the values of the society or nation is a central idea.

This has very important implications for education. Benedict Anderson writes in *Imagined Communities*, his ground-breaking book on the study of nationalism, that the growth of mass education, often funded and guided by the state, played a major part in creating a sense of national identity in nineteenth century Europe (Anderson 1983). Populist nationalists today, such as Donald Trump or Viktor Orbán, argue that they face a different situation where mass education has long been guided by a cosmopolitan elite who decry much of their own history and culture and advocate replacing them with liberal principles which ignore or undermine national values and identities. Reclaiming education for the nation thus becomes an important part of populism, which is why the appointment of someone like Betsy DeVos as President Trump's Secretary of Education and the Hungarian government's criticism of the CEU, far from being peripheral matters, reflect values and beliefs which are at the heart of populist agendas for government.

It is important to point out, though, that there are varieties of nationalism that its advocates regard as being inextricably linked to liberalism and liberal democracy. Indeed, in the nineteenth century, nationalism was most often associated with liberalism, a position exemplified in the writings and political practice of the Italian nationalist Mazzini. Contemporary writers such as John B. Judis (2018) and Francis Fukuyama (2018a; 2018b), both of whom are critical of much about populism, nevertheless see a recognition of the potential overlaps between liberalism and some forms of nationalism as an important counter to populist nationalism. In arguing this way, they are effectively echoing not so much Mazzini's liberal nationalism in his *The Duties of Man* (1907) which ultimately prioritises nationalism over liberalism, but a widely held interpretation of John Stuart Mill's defence of nationalism which holds that national identity might, as a matter of contingent, historical fact, form the basis of a settled community within which liberal ideas can flourish. Mill's discussion of nationality (to use his term) in *Considerations on Representative Government* (1865) is rather more nuanced than this but, as we will see in more detail in Chapters 5 and 6, is important both in the context of the development of Mill's own relationship to nineteenth century liberal thought and in relation to the nationalist strand in twenty-first century populism.

Populism and liberalism

The argument that the most fundamental part of the threat to liberal democracy is at the level of a challenge to its values by alternative values found, among other places, in the writings of Rousseau and their influence on later populists, might suggest, as many discussions of liberal democracy and populism do, that liberalism and populism are binary opposites. Some critics of populism do not go this far but suggest instead that it is either a deviation from liberal democracy or that it represents an immature version of it. The deviation interpretation is perhaps reflected in Müller's description of populism as the shadow of liberal democracy (2016: 101). The immature version is well captured by Francis Fukuyama during a discussion of democracies at an early stage of their development. In such circumstances, he argues, they sometimes embrace a 'spoils' system to help reward supporters before the society develops a more sophisticated and ethical framework. Fukuyama refers to, among others, Andrew Jackson as an example of a practitioner of such as system: a president who Steve Bannon has suggested offers a close parallel to Donald Trump, and whose portrait currently hangs in the oval office (Fukuyama 2014: 140–3).

These views all suggest that populist democracy is inferior to liberal democracy. It may be, though, that populism represents an alternative understanding of democracy which, particularly under certain circumstances, may offer an important counterbalance to limitations within liberal democracy. In this context, a distinction needs to be made between populists and more radical critics of liberal democracy such as Karl Marx. Marx regards liberal democracy as merely a mask for concealing the oppression of one class by another, and argues throughout his writings for the overthrow of liberal democratic institutions in favour of a political system based on the dictatorship of the proletariat. By contrast, populists do not want to replace democratic institutions but capture them for their own purposes. In particular, although they may have reservations about some of the restrictions imposed by liberal principles such as respect for minorities or, more particularly, tolerance for those who dissent from what they understand to be the fundamental values of society, populists do regard elections as a vital means of legitimising government.

Indeed, taken by themselves, many of the strands which contribute to a populist perspective are unremarkable in a democratic society. Distrust of experts, for example, is not unusual, nor is it restricted to those who might be classed, fairly or unfairly, as people lacking in specialist expertise. This is apparent in the way that experts in one area may be disdainful of experts in another, as neuroscientists are often dismissive of psychoanalysts, or natural scientists such as physicists or chemists often reject the claim to scientific rigour of social scientists. With respect to practice based on expertise in politics or economics, or in the practice of social work, it is often considered part of a healthy democracy that the theory and practice of these experts should be sufficiently transparent for active citizens who take an interest in such matters to be able to offer reasonable and practical criticisms.

Despite these comments about areas of overlap it remains true that there are substantial differences between liberal democracy and populism which go beyond mere political styles or stances. The basis of these differences is to be found particularly in the contrast between the conflicting views of society and of the role of the individual. Educating people for their role in society is crucial to both these approaches and to see how different in principle, and on occasion in practice, these are it will be helpful to turn to return in greater detail to the conflict between the populist government of Hungary and the liberal CEU.

Populist versus liberal education: the case of the CEU

For several years the populist-nationalist Hungarian government led by Prime Minister Viktor Orbán has been in conflict with the CEU, an institution founded on avowedly liberal and cosmopolitan principles and which has been based for many years in Budapest. I will use this as a case study to help clarify some of the ways in which liberals and populists disagree over the nature and purpose of education. I will not discuss at this point the merits and demerits of the two sides but use the arguments each make as examples of how liberal and populist approaches to education differ from each other. This is particularly important because, as discussed previously (p. 10), there is very little in the way of positive articulation of contemporary populist theory in general and its attitude to education in particular. This is not to say that all populists will agree with every aspect of Orbán's education policy, nor that all liberals would agree with all the educational policies of the CEU, but their relative positions do show the broad areas of policy differences which populists and liberals would take. Drawing out some of these broad areas will help guide the discussion in the following chapters.

The dispute, and the larger political issues of which it is a part, has been the subject of intense debate in the Western media, much of it highly emotive. Following the CEU's initial public announcement on 1st November 2018 that it was transferring most of its teaching and research from Budapest to Vienna, the *Washington Post* reported the decision under the headline 'Soros-founded University Says it has been Kicked out of Hungary as Autocrat Tightens his Grip' (Witte 2018). The headline captures some of the drama of the confrontation and also highlights the two most important figures, George Soros and the allegedly autocratic Orbán.

The CEU was founded in 1991, in the aftermath of the fall of the Berlin Wall and the collapse of Soviet control over its empire in Eastern and Central Europe. It had wide-spread support both in the region and elsewhere from intellectuals and politicians, including the then President of Czechoslovakia Vaclev Havel, and with funding from the Soros Open Society Foundation. At Havel's invitation the University was first based in Prague but it moved in 1993 to Budapest. In the following years the University developed a global reputation for the quality of its reaching and research, being placed in the top 200 universities by QS in 2017, where it is also rated at equal 42 for Politics and International Studies.[8] It is a graduate level institution with some 80 per cent of its courses, including Gender Studies, a subject of which the Hungarian government strongly disapproves, validated by Bard College in the state of New York and the remainder by the Hungarian Ministry of Education.

Following the end of Soviet rule Hungary adopted a democratic government and cemented its break with Russia and identification with the West by joining the European Union and the North Atlantic Treaty Organization. In 1998 Fidesz, in alliance with the Christian Democrats, won the general election and Viktor Orbán became Prime Minister. Fidesz and their allies lost the election to the Socialist Party in 2002 and again in 2006 but were returned to power in 2010, 2014 and 2018, each time gaining, in alliance with their junior partners, a supermajority of seats in the Hungarian parliament which allowed them to make changes to the Constitution.

Orbán first came to prominence as a distinguished and courageous dissident against the old Soviet-controlled Communist governments of Hungary.[9] To his critics this makes all the more surprising his subsequent emergence as the leader of a populist nationalist governing party and even more his outspoken criticisms of liberal policies, particularly on immigration. In a speech at the 25th Bálványos Summer Free University and Student Camp in 2014, widely reported and much discussed in the Western media, he claimed that his government was building an illiberal society.[10]

Orbán argues that there are three great moments of change in the twentieth century – the end of the First World War, the end of the Second World War and the collapse of communism. We are now in the midst of a fourth such change which became dramatically apparent during the financial crisis of 2008.

When he attacks the liberal world view in his speech, he is referring primarily to neo-liberal economic policies which were in the ascendant before 2008.

He claims that many individuals and institutions which were proponents of neo-liberalism have come to question some of its basic tenets. Referring to criticisms by the then United States President Barack Obama, and others, of the neo-liberal economic system he argues that they suggest the need for a more national economic system. He claims that forces that were once seen as conducive to freedom have changed, and cites as an example the internet, which 'has been colonised by large corporations' which he claims are threatening the neutrality of the internet.

Neither of these criticisms would be particularly alarming – or even novel – to many left-wing Western liberals, though some might be less happy with his approving reference to another analysts' attack on the decadence of much Western life in which he argues that 'the strength of American soft power is in decline and liberal values today embody corruption, sex and violence, and as such discredit America and American modernisation', nor to his approval of the then British Prime Minister David Cameron's defence of Britain's Christian identity.

But there are implications in what Orbán says that go beyond purely economic issues. John O'Sullivan seeks to defend Orbán by arguing that he is not attacking liberalism as such but a new system which is gradually replacing 'old-fashioned majoritarian democracy'.

> This system is one in which 'rights', devised and enforced by courts and international agencies, are placed beyond the control of elected parliaments, so that over time the voters lose influence over how they are governed.... A better name for it would be 'undemocratic liberalism'.
> (O'Sullivan and Pócza 2015: xviii)

But this interpretation is undermined by Orbán's argument that the primary purpose of the state is 'to make a nation and community internationally competitive', and that the most successful models of how to do this are the non-liberal and, as he admits, in most cases non-democratic states of Singapore, China, India, Russia and Turkey.

Orbán goes further in a direct attack on a major liberal principle which forms the heart of John Stuart Mill's *On Liberty*, that 'the sole end for which mankind are warranted, individually or collectively, in interfering with the liberty of action of any of their number, is self-protection'.

'The principle around which Hungarian society is organised', Orbán contends, 'should not be that everything is allowed that does not infringe on the other party's freedom, but instead should be that one should not do unto others what one does not want others to do unto you'. This, he claims, should be a fundamental principle of Hungarian society and central to the education it provides.

In language that we will find anticipated in Rousseau, Orbán argues that 'the Hungarian nation is not simply a group of individuals but a community that must be organised, reinforced and in fact constructed'. And so in this sense, the new state that we are constructing in Hungary is an illiberal state, a non-liberal state. It does not reject the fundamental principles of liberalism such as freedom, and I could list a few more, but it does not make this ideology the central element of state organisation, but instead includes a different, special, national approach.

Since the second victory of Fidesz in 2012 the CEU has come under intense pressure by the Hungarian government to modify what it teaches to bring it into line with the nationalistic education system of Hungary as a whole. One of the chief criticisms levelled against the CEU by the Hungarian government is that its teaching reflects a liberal cosmopolitan perspective that is widespread in Western European and American universities and which undermines commitment to the particular intellectual and cultural traditions of Hungary. Stefan Roch quotes the historian and Orbán supporter Mária Schmidt's criticism that a liberal open society "would require Europeans to sacrifice the remnants of their identity at the altar of openness and renounce everything that made them what they are" (Roch 2018: 56).

This criticism is overly harsh but in its Mission Statement, the University does emphasise its explicitly liberal and cosmopolitan approach to education. It acknowledges that its 'distinctive educational program builds on the research tradition of the great American universities', as well as 'on the most valuable Central European intellectual traditions', and it claims that one of its great strengths lies in 'the international diversity of its faculty and students …'. It refers to 'its own history of academic and policy achievements in transforming the closed communist inheritance' and in doing so proclaims that it is 'committed to promoting the values of open society and self-reflective critical thinking'. To underline its mission as a cosmopolitan University it argues that the 'CEU is a new model for international education, a center for study of contemporary economic, social and political challenges, and a source of support for building open and democratic societies that respect human rights and human dignity'.[11]

What is important here is the criticism that notwithstanding its claim to openness, the CEU is consciously offering a set of values which it acknowledges is central to its mission and which in a sense transcends the values of the nation where it happens to be situated. Except, of course, the CEU does not just happen to be situated in Eastern Europe, it was created and placed there for a reason, namely because of a wish to see the ex-Communist countries of Eastern and Central Europe become liberal democratic societies with a pronounced cosmopolitan attitude. That may be a wholly laudable ideal, but it is an ideal which the Hungarian government clearly believes is problematic because, in its view, the CEU undermines the primacy of national values.

These pronounced differences between a liberal and a populist help to explain the four ways mentioned earlier (pp. 4–7) in which liberals and populists disagree over the role of education in society. These are, the role of education in promoting a stable society, the place of expertise in education and political life, the encouragement of critical thinking and the promotion of autonomy.

On the role of education in promoting a stable society, the populist view understands this primarily in terms of defending the values of the nation, with its distinctive traditions and values.[12] The liberal view contends that the most stable society is one in which students are taught the principles of liberty which are universal. The CEU at its inception took this a stage further when it declared that its purpose was to train leaders who would guide the transition of the newly free countries of central and eastern Europe to liberal democracy. Stefan Roch argues that this was very close to the Platonic view and suggests that although the CEU has shifted its policies to a more open, enquiring view of society, the tension remains (Roch 2018: 52–7). This criticism of the ambiguity in the liberal position is by no means new and in Chapter 3 we will discuss criticisms of Locke's liberal theory of education along these lines.

This leads on to the second issue, of the place of the education of experts in a democratic society. Some liberals, such as George Soros, believe that it is necessary to train certain people to guide the rest of society. In this, as we shall see, they echo a central argument of Plato's; that ruling is a skill like any other in which people can and should be trained.[13] They also argue that the principles which should guide this training are universal liberal values, and that educational institutions should be internationalist in outlook. The CEU claims this as an explicit part of its mission, and regards the recruitment of scholars and students from many different countries as an important means of achieving this. Populists like Orbán do not disagree that certain kinds of experts are useful in society but they differ in that they think – and in this they follow a different point of Plato's – that experts should be grounded in the culture of their own society so that they can apply their skills in a way that is in harmony with the interests of society. We will see in Chapter 4 that this is also Rousseau's view, and that Rousseau believes that teachers should be drawn only from the country in which they are citizens.

It is not surprising given their differing views of stability in society and expertise that populists and liberals will disagree over the role of critical thinking in education. Populists are not necessarily opposed to critical thinking as such, what they are opposed to is an education process (or individual teachers) who encourage a negative attitude towards the fundamental values of their own society. As we have already seen, liberalism is sometimes torn, as the CEU is, between its founding principles and its current mission, between an education which aims to train people to be good liberal leaders and citizens and one which encourages open-ended criticism.

It might be thought that liberal education is superior to populist education because it promotes autonomy by prioritising the values associated with individual freedom. But the meaning of autonomy is not so straightforward as this claim would suggest. We will leave aside, for the present, the element in liberal thought which aims to train people to become good liberals,[14] the idea which the CEU was originally designed to implement. The contemporary CEU is closer to the position of liberals such as John Stuart Mill, who place the greatest importance on individuality and the right to choose how to live one's own life. Mill's view is summed up in the phrase from *On Liberty* which Orbán singles out for criticism: 'the sole end for which mankind are warranted, individually, or collectively, in interfering with the liberty of action of any of their number, is self-protection' (Mill CW, XVIII: 223). As one consequence of this principle, Mill argues that education provision should be as diverse as possible and that there should be no state-regulated curriculum. It is not surprising that, in language that we will find anticipated in Rousseau, Orbán attacks this principle in his speech of 2014, arguing that instead the guiding principle should be the good of the community.

On this understanding we are free only in so far as we are part of a just community. This leads to the view that the ideal education is not one that, as Locke argues, promotes the independence of the individual but one which, in Rousseau's words in *Considerations on the Government of Poland*, seeks to 'give souls the national form, and so direct their opinions and their tastes that they may be patriotic by inclination, passion, necessity' (Rousseau 2019b: 193). The contrast could not be starker, either between Locke and Rousseau or the government of Viktor Orbán and the values of the CEU. Nor is this the only example of such opposing views. As we will see in what follows, these differences lie deep in the history of Western culture.

Three points of clarification

Before discussing the four thinkers it will be helpful to clarify three general points about the purpose and aims of the book.

First, this is a book about the broader political and philosophical aspects of education. It does not offer detailed suggestions on the curriculum or on the organisation of educational institutions. Rousseau may be appealed to in part in justification of this approach – in the Preface to *Emile* (1979) he argues that there are two things to consider when trying to understand the nature of education. The first is whether the fundamental principles underlying the analysis is correct, the second is how those principles might be put into practice. The methods of application, he says, will differ considerably from place to place and between different groups in society, and have to be worked out in detail by those who have a knowledge of and interest in those particular circumstances. There will be occasions during the course of my argument where I will disagree with Rousseau, but on this point he is, I think, correct.

Second, I have already referred on a number of occasions to the historical context in which these philosophers wrote and I will do so again in the following chapters. Two things need to be said about this. I do not wish to argue that we can find straightforward parallels between contemporary events and those of the past, and the currently popular attempts to explain contemporary populism by reference to the 1930s in Europe often give rise to more misunderstanding than clarity. I do, though, argue that looking at past responses to particular issues – especially when they are of as searching a nature as Mill's analysis of the growth of democracy and the threat of popular threats to individual liberty – can help provide valuable perspectives on the present. Nevertheless, it is the philosophical rather than the historical which is my primary concern.

The final point is that I have tried to follow the principle of charity in assessing the arguments of the various authors whose work I discuss. That is to say, I have taken as a working hypothesis that each of these thinkers should be read as having produced coherent bodies of work which should be treated seriously. This is not meant to suggest that there are no inconsistencies or bad arguments in their work. What it does imply is the need to read the texts in what Rousseau describes as 'good faith' (Rousseau 1960: 11) and to take seriously a comment of Mill's, born as is Rousseau's comment, out of exasperation with critics who impugn the worst intentions: 'There is no difficulty in proving any ethical standard whatever to work ill, if we suppose universal idiocy to be conjoined with it ...' (Mill CW, X: 224). Reading and listening to the arguments between liberals and populists, one quickly becomes aware how lack of good faith and strident accusations are all too prevalent.

Notes

1 On some problems associated with giving insufficient attention to the historical contexts in which different uses of the term 'rights' are used see Moyn 2010; Moyn 2014. Mill does not appeal to a concept of rights but does argue for the moral primacy of the individual.
2 Whitehead's sentiments are not as backward looking as the analogy might at first make them seem. The comments are made in the context of universities needing to adapt and become more open to a much wider variety of people than hitherto (they were written in 1941). He refers particularly to London University's innovative attempts to meet the needs 'of artisans seeking intellectual enlightenment, of young people from every social grade craving for adequate knowledge' and characterises the dismissive response to such aspirations by traditionalists in Oxford and Cambridge as 'ignorant contempt' (Whitehead 1941: 14). The relationship between widening democratic participation and opening up access to education at all levels is one that will be discussed in more detail later, particularly in Chapters 5 and 6.
3 Mill thinks that times of intellectual change may provide great opportunities for societies to advance morally and politically – see Chapter 5 of this volume.
4 'Two Concepts of Liberty', delivered as his inaugural lecture as Chichele Professor of Political Theory at Oxford in 1958 is reprinted in *Four Essays on Liberty* (Berlin 1969a) and in *Liberty* (Berlin 2002) This liberal pluralism is a central theme in Berlin's writings and continued to preoccupy him throughout his life – see for example, 'The Pursuit of the Ideal', first published in 1988 and reprinted in *The Crooked Timber of Humanity* (Berlin 1990b). Michael Ignatieff, the Rector of the CEU, is the author of the authorised biography of Berlin in which he provides a detailed analysis of Berlin's argument (Ignatieff 1998: 225–9).
5 Federico Finchelstein has argued that treating populism as a European-North American phenomenon risks losing sight of some important aspects of the movement (Finchelstein 2017). I agree with his point as a commentary on general historical or sociological discussions of populism but my focus is narrower than this. I discuss populism as a phenomenon in established European and North American democracies (including the 'new democracies' which emerged in Central Europe after the end of the Cold War) and its relevance to the educational systems of those countries. I certainly agree that a study of education, liberal democracy and pluralism in other parts of the world, particularly Latin America, would be very valuable, but that would require another book.
6 The classic argument for this view of shifting majorities and alliances within society, the basis of what was later termed pluralism, is James Madison's in *The Federalist Papers*, Number 10 (Madison, Hamilton and Jay 1987).

7 It might, of course, be pointed out that some of the most incisive criticisms of these events has come from experts who disagreed with the actions taken – such as Hans Morgenthau and Michael Walzer over the conduct of the Vietnam War (Scheuerman 2009: Chapter 6; Walzer 1977/2015) and the Neo-Realist foreign policy experts such as John Mearsheimer who took out a full-page advertisement in the New York Times on 22nd September 2002 to warn against the invasion of Iraq.
8 QS Top Universities (2017) 'Politics and International Studies', www.topuniversities.com/university-rankings/university-subject-rankings/2017/politics
9 For a discussion of Orbán's role in the peaceful overthrow of Communism in 1989 and his subsequent rise to power see Paul Lendvai's critical biography *Orbán Europe's New Strongman* (2017) and, for a more sympathetic account written after his election victory in 2014, the collection of essays edited by John O'Sullivan and Kálmán Pócza, *The Second Term of Viktor Orbán: Beyond Prejudice and Enthusiasm* (2015). Péter Krekó and Zsolt Enyedi offer an illuminating analysis of what they term 'Orbán's Laboratory of Illiberalism' (Krekó and Enyedi 2018) and his problematic relationship with democracy. They argue that 'Orbán's political character cannot be understood apart from the logic of competitive electoral politics ...' and that while the methods he uses 'are often nondemocratic ... the logic of his behavior is quintessentially competitive....' and that he is 'at home with democratic electoral contests' (Krekó and Enyedi 2018: 43). Norman Stone provides a deeper background to the rise of Orbán in his *Hungary: A Short History* (2019: Preface and Chapter 8, especially 230–44).
10 The speech is available at the Hungarian government website, see Website of the Hungarian Government (2014) 'Prime Minister Viktor Orbán's Speech at the 25th Bálványos Summer Free University and Student Camp', www.kormany.hu/en/the-prime-minister/the-prime-minister-s-speeches/prime-minister-viktor-orban-s-speech-at-the-25th-balvanyos-summer-free-university-and-student-camp. All quotations from the speech are taken from this source.
11 Central European University (date unknown) 'Our Mission', www.ceu.edu/about/our-mission
12 See Orbán's comments on education in his State of the Nation Address in 2017:

> It is also good that children are entering the nursery school education system at the age of three, and that the state is paying for school meals and textbooks. But in the meantime are we raising them to love their homeland, to be patriotic and to have a patriotic frame of mind? Will Hungary be their shared passion, as it is ours? Will they too have a sense of national justice, which is fuelled by patriotism? Will they understand that the only way we can avoid being the slaves of other peoples – and the only way we can remain an independent nation – is if, first and foremost, we declare ourselves to be Hungarian? These are all things that we should take care to teach children in school, because it is only through this that our children can understand what links and binds us together.
> (the full speech is available at Viktor Orbán (2017) 'Prime Minister Viktor Orbán's State of the Nation Address', www.kormany.hu/en/the-prime-minister/the-prime-minister-s-speeches/prime-minister-viktor-orban-s-state-of-the-nation-address-20170214)

13 There is a certain irony in that Soros himself is deeply influenced by Karl Popper who was highly critical of Plato. What this shows is not any double-thinking on Soros' part but the complexity of the interpretation and application of sophisticated ideas such as Plato's.
14 This rather negative way of putting it is rather unfair, and as we will see, Locke has a good argument against the views underpinning what could be taken as a rather snide remark, but it is worth expressing it this way here to show that there is at least a problem for an important aspect of a liberal theory of education.

2 Plato
Two philosophies of education?

Plato and skilled experts

In his *Republic* Plato sets out a long and detailed argument in favour of a strong, stable society ruled by experts as the only possible basis for a truly just society. In this society critical thinking is to be banished, as is any notion that individual members of society should strive for personal autonomy. One of the chief ways in which this society is to be established and maintained is through a highly selective and rigidly controlled education system.

It might seem out of place in a book on education, liberal democracy and populism to devote a chapter to Plato, who was implacably opposed to democracy and was neither a liberal nor a populist. Plato claims that democracy is the worst form of government other than tyranny, and, moreover, that it paves the way for tyranny (*Republic* 564a).[1] The most desirable, as we will see, is rule by the wise whose decisions should never be discussed, let alone dissented from, by the great majority of people.

Despite this attack on democracy, Plato's political philosophy, and especially his view of the central importance of education in creating a just political society is fundamentally important for our discussion. This is partly because of the place of Plato's thought in Western society since the Renaissance. Plato's philosophy of education and society has been frequently rejected in modern liberal democracies, but that is a very recent phenomenon; for much of the last four centuries his ideas have been directly or indirectly very influential. Two of the other three writers we are discussing, Rousseau and Mill, regard Plato's discussion of the role of education in society as of the first importance, and both claim to have been deeply influenced by him.

I have already alluded in the Introduction to a second reason for discussing Plato at some length, which is that his work contains arguments which resurface in contemporary discussions of democracy. One of these is the way in which some democratic opponents of populism, such as Andrew Sullivan (2016), appeal to Plato's argument of the need for wise rulers to guide the less enlightened majority. This view is widely rejected by current populists who disparage experts and out-of-touch elites, but it is far from new. It has an eminent antecedent in Mill's appeal to Plato during the course of his claims for the importance of experts in a liberal democratic society.

There is also a quite different way in which an aspect of Plato's thought is reflected in the populist argument for the need to transform society by appealing to a deeper understanding of justice. Although populists do not directly derive this idea from Plato, it is a prominent feature of Rousseau's interpretation of Plato, as will be discussed further in Chapter 4.

This point about how one reads Plato, and the contradictory ways in which he is read by philosophers as sophisticated as Mill and Rousseau, is a reminder that interpreting Plato is no easy matter. This is in part because almost all of Plato's extant works are dialogues, with the ambiguity that type of writing entails. To this is added the enormous weight of scholarly discussion over the past two and a half millennia, from Aristotle to the present day. In view of this I will indicate two principles which I have followed in my discussion of Plato.

The first is that there are a number of key themes in the *Republic* over which there is widespread (though by no means universal) agreement, two of which are especially significant for our present discussion. The first of these is the theory of 'Forms', in which Plato argues that there are universal truths which can be discovered by reason, though only after a long and arduous period of study stretching over many years. The second is the claim that only a society ruled by philosophers, who alone are sufficiently highly educated to learn the Forms, can be just – and that democracy, which is the rule of the masses, must invariably be unjust. The widespread acceptance of these and related themes is central to what is often referred to as Platonism, or as the traditional interpretation of Plato (Fronterotta 2010: 136). Most importantly, for our present purposes, this reading of Plato has been the one which people have often attempted to relate to the education and politics of their own day and as such provides a focus for the discussion of Plato's view throughout the book. Rousseau is a prime example of a major philosopher who seeks to embrace and apply Plato's ideas, as we will see in detail in Chapter 4, but the influence is apparent too, though in a different way, in Victorian thinkers and reformers like Benjamin Jowett and George Grote, who will be discussed in Chapter 5. Mill rejected some of these ideas as inappropriate (or just downright dangerous) but also thought that something of great importance could be found in the Platonic dialogues and in the teachings of Socrates and especially his method of a radical and 'liberal' Socratic Method.

The other principle concerns the relationship between the *Republic* and the discussion of education and politics in two other Platonic dialogues, the *Statesman* and the *Laws*. The *Statesman* was written some time after the *Republic* and the *Laws* was, according to the current scholarly consensus, the last of Plato's works. Some writers have argued that the views of the *Statesman* and the *Laws* supersede those of the *Republic* – this was Jowett's view, for example (Plato 1875), and also the view of the eminent modern Plato scholar Julia Annas (Annas 1995). Others have suggested that the two later dialogues merely expand on the ideas of the *Republic* without undermining them (Laks 1990; Rowe 1999; Schofield 2016). This interpretation is reflected in my occasional references to the *Laws*, particularly in Chapter 4 in relation to Rousseau's reading of this work. The main focus in this chapter is, though, on the *Republic* because of its great influence on thinking about, and practising, education in the Western world.

Although I will refer to some contemporary scholarly discussions about the interpretation of Plato, I will particularly focus on the ways in which Rousseau and Mill, analysed, criticised and used Plato's arguments. Locke wrote little about Plato whereas Rousseau and Mill, by contrast, both claimed to have been strongly influenced by Plato, despite their interpretations of what was important and significant in his work differing sharply. These differences of interpretation are not inconsequential and reflect in part their very different views of education and democracy.

Plato and democracy

The Athenian society in which Plato lived was a democracy, in which all citizens, meeting face to face in the Assembly, participated in the discussions over all important policy matters and voted upon them. Compared with modern liberal democracies that of Athens had its limitations. Women played no part in the democratic process as only men could be citizens – Plato is very unusual as an Athenian who rejected the idea that women could not be rulers (*Republic* 540c–d) – and the Athenian economy rested on slavery. Yet Athenian democracy may, from a different perspective, be seen as more democratic in some respects than modern liberal democracies because of the direct involvement of all citizens in decision making (Arblaster 2002: Chapter 2). The claim that all citizens should be entitled to have a direct input into decisions is one populists often make.

Plato was neither a liberal nor a democrat. It is sometimes argued that Plato could not have been a liberal because liberal ideas, such as John Locke's defence of natural, or human, rights or John Stuart Mill's advocacy of the principle of liberty would not have made sense either in the context of the way democracy was practised in Athens or, more generally, in terms of the concepts and structure of Greek political thought. That argument has been challenged by Thomas Mitchell, who provides powerful evidence to show that democratic Athens, both under Pericles and after the restoration of democracy following the fall of the Thirty Tyrants,[2] espoused a set of values which would have been recognised as liberal by liberal philosophers such as Mill. The ideals of democracy which first emerged in Athens, Mitchell argues, entailed 'a new vision of the state as a community or partnership of political equals, equal in freedom, equal in political rights, equal in justice under a communally sanctioned rule of law …' (Mitchell 2015: 4). He also argues that there is a 'striking ethos of Liberalism' in Pericles' Funeral Oration, as recorded by Thucydides in *The Peloponnesian War*. The

> … leitmotif is freedom, not only the freedom of that bestowed legal and political equality; but a freedom that permeated the entire life of citizens, public and private. It was a freedom that respected a right to a private space and private possessions. It also protected freedom of speech, which was deemed essential to the functioning of the democracy.
>
> (Mitchell 2015: 69)

As Mitchell acknowledges, this is a controversial interpretation, but as we will see in Chapter 5, Mill explicitly draws parallels between the liberal values, as he interprets them, of ancient Athenian society and his own liberalism.[3]

However one assesses the evidence for a liberal ethos in Athens there is no doubt that Plato could have been a democrat. The Athens in which he wrote the *Republic* was, as Paul Cartledge argues, the most radical of the several hundred democracies which had existed among the Greek city states over several hundred years (Cartledge 2016: 145–6, 199–202). It is in part for this reason that his argument in the *Republic* for a hierarchical society based on the rule of a highly educated elite and for the rejection of democracy as anarchic (*Republic* 558c), presenting as it does a fundamental challenge to the democracy of his own society, Athens in the fifth century BC, also retains the power to unsettle and challenge advocates of both liberal and populist democracy in the twenty-first century.

Plato's criticisms of Athenian democracy lead directly to his challenge to another Athenian view of the time, that the education of children was largely a private matter. This practice was in direct contrast to that of Sparta, Athens' great rival ideologically as well as militarily, which was resolutely anti-democratic and where education was rigorously controlled by the state. Plato was an admirer of Sparta and his argument that the state should take full and exclusive responsibility for education would have been greeted with considerable suspicion by most Athenian citizens. Rousseau, as we will discuss in Chapter 4, defended Plato and argued that Spartan education at its best was superior to that of Athens.

Education and expertise

The central problem to be resolved in the *Republic* is: 'What is justice?'. This is not meant to be construed primarily in terms of political institutions or laws but rather what leads us to consider someone a just person. It is easier, though, Socrates tells his interlocuters, to see justice on a large scale first (in the state) and then having seen the large picture (or read the larger writing, as he puts it) to understand what justice is in the individual (*Republic* 368c–69a).

According to Plato, a just society would be divided into three groups of people. Following a well-established convention by modern translators and commentators I will refer to these as three classes, though this notion of class is quite distinct from modern Western notions of class based on economics. The three classes are the philosopher rulers, the soldiers (often translated as the auxiliaries) and the rest of society, the workers, which make up the largest group. The society is to be governed by the wise philosophical rulers who have a profound knowledge of timeless, universal values, or Forms (*Republic* 504d–511e).[4] This understanding is required in order to provide the philosopher rulers not only with a clear understanding of the true nature of justice in society but also what would be required to achieve it (*Republic* 427c–34c). By contrast, the great majority of people are incapable of achieving such understanding and are, therefore, incapable of making rational decisions about how society should be governed. Plato stresses that those who are to become rulers need to be educated to develop the skill of ruling – they need to become experts in government. It would be just as absurd, he says, to allow people to rule a city if they lack the necessary skills, based on many years of study and practice, as it would be to permit sailors who lack the skills to steer a ship to overthrow the trained pilot and take control themselves (*Republic* 488a–89a).

Those young men and women who display the potential to become philosopher rulers are to be selected for a long and rigorous education in order to prepare them for their duties. The remaining members of society should receive a far more rudimentary education to prepare them for work in trades such as farming, commerce and manufacturing (*Republic* 373d–6e, 473d–4c). Plato stresses that the members of this large majority, who would have formed the ruling group in a democracy, would be incapable of benefitting from higher education and would be far happier receiving an education tailored to their particular skills and abilities. Having completed their education, they would gladly spend their lives honing and developing their skills in activities that best suited their character and intellect. This explains why, in Plato's opinion, the Athenian democracy of his day, in which all citizens directly participated in the major decisions of state, so often lurched from crisis to crisis and why there was so much social injustice. What else could one expect when the mass of the people, wholly untrained for government and dissatisfied with their lot in a society which failed to provide them with an education suited to their needs, were given the opportunity to exercise power?

Almost all of Plato's discussion of education in the *Republic* concerns the education of the auxiliaries and the philosopher rulers but it is worth pausing for a moment to look more closely at the situation of the remainder of the population. A common criticism is that these people have no choice in what occupation they are to follow, nor in the education that is intended to prepare them for that role in society. Karl Popper claims that this is an example of what he describes as the totalitarianism, of the *Republic* (Popper 1945: 86–7).[5] It is possible to look at this in a more positive way, as John Dewey does in *Democracy and Education* where he writes that it

> would be impossible to find in any scheme of philosophic thought a more adequate recognition on one hand of the educational significance of social arrangements and, on the other, of the dependence of those arrangements upon the means used to educate the young. It would be impossible to find a deeper sense of the function of education in discovering and developing personal capacities, and training them so that they would connect with the activities of others.
>
> (1916: 56)

Although Dewey argues that Plato was unable to see the wide range of possibilities open to each individual,[6] his reading of Plato highlights the problem of the enormous waste of potential when children are offered no clear guidance on what is best suited to their talents and abilities or support in how to achieve this.

This lack of guidance might be the result of an overemphasis on encouraging children to discover things for themselves; Dewey, as we will see in Chapter 4, is critical of what he regards as Rousseau's excessive concentration (at least in *Emile*) on the self-discovery of the individual child. It may, though, be due to less benign and more impersonal forces in the form of a lack of resources to children in economically deprived conditions. It is a criticism of Locke that he largely ignores the plight of the poor in this regard, though his historical context makes such attitudes at least understandable.[7] Nineteenth century educational reformers such as Jowett seek to use Plato's argument as justification for the provision of elite education, and although Mill does not share all their prejudices (least of all in the case of education for women), he does not fully embrace an egalitarian education system. In offering the possibility of a more equitable system Dewey illustrates the potential in liberal thought and practice for critical reflection and the development of new insights.

The discussion of the education of the auxiliaries and the philosopher rulers in the *Republic* is divided into two sections. The first, in Books II and III, discusses the education of those selected to become auxiliaries. The second, which takes up most of Book VII, is concerned with the education of those auxiliaries who have been identified as having the temperament and intellectual skills to receive higher education, with the aim of their becoming philosopher rulers.

An important feature of the education of the auxiliaries is that they are closely guided and monitored in what they learn and that their reading of poetry and their exposure to other types of artistic expression, including what is for Plato the extremely important element of music, are heavily censored. Poets are permitted in the *Republic* only if they write according to standards set out by the philosopher rulers and will, therefore, present a positive and ennobling view of the world. This censorship extends beyond the formal education of the auxiliaries to control over the artists who should also be guided in what they produce (such as buildings and sculpture) so that their products reflect what is good and decent rather than what is bad and unseemly (*Republic* 401b–c). Later in the *Republic*, Plato argues that the skilled carpenter seeks to create a couch or table according to the form of a couch or the form of a table (*Republic* 596b), which suggests that their work too comes under the oversight of the philosopher rulers.

This desire to control the products of the artisans reflects Plato's belief that it is important to control informal education as well as formal. This is further demonstrated in Plato's banning of the theatre which he regards as harmful because drama manipulates feelings and desires and unsettles what the members of the audience have been taught during their education by the state.[8]

This raises issues about the relationship between formal and informal education and the way in which non-liberal regimes, such as the medieval Catholic Church in England or the Puritan colonies of New England frequently sought to censor expression of dissident, or even merely divergent views (for example, those of quietist, non-proselytising religious groups) as well as controlling the curriculum in formal education. It is also an area in which the advocacy by Locke and Mill of toleration and critical thinking, and their essential place in education, brings them into conflict with Plato.

The second discussion of education, that relating to the higher education of the auxiliaries, also addresses the selection of those who are to become philosophers, and hence rulers in the state. The first stage of this higher education involves education in arithmetic, plane geometry, astronomy and harmonics and has two purposes. The first of these is to provide the auxiliaries with the mathematical skills that are beneficial to military life, such as the use of arithmetic in calculating (*Republic* 525b) and geometry in helping pitching camp and planning manoeuvres (*Republic* 526d). The second, is to lay a foundation of abstract thinking in the most philosophically gifted of the auxiliaries as preparation for their final training as philosophers. Plato contrasts the use of mathematical skills by the auxiliaries and the potential philosophers with the practical and intellectually far less sophisticated use of mathematics in commerce (*Republic* 525c).

Those who excel at the sophisticated study of mathematics will finally, at the age of 30 (*Republic* 537d) be initiated into dialectic, the study of intensely abstract argument which will ultimately lead, through questioning and debate, to the knowledge of the Forms, and most particularly the Form of the Good (*Republic* 543c–d). After an initial period of training in dialectic they will then undergo a further period of physical training for five years (*Republic* 539e), followed by another 15 years of being tested in positions of military authority or other offices suitable for the young (*Republic* 540a). Only at the age of 50 years will those who have proved their worth finally ascend to knowledge of the Forms.[9] After this they will spend their lives doing philosophy and, from time to time, in rotation, they will serve terms as rulers of the republic.

In terms of the four themes outlined in the Introduction of this volume, Plato stresses the importance of education in establishing and preserving order and stability in society. His belief in the need for strict control in society, and especially his argument for the need to educate a class of elite experts to ensure this, places him at odds with populists. Yet some of the most powerful criticisms of Plato have been made by liberals, of whom Popper is among the most prominent.[10] As we saw in the Chapter 1, one irony of this is that the CEU, of which the populist government of Hungary is so critical, is funded by, and supports the aims of the Open Society Forum which seeks to further the principles of Popper's liberalism.

Challenging the experts: the Socratic Method

One of Karl Popper's major criticisms of Plato is that he banishes freedom of speech, and freedom of thought, from the Republic and that his education system seeks to reinforce this by stifling, at least for the great mass of the people who do not become philosophers, both critical thinking and the autonomy of the individual.

Some thinkers, however, have found the basis of a quite different approach to education in other parts of Plato's writings. The *Republic* belongs to a later stage in Plato's intellectual development – usually attributed to the middle dialogues[11] – but whereas much of the *Republic* is largely a monologue in which

Socrates offers a fully worked out system of thought, culminating in the theory of forms and a strictly hierarchical view of society, many of Plato's earlier works are very different in tone and content. These early dialogues, such as *Euthrypho*, *Crito*, *Phaedo*, *Charmides*, *Laches* and *Lysis* take the form of discussions between Socrates, who had been Plato's mentor and teacher until his trial and execution, and one or more protagonists on a particular topic, such as beauty, love and goodness. In these dialogues, unlike in the *Republic*, Socrates does not offer any answers to the questions himself but simply draws out the views of other people – they read very much like genuine dialogues, as if neither Socrates, who is speaking, or Plato, who is writing, knows the answers and both are genuinely curious to know where the questioning will lead. The discussions take place in a variety of locations, in private houses, outside the courthouse, in the market place, and Socrates particularly seeks out those who are widely regarded as experts in the particular topics he wants to discuss. Socrates' method begins by asking an expert for their definition of the topic in hand, such as beauty or love. When the definition has been given Socrates asks further questions to make people think through the implications of the beliefs they hold, with the result that those with whom he is talking are forced to admit inconsistencies in their beliefs. This newly arrived at definition then forms the basis for the next stage of the discussion in which the process is repeated. This is the Socratic Method,[12] and applied to education it has often been understood as suggesting an open-ended and critical approach to problem solving. It also seems to draw upon the method of dialectic which Plato discusses in the *Republic*.

This interpretation of the Socratic Method is very much to the fore in the way in which several recent writers have drawn comparisons with the work of the influential radical Brazilian educational theorist and adult educator Paulo Freire (Brown 2012; Irwin 2012), especially his notion of dialogics in *The Pedagogy of the Oppressed* (Freire 1993: Chapter 3; see also Jarvis 2010: 97–101). The Socratic Method is often contrasted, as well, with Confucianism in comparing the teaching and learning styles of Western liberal democracies with those of the allegedly authoritarian (or illiberal) China (Peters 2015). One of the most important writers to suggest a radical disjunction between the early 'liberal' Socratic Plato and the later 'dogmatic' Plato is John Stuart Mill, who argues, that there are 'two complete Platos in Plato – the Sokratist and the dogmatist – of whom the former is by far the most valuable to mankind, but the latter has obtained from them much the greater honour' (Mill CW, XI: 451).

We will discuss Mill's argument more fully in Chapter 5. However, despite such illustrious championing of the prioritising of the Socratic Method because of its supposed critical and democratic aspects, there are two important reasons why such an approach is problematic.

The first problem is that the historical Socrates' support for democracy was, to say the least, ambiguous. Waterfield (2009: 178–81) and Mitchell (2015: 196–201) both point to Socrates' own misgivings about aspects of Athenian democracy and they refer to his association with those like Alcibiades who violently opposed Athenian democracy as a reason for the persecution which led to his trial and execution.

Of course, even if Socrates himself were opposed to democracy that does not mean that his method cannot be used profitably for education in a democratic society. To see why we should be cautious, at least in how the method should be applied, we need to return to Plato's primary purpose in putting forward the educational theory of the *Republic*. It was, in Rousseau's striking phrase, to have 'purified the heart of man' (Rousseau 1979: 40). Repulsed by what he sees as the corruption of Athenian society, Plato offers a radical solution – replace the current democratic order with a wholly different one which will be based not on acquisitiveness and competition but on order and harmony, with each person living contentedly in a society that emphasises simplicity and the natural order. The belief in the need to purify the present corrupt political and economic system and transform it into a more natural society is familiar in populist politics and looked at from this perspective Socrates' constant questioning of the so-called experts could be seen not as an exercise of democratic citizenship but a radical undermining of democratic order to help pave the way for a new and more just rule.

This point can be seen more forcefully when we consider an apparent contradiction between Socrates' criticism of experts in the *Apology* and his defence of the theory of the philosopher rulers (who are, of course, experts par excellence) which Plato attributes to Socrates in the *Republic*. There is much debate over the precise relationship between the Socrates of the early dialogues and the views which Plato attributes to him in the middle and later dialogues, but in this case suggesting a possible difference between different stages in Plato's writing is in danger of obscuring a more important philosophical point. The experts whom Socrates attacks in the *Apology* have an understanding which is only partial and incomplete, which is why Socrates is able to undermine their claims to true expertise (*Apology* 21b–4a). However, the philosopher rulers in the *Republic* have a complete knowledge of reality, based on an understanding of the Forms. Moreover, unlike that of the alleged experts, the knowledge of the philosopher rulers has, so to speak, become internalised and, therefore, has transformed them ethically as well as intellectually, as the prisoner who leaves the cave has his sight illuminated by the Sun (*Republic* 516a–c and compare 508b–e). The philosopher who knows the Form of justice cannot but act justly.

The attack on experts in the *Apology* is best understood as an attack on those whose claims to expertise are false. The attack is negative and the account of true expertise has to wait until later writings. But in the *Republic*, once it has been established who the true experts are there is no question of challenging their authority.

There is a further reason why we should treat Socrates' use of the dialectic with some care. In the discussion of the education of the philosophers Plato warns against the dangers of the misuse of dialectic by those who are young and inexperienced. The dialectic is by its very nature critical and in challenging accepted opinions and beliefs without offering positive alternatives it can be dangerously destructive both for the soul of the individual who uses it and for the society of which he (or she) is a part. This danger is one reason why, having been taught the elements of dialectic and learnt to use its method, the prospective philosophers are forced to undergo five years of hard physical training followed by 15 years of administration to give them the time to mature to a point where they can be entrusted to use the dialectic wisely (*Republic* 539a–40b).

There are some similarities with populism here. One is the rejection of false claims to an expertise which privileges the expert to the extent that they lay claim to a superior role in society. The claim is false because the expert has at best only a partial understanding. This is a particularly important aspect of the Socratic Method which draws attention to its negative, destructive potential. There are good examples of this in the first part of Book I of the *Republic* where Socrates shows the inconsistency first in Cephalus' definition of justice and then in Polemarchus' amended version. In dismissing the expertise of his interlocutors because they are incomplete, Socrates is implicitly saying in Book I what he argues for explicitly for in the later books of the *Republic*, which is that only those with a complete understanding of the truth can legitimately be leaders of society. It follows from this that democracy is a bad type of government because, among other reasons, it encourages debate and eventual compromise whereas in the Republic the great majority of people should only listen and acquiesce. Mill, in common with many later philosophers and educators, highlighted what he took to be the directly opposite benefit of the Socratic Method, which was to encourage fierce debate and argument in order to achieve compromise and to get closer to a semblance of an always unreachable truth. It is no surprise that Mill rejected the theory of Forms as metaphysical nonsense. These two views of the Socratic Method imply very different educational values and systems as well as different fundamental assumptions about the place of reason in politics.

A second similarity with populism, closely linked to the first, is the rejection of an expertise which, while genuine, is self-serving rather than at the service of the community. A prime example of this kind of expert is Thrasymachus in Book I of the *Republic* who argues for the cynical view that politicians always rule in their own self-interest. Part of the dramatic purpose of Thrasymachus in the dialogue is to reveal the true nature of rulers in democracies like Athens, a view which finds echoes in contemporary populist criticism of the alleged corruption and incompetence of many politicians. But Thrasymachus not only lays bare the nature of such rulers, he also exemplifies them in his own person. Thrasymachus is a Sophist and Sophists are often portrayed by Plato as a prime example of the pernicious effect of having some genuine skill in dialectic which is nevertheless incomplete. This is because they have been partly, though inadequately, trained in philosophy and, having become corrupted, sell their expertise in argument to the highest bidder. That is what so-called experts in democratic societies are like, Plato is arguing: their claim to expertise is a sham.

For Plato the lack of true expertise is fundamentally a matter of intellect, of the long, hard, self-denying education that ultimately, in the most famous metaphor of the *Republic*, allows a person to leave the cave with its shadows and illusions and become illuminated by the true light of the sun. But the person so illuminated realises a duty to go into the cave and try to guide those still caught up in illusions (*Republic* 514a–17c). This is a powerful image which resonates with much populist thought: the view of the rightful rulers as members of the community, not above it, not seeking to benefit from their rule but willing to sacrifice their own happiness for the greater good of the community. The philosopher rulers have no private property, wealth or family life: they sacrifice all that for the greater good of serving the community (*Republic* 415d–27c). Moreover, they are not cosmopolitans, their commitment is wholly focused on the community of the republic they govern. Populists who are nationalists often share Plato's view that only those who have a complete understanding should rule, but they amend the argument to define such an understanding of the truth to at least partly redefine the communal identity of the ruler in terms of nationalism. On this view, one cannot expect someone who is not in harmony with the nation (someone who is a foreigner by birth or who is cosmopolitan in outlook) to sufficiently understand the values and principles of the nation. There are powerful, consciously Platonic, echoes of this in Rousseau's view of the importance of small communities and civic obligation.[13]

Because, unlike Plato, populists are not opposed to democracy they might in some respects appear to be closer to the Athenian democracy of Plato's day than to modern representative democracy, with an emphasis on trusting the views of the ordinary people. But, like Rousseau, they might believe that only a democracy which expresses the general will (which Rousseau thought Athenian democracy had ceased to do by the time of Plato) is legitimate. Those who do not share the values of the general will cannot be members of the community.

The significance of the Socratic Method is of great importance to any debate about the proper nature of education and of the relationship between education and society. The Method has been seen, and rightly so, as an extremely helpful model when teaching critical thinking, which is a fundamental part of education in a liberal democratic society. It is, however, crucial to differentiate between good teaching methods and the claim that the application of such methods inevitably leads to particular kinds of political societies. Taken in isolation as a method, through the relentless negative criticism of the ideas of others,[14] it can also have a powerful impact as a tool of illiberal politics and illiberal education. In this way it illustrates the point that critical thinking divorced from a respect for evidence and from the idea of civility, both ideas which will be discussed in the next chapter as they appear in Locke's work, may actually contribute to the development of illiberal education

Plato would have rejected many populist arguments, and populist movements, and would have seen them as pandering to the worst aspects of democracy and the democratic soul. Plato's ideal republic, with its highly educated rulers guiding a docile and politically uninvolved society, might also seem to embody a populist's worst nightmare. As we will see in Chapters 3 and 5, liberal thinkers such as Locke and Mill shared some of Plato's misgivings about democracy, partly because they believed in the importance of rulers being well-educated and being able to make the kind of skilled judgments which would be beyond the ability of the untrained majority. In that respect the successes of liberal democracy and representative government in the nineteenth and twentieth centuries at the expense of the majority of people being able to have a more direct say in policy making laid some of the foundations for the re-emergence of populism in the twenty-first century. This was particularly because experts seemed to lose control of the economy during the financial crisis of 2008, but it also drew on longer term concerns, such as the perceived democratic deficit in the governance of the European Union.

Despite Plato's dislike of democracy there are aspects of his thinking which have some similarities with populism. It would be wrong to argue that there is any direct link between contemporary populists and Plato's *Republic*, but there is an indirect route through Plato's influence on Rousseau and Rousseau's own contribution to the foundations of populism. One way this is apparent is in the use of the Socratic Method to undermine expert opinion leading to an erosion of support for experts, which could feed into populism. Closely linked to this is Plato's argument that current society cannot be reformed but must be recreated – an idea which profoundly influenced Rousseau and which has echoes in much populist thought. In both these cases education is key to ensuring that only the wrong kinds of experts, or ideas, or values are questioned and to lay the foundations of the newer and better society which is to come.

Notes

1 The *Republic* is conventionally divided into ten 'Books', though this is the work of later editors. I follow the standard practice by referring to Plato's works using Staphanus' numbering system. The best modern edition of Plato's work in English translation is the *Complete Works* edited by John M. Cooper (1997). The edition of *Republic* in the Cambridge Texts in the History of Political Thought series (2000) has a very useful introduction and notes.
2 The rule of the Thirty Tyrants was a period of dictatorship imposed by Sparta as part of its conditions for peace following its defeat of Athens at the end of the Peloponnesian War. As we will see below (pp. 38–9), Socrates was accused by some critics of being more in sympathy with the values, though not the particular practice, of the Tyrants than with the values of Athenian democracy.
3 For a critical review of Mitchell's argument see Atack 2017: 578–80.
4 Following his account of the three parts of the state, Plato describes the three parts of the soul as reason, spiritedness (or honour) and desire (*Republic* 434d–41c). The just person is one who is ruled by reason which controls spiritedness and desire. Democratic societies are marked by people in whom the three parts of the soul are in constant competition and so their lives are chaotic, with no settled purpose (*Republic* 561c–2a).
5 From the time of the publication of *The Open Society and Its Enemies* Popper has been heavily criticised for his characterisation of Plato as a totalitarian, but see Blackburn 2006: 52–8 for a recent sympathetic discussion of Popper's views.
6 A fuller analysis of Plato's apparent relegation of most people to a life devoid of intellectual enlightenment has to be balanced by his metaphysical view of human being as living many lives through reincarnation, especially in the myth of Er in the *Republic* Book X, though that is beyond the scope of our present discussion.
7 This is discussed further in Chapter 3.
8 Rousseau in his *Letter to M. d'Alembert on the Theatre* (1960), appeals to these arguments in his attempt to prevent a theatre being established in Geneva – see Chapter 4.
9 It is an important feature of this education that it relegates empirical information to the realm of belief rather than knowledge. Plato believes that the physical world is constantly changing and so there cannot be any certainty based on our experience of

any part of it. In his dialogue *Cratylus* he has Socrates refer to Heraclitus who expresses this idea by saying that because the water in a river is always flowing it is impossible to step into the same river twice (*Cratylus* 402a). This is one of the basic differences between the philosophies of Plato and Locke, and a source of their contrasting theories of education.

10 See also Blackburn 2006: 52–8; Cartledge 2016: 98. Liberal defenders of Plato against Popper include Annas 1981: Chapter 7, especially 74–6; Pappas 1995: 195–200; Ryan 2012: 47–70.
11 For a succinct account of the questions surrounding the chronological order of Plato's works see Cooper's 'Introduction' to Plato 1997: viii–xviii.
12 It is also referred to by the technical term *Elenchus*.
13 We will discuss in Chapter 4 similarities with Rousseau's theory of education in *Emile*, which emphasises the need for the purity of the soul to be a good person and a good citizen and also with his account of the education of citizens in *Considerations on the Government of Poland* (2019b).
14 Judith Shklar argues, in *Men and Citizens*, that Rousseau is a social critic, not someone who is a political activist or even envisages radical change. In the Preface to the second edition she writes: 'His great aim was to disturb, awaken and so shake us into recognising the actualities of our lives' (Shklar 1985: vii) There is a similar problem with Rousseau's approach as there is with Plato's; that radical criticism without the mechanism for bringing about positive alternatives, and the means of putting that alternative in practice, has the potential of being wholly destructive. It also opens the door to the possibility of scapegoating certain individuals or groups if things go wrong. Because the ideas of the philosophers or of the general will cannot be wrong, the explanation must lie elsewhere, with those who are not prepared – or not able – to submit to the superior wisdom or be in harmony with the general will. Education is one of the keys to ensuring that people do not deviate from the correct path.

3 John Locke
A liberal philosophy of education

Locke's writings

The political and educational philosophy of John Locke offers a stark contrast to that of Plato. Locke was a medical scientist and an active member of the Royal Society of London, as well as a philosopher, and his theory of knowledge, based upon a defence of the primacy of empirical knowledge, reflects his commitment to the scientific method which was developing in the seventeenth century. His liberal defence of political freedom, based on the moral autonomy of the individual, and his empiricist epistemology are fundamentally opposed to Plato's ideal of a strictly hierarchical society ruled by philosophers in possession of absolute truth arrived at by abstract reasoning and for whom information acquired through the senses leads most frequently to error and confusion.

Locke's work, published in the latter part of the seventeenth century, had a profound effect on the Enlightenment thinkers of the eighteenth century (Pagden 2013: 63–4) and on the development of liberalism in Europe and North America. Like Locke, Enlightenment thinkers such as the French *philosophes* Voltaire and Denis Diderot and the Americans Thomas Jefferson and James Madison stress the importance of reason being informed by empirical knowledge, and the relevance of such knowledge to the development of liberal political principles and practice.[1] In arguing this way, they are often very critical of the governments of their own day[2] which, they claim, frequently fall short of these standards. At the same time, many Enlightenment thinkers are also wary of placing too much power in the hands of what they see as the irrational and uneducated masses. Appeals to the natural wisdom of the great majority of 'ordinary people', lacking education and guided by feelings and emotions as they are perceived to be, are rejected by those like Voltaire who believe in the superior power of educated reason.[3]

In contrast to those people who held Locke in such high esteem, Rousseau's argument, that a truly just society would not be one based primarily on reason and specialised knowledge but on the deeper values of society expressed through the general will, means that his relationship to the Enlightenment, and to liberalism, is, to say the least, ambiguous. This conflict between the liberal ideals of the Enlightenment, strongly influenced by Locke, and the contrasting emphasis on the value of the untarnished expression of the deep values of particular societies, underlie two distinct ways of thinking about political societies, and of the type of education they require, throughout modern European and North American history. The current conflict between liberalism and populism is the most recent manifestation of this.

Today, Locke's best known, and still widely studied, books are *An Essay Concerning Human Understanding* (henceforth *Essay*)[4] (Locke 1975) and *Two Treatises of Government* (henceforth *Two Treatises*) (Locke 1988) along with his *A Letter Concerning Toleration* (1993), first published in Latin as *Epistola de Tolerantia*. All three were extensively read in the eighteenth century but his *Some Thoughts Concerning Education* (henceforth *Some Thoughts*) (Locke 1968; 1989; 1996) was at least as popular and played a significant role in shaping progressive thinking about education in a liberal society. It was also read closely by Rousseau who discusses it frequently in *Emile*, sometimes agreeing with Locke, but often criticising him for what he regards as the Englishman's shortcomings. Rousseau's ambiguous attitude towards Locke's work reflects not only a similar ambiguity on his part towards the Enlightenment but also, as I will argue in Chapter 4, to many of the central principles of liberalism. In this chapter I will refer to the *Two Treatises* and other of Locke's political writings, including his work on toleration, but the primary focus will be on *Some Thoughts* and *Of the Conduct of the Understanding* (henceforth *Conduct*) (Locke 1996). *Conduct* is a short work which was originally intended by Locke as an additional chapter for later editions of the *Essay* but was only published posthumously and separately. As the title implies, *Of the Conduct of the Understanding* is concerned with how to think correctly and in the book Locke often relates this to education and to the importance of education for helping to develop mature and responsible citizens.

The question of the relationship between Locke's writings, and the permissibility of drawing upon several texts to develop a single argument, was regarded as problematic during Locke's lifetime and continues to be much discussed. Some have argued that Locke wrote what were often effectively discrete works with little or no overlap – the *Essay* and the *Two Treatises* are often cited, for example, as having incompatible theories of innate ideas. This view began with Voltaire and has been followed by recent writers such as David Lay Williams (Williams 2007: 20–3). Other writers, such as John Yolton and Jean Yolton, have argued that while Locke's work is not systematic there are many connections between his different writings. They note especially the closeness between *Some Thoughts* and the *Two Treatises*, arguing that the latter work is concerned with the role of the citizen in society while *Some Thoughts* is concerned (at least in significant part) with preparing a young person to take his place in that society as a good citizen ('Introduction' in Locke 1989: 18). More recently, Nicholas Jolley argues in *Toleration and Understanding in Locke* (Jolley 2016) that although there are some inconsistencies between Locke's works there is a greater unity in his thought than has often been recognised and that the concept of toleration, which preoccupied Locke throughout his life, affords the best way to seeing these connections. In what follows I will treat Locke's work as broadly consistent.

That said, it is also important to stress that *Some Thoughts* is written in a different style, and with a different purpose, to that of the *Essay*, the *Two Treatises* and the *Letter on Toleration*. *Some Thoughts* began as a series of letters which Locke wrote to his friend Edward Clarke in reply to Clarke's request for advice on the education of his son. Locke's advice both to Clarke and to other friends became well known and, as Locke says in the epistle dedicatory, he has been 'consulted of late by so many ... who profess themselves at a loss how to breed their children ...'. It is not particularly surprising that Locke was seen this way as he had considerable experience of teaching children and young men. His experience as a university teacher at Christ Church College, Oxford meant that he had close pastoral as well as teaching responsibilities with respect to those in his charge (Cranston 1957: 70–3; Woolhouse 2007: 47–9; Axtell's comments in Locke 1968: 37–41). In addition, he later became tutor to a number of children. The education of Edward Clarke's son seems not to have been the success that Locke claimed it was in the epistle dedicatory to *Some Thoughts* (Woolhouse 2007: 306–8, 416–17) but there were other notable achievements, the most significant of whom was the grandson of Ashley Cooper. Locke acted as director of education for the boy who later, as the third Earl of Shaftsbury, became a philosopher of some distinction. In his published philosophical work, the third Earl disagreed on important points with Locke but nevertheless still referred to him with affection and respect as 'my friend and foster father' (quoted in Woolhouse 2007: 97; see also Koganzon 2016: 556). Locke would regard Shaftsbury's independence of thought as an indication of the success of his education.

Locke was critical of much of the education of his own day. From his time as a pupil at Westminster School, where he was championed by the headmaster, Richard Busby (Woolhouse 2007: 15; Cranston 1957: 18–28), and through which he gained a scholarship to Christ Church College, Oxford, he retained a dislike of parts of the curriculum, such as rhetoric and, perhaps more fundamentally, a disapproval of many of the methods used in teaching, including the practice of corporal punishment (Woolhouse 2007: 14–15). This disapproval is reflected in his argument in *Some Thoughts* that corporal punishment should be used sparingly, in only the most exceptional cases (Locke 1989: 112–13, 144–6) He was also highly critical of the scholasticism and Aristotelianism which were dominant in Oxford at the time when he was a student, and which his own later philosophical work did much to undermine.

Education and epistemology

Locke's eminence in the latter part of his life was built to a considerable extent upon the success of the *Essay* following its publication in 1689, and the reception of *Some Thoughts* on its publication some years later benefited considerably from the knowledge that both were written by the same author. These two books were rare among Locke's works in that he acknowledged his authorship of both of them, reinforcing the view that his work on education draws upon the epistemological views of the *Essay*.[5]

Central to Locke's epistemology is his argument concerning the basis of knowledge. What, he asks at the beginning of Book II of the *Essay* is the source of our claims to know anything? His answer forms one of the most celebrated passages in early modern philosophy.

> Let us then suppose the mind to be, as we say, white paper, void of all characters, without any ideas; how comes it to be furnished? Whence comes it by that vast store which the busy and boundless fancy of man has painted on it, with an almost endless variety? Whence has it all the materials of reason and knowledge? To this I answer, in one word, from experience; in all that our knowledge is founded, and from that it ultimately derives itself. Our observation employed either about external sensible objects, or about the internal operations of our minds, perceived and reflected on by ourselves, is that which supplies our understandings with all the materials of thinking. These two are the fountains of knowledge, from whence all the ideas we have, or can naturally have, do spring.
> (Locke 1824: *Essay*, Book II, Chapter 1, Section 2)

It follows from the claim that knowledge of the external world is dependent on our senses that the mind at birth is, in the metaphor he employs at the beginning of the above quotation, a sheet of empty white paper 'void of all characters without any ideas'. One inference that has been drawn from this picture of the mind has had considerable implications for education. Some later liberal thinkers have argued that if all minds are equally empty at birth, all children are in principle intellectually equal and that therefore they could, and arguably should, have the same educational experience and opportunities (see Tarcov 1984: 109). A particularly radical, though less liberal, version of this argument is to be found in the writings of Behaviourists such as John Watson.

> Give me a dozen healthy infants, well-formed, and my own specified world to bring them up in and I'll guarantee to take any one at random and train him to become any type of specialist I might select – doctor, lawyer, artist, merchant-chief and, yes, even beggar-man and thief, regardless of his talents, penchants, tendencies, abilities, vocations, and race of his ancestors.
> (Watson 1970: 82)

Locke's account of the mind is rather subtler than many eighteenth and nineteenth century empiricist interpretations suggest, and far from the views of twentieth century Behaviourists like Watson. The passage quoted above, which compares the mind of a new born infant to an empty sheet of paper, has to be read in the context of its place in the *Essay*. Coming at the beginning of Book II, it follows on immediately from Locke's criticism of the theory of innate ideas in Book I, where he attacks the view that the mind is born fully equipped with distinct principles, or ideas, particularly of morality, theology, mathematics and logic. The theory of innate ideas was widely held by those who regarded themselves as Platonists – philosophers such as Descartes and Leibniz and the Cambridge Platonists – who argue that the evidence of the senses is too unreliable to serve as the basis of knowledge. This being the case, the only sure source of knowledge must be innate ideas implanted by God in the human mind, without which neither the truth of theology or morality, nor of mathematics and logic, could be established. Locke's attack on this theory, and his use of the metaphor of the white sheet of paper as part of his strategy, has to be understood as an attack on a particular theory of epistemology, not a direct statement on the structure of the mind.

John Yolton and Jean Yolton argue that Locke never intended the metaphor of a white sheet to be taken to mean that everyone's mind at birth was the same. In their introduction to the Clarendon edition of *Some Thoughts*, they maintain that Locke was fully aware of the differences of character between children at birth, a point they make in the context of Locke's discussion of the need for parents to recognise the differences in 'Temper and the particular Constitution of [each child's] Mind ...' (Locke 1989: Section 100; for Yolton and Yolton's discussion see note 39 on page 162). To reinforce this point, we can point to the final section of *Some Thoughts* where Locke uses the terms 'white Paper' and 'Wax' to describe how children might be moulded through their education, but each needs to be treated differently because of the variety of 'Tempers ... Inclinations and particular Defaults that are to be found in Children' (Locke 1989: Section 217)

A good deal of the discussion of *Some Thoughts* makes no sense if we read Locke as arguing that education is simply a matter of inputting information to a passive mind; indeed such a reading of Locke is profoundly misleading in that it undermines his liberal purposes in seeing education as a means of developing children's minds to be active and critical. Locke constantly emphasises the importance of the teacher understanding and responding to what he refers to as a child's 'natural genius and constitution' (Locke 1824: *Some Thoughts*, Section 66). Although he claims that education contributes more than anything else to the differences in the manners and abilities of men (*Some Thoughts*, Section 32), he argues that it would be wrong to try to alter these fundamental traits.

> We must not hope wholly to change their original tempers, nor make the gay pensive and grave, nor the melancholy sportive, without spoiling them. God has stamped certain characters upon men's minds, which, like their shapes, may perhaps be a little mended; but can hardly be totally altered and transformed into the contrary.
>
> (Locke 1824: *Some Thoughts*, Section 66)

Locke's reference to the varying characters stamped upon different men's minds indicates that although empty of particular ideas at birth, individual minds already have particular features which predispose them to interact with the world in different ways. This links to a related argument which is of great importance in Locke's thinking, an emphasis on the importance of active, rather than passive, thinking. This is illustrated in his discussion of reading in *Conduct*, where he refers to the importance of an active engagement with what one reads.

'Reading furnishes the mind only with materials of knowledge, it is thinking makes what we read ours' (Locke 1824: *Conduct*, Section 20). Children should be taught to read in this way, so that they learn the habit of questioning what they read. Education of the young is vitally important because, properly conducted, it inculcates into them the ideals of critical thinking which should enrich their own lives in adulthood and allow them to in turn enrich and strengthen the society of which they are a part.

> This is that which I think great readers are apt to be mistaken in. Those who have read of every thing, are thought to understand every thing too; but it is not always so. Reading furnishes the mind only with materials of knowledge, it is thinking makes what we read ours. We are of the ruminating kind, and it is not enough to cram ourselves with a great load of collections; unless we chew them over again, they will not give us strength and nourishment.
> (Locke 1824: *Conduct*, Section 20)

This is an argument which has echoes in Friere's criticism, referred to in Chapter 2 of this volume, of the banking view of education in *The Pedagogy of the Oppressed*. Offering a radical critique based on a strongly Marxist influenced version of Liberation Theology, of what he considers to be the corrupt, hierarchical society in his native Brazil, Freire claims that education in Brazil, as in many other places, consists in educators 'depositing' information in children's heads, as a person might deposit money in a bank (Freire 1993: 53). The information is there to be retrieved when needed, to enable workers to fulfil their roles in the economy, but the dogmatic way in which it is taught, and the passive way in which it is received, means that those who have been schooled in this way lack the skills and understanding to be critical of what they have learnt.

This banking view of education is based on an empiricist epistemology which sees young minds as malleable and education as a form of social conditioning, a view not unlike that expressed in the quotation from John Watson's *Behaviorism* (1970), referred to above (p. 47). It is important to emphasise that Locke's epistemology does not support such a view and is, on the contrary, strongly opposed to it. In this respect Locke's liberal theory of education, although very different from Freire's theory in other ways, has a similar potential for being critical of the status quo; an important reminder of the radical potential in his liberalism.

Some limits of Locke's liberal philosophy of education

Locke's epistemology, then, does not imply a passive view of education. There are, though, other differences between Locke and Freire. Chief of these is that unlike, Freire, Locke is not a revolutionary, in the sense of wanting to overthrow the established economic and social order. He argues for a defence of calm, steady thought, in which the individual has the ultimate responsibility for his own opinions, and that these opinions should be frequently and carefully analysed, reappraised and, where appropriate, corrected. Marxist critics of Locke's liberal individualism have sometimes attacked him, at this point as elsewhere, for what Marx himself characterises as Locke's atomistic view of the individual and society. Yet this misunderstands Locke, for whom thinking should not be a solitary matter and who argues that the person who neglects to listen to others, and engage in open and frank discussion, seriously narrows the scope of his knowledge and the development of his critical abilities.

It is tempting to see a contrast between Freire's revolutionary fervour and Locke's more sedate approach as a contrast between the rebel Freire, forced to flee his home country under pressure from an oppressive government, with Locke the respectable English gentleman and, late in life, a pillar of the establishment. Such a view would be seriously misleading. Locke was deeply involved in the opposition politics of the 1680s and had to flee to Holland after the fall of his patron Lord Shaftsbury. As John Dunn has written, by '1682, if not before, Shaftsbury himself, and Locke, Algernon Sydney Lord William Russell and the Earl of Essex were all gambling with their lives' (Dunn 1984: 9). Locke is powerfully committed to change and unless this is appreciated, the radical nature of his approach to education, as much as to politics as a whole, cannot be fully understood.

There is, though, another contrast with Freire which is more problematic. Locke's political philosophy is radical and subversive when understood in the context of late Restoration England, but as even the most sympathetic of commentators on Locke's writings on education, including Tarcov (1984: 5), point out, his advice was aimed at the gentry, not at the lower orders. In Section 7 of *Conduct*, Locke contrasts the narrow mindedness of the ploughman with the greater intellectual flexibility of the man of leisure, explaining that scientific knowledge is available only to those who have the time to devote to it. This might seem to imply a defence of class divisions, a view which could be taken to reinforce C. B. McPherson's criticisms of Locke in his *Political Theory of Possessive Individualism* for whom Locke's theory of individualism renders class divisions inevitable (1962). It might also suggest an elitism in one of the founders of liberal thought which populists could see as indicating a fundamental flaw at the heart of liberalism, present from its foundations in the early modern period and carrying over into the mainstream thinking of Enlightenment *philosophes* such as Voltaire, and, with more far reaching consequences, founders of the American Republic such as Jefferson and Madison. As we will see in the next chapter, Rousseau thought criticisms along these lines were very significant.

Such criticisms, though, are misplaced. While it is true that Locke does not question the social order which leaves the ploughman without time or opportunity to improve his understanding this does not mean that he believes the ploughman is necessarily inherently inferior to the man of leisure. Rather it reflects the different opportunities in life. It becomes clearer that Locke does not think that members of the leisured class are inherently more skilled at thinking and reflection when in *Conduct* Section 8 he discusses the importance for all Christians to come to a clear understanding of the fundamental principles of their faith. In a particularly telling example he refers to the Huguenot Protestants among the skilled artisans and peasants of France who, he claims, often have a deeper and more sophisticated understanding of theological issues than many of the more highly educated and leisured Protestants in England. This is because the Huguenots, under intense pressure from the French government to convert to Roman Catholicism, have a much greater incentive to think through the principles and implications of their faith. Locke broadens this argument in *Conduct* Section 23 where he argues that the study of theology is the duty of every man and something which all rational people are capable of. He goes on to argue, in a manner familiar from his writings on toleration, that in a free society people should be at liberty to work out and express their opinions on religion:

> This is that science [i.e. theology] which would truly enlarge men's minds, were it studied, or permitted to be studied every where, with that freedom love of truth and charity which it teaches, and were not made, contrary to its nature, the occasion of strife, faction, malignity, and narrow impositions.
> (Locke 1824: *Conduct*, Section 23)

Locke's arguments do not logically commit him to the belief that working-class men might never have the time and formal education to be able to take part in political debate and to vote. That is not to say that he envisaged this happening and indeed, to use one of his own arguments in part against him, he suffered from the prejudices of his day. From a broader liberal perspective it is important to bear in mind the later liberal view, discussed in Chapter 1, of the need to allow for development of liberal principles, a point reinforced by Locke's own general epistemological view on the need to revise one's opinions in the light of new evidence and experience. This liberal argument about the need to be willing to revise principles recurs, for example, in Mill's contribution to the debates about the ability of working-class people to acquire sufficient education to be able to vote in a serious and responsible manner. For much of the nineteenth century even liberals such as the Liberal Prime Minister William Gladstone were uncertain as to whether this was possible and it was only with the extension of the franchise in the Second Reform Act that prominent members of the Liberal Party, including Gladstone himself, came to accept that the working classes were able to make measured and responsible judgements about politics. This point will be returned to in the discussion of Mill in Chapter 5 but for the moment it is important to stress that a rational, liberal-minded person of the nineteenth century (a John Stuart Mill or a Harriet Taylor Mill, for example) would in part be building on Locke's own insights in examining his or her opinions to welcome the extension of the franchise and the wider political participation of adult citizens as a whole. While populists are correct to argue that liberals sometimes defend the power and privileges of wealthy elites, they are wrong to suggest that this is an inherent defect of liberalism. The critical thinking which liberals stress as vital to a healthy political system, and which they argue should be taught as part of the education required by a liberal state, ought always to involve a critical re-evaluation of how liberal ideas are applied.

This raises two questions which now need to be addressed. The first is: what precisely does Locke mean by critical thinking? The second raises a broader question that is potentially problematic for all liberal thought: is a liberal education which provides learners with the ability to think critically able to avoid the charge that it will still inevitably reinforce an uncritical acceptance of those liberal values which are essential parts of the foundations of a liberal society?

Critical thinking and expertise

Locke's discussion of critical thinking rests on two of his most important philosophical beliefs, the empiricist theory of knowledge and the responsibility of individuals to do their civic duty.

Empiricism, in Locke's understanding, requires intellectual modesty. The theory that all claims to knowledge rest upon evidence places considerable limits on what a person can claim to know, as opposed to what they merely believe to be the case. Even when a theory is based on a large body of evidence, new information may be discovered which will force a re-evaluation, or even a rejection, of the theory. Empiricism can never lead to certainty of the kind which Plato envisages in the *Republic*. Indeed, it is fear of the instability of claims to knowledge based upon empirical evidence that lies behind Plato's rejection of empiricism, and the position of seventeenth century philosophers like Descartes, Leibniz and the Cambridge Platonists who followed him at this point.

Locke, by contrast, embraces the lack of certainty. In the 'Epistle to the Reader', which serves as his preface to the *Essay*, he writes: 'Every step which the mind takes in its progress towards knowledge, makes some discovery, which is not only new, but the best too, for the time at least'. In maintaining that all claims to knowledge are provisional and subject to revision, and thereby rejecting the Platonic view that it is possible to arrive at an understanding of unchanging, timeless truths, he also rejects the basis of Plato's theory of education. Plato argues that the purpose of education is for those who have true knowledge to guide people to take their place uncritically in a rigidly ordered society. By contrast, Locke's theory of knowledge leads to a view of education which encourages learners to be open-minded and critical of received opinions, both when they are engaged in formal study and as a preparation for their lives as citizens.

How is this open-mindedness to be promoted? There are, Locke says, two things which are essential. These are to maintain an attitude of indifference between the claims of alternative propositions to being true until one has good, sound well-argued and well-evidenced reasons for choosing between them and when (or if) one has made such a decision to be willing to re-examine one's reasons in the light of new arguments and new evidence. These two things, being of such great importance to the way in which a person leads his life, should be of particular concern in education.

Locke says a good deal about the benefits of indifference between theories because he believes that most people are brought up from childhood simply believing the widely held views in their society without ever examining them, or thinking through what reasons there might be for holding them. Yet indifference might seem a strange value to emphasise – surely, one might argue, indifference is a curse of political and social life – one should be committed to improving the lot of one's fellow citizens not standing idly by while others suffer injustice. It is important to distinguish between two different senses of indifference. The first sense is that of epistemological indifference where we have no good grounds for either assenting to or dissenting from the truth claims of a particular proposition. The second is moral or political indifference to the attitudes, actions or sufferings of another when we nevertheless are aware of an obligation to that person. Locke does not argue that we should be indifferent in the second sense, but he does maintain that a true moral obligation is only possible once we have a clear, rational knowledge of the underlying principle and an understanding of how that obligation should be discharged.

On the face of it this seems cold and unfeeling but there are two ways of defending Locke from such a criticism. The first is that acting without a proper understanding may lead to unfortunate consequences. The other is that moral decision making of this kind does not take place in a vacuum and it is one of the areas in which the education of a good person and a good citizen are intertwined. We learn to think and act morally as we develop as moral beings in society with others but also as we learn to think analytically and to critically evaluate the situations in which we find ourselves.

This argument is reflected in some of the current discussion of the relationship between indifference, in the second sense, and populism. People have become indifferent about politics, and between different political values and ideals, because, it is argued, they have been disillusioned by the way in which the elites which have come to dominate institutions in representative democracies use education and the media to mislead them. Convinced that there is no way of discovering the truth even about the things which affect them most, such as the economy, they stop trying to understand and lose interest. Having become disillusioned, the argument continues, they are then more susceptible to populist rhetoric which appeals to feelings of anger and disillusionment and promises to take radical steps to address their grievances. Locke's response to this is to say that under these circumstances it is essential to reserve judgement.

For Locke, appealing to feelings rather than reason sacrifices one of the greatest strengths of a just society – the ability of its individual members, through thinking rationally and critically, to challenge the policies of its rulers. Early on in Section 3 of *Conduct* Locke argues that reason is the most important element in human conduct but that it is often abused. He suggests three reasons why people do not use their reason properly.

They allow their ideas and beliefs to be guided by others, such as 'parents, neighbours, ministers …', they are guided by their passion rather than reason and they have too narrow an understanding of the world beyond their own particular interests and prejudices. In essence, they do not enter into debate and discussion with a wide variety of people of different opinions. 'Thus', he writes in a later section, 'we are taught to clothe our minds as we do our bodies, after the fashion in vogue, and it is accounted fantasticalness, or something worse, not to do so' (Locke 1824: *Conduct*, Section 34).

The first reason points to the danger of relying on the views of others, a principle which was to become a staple of Enlightenment thought. Although it warns against relying on anyone else's opinions, it might be applied particularly to experts. This is not to say that the opinions of experts are worthless, or to be ignored, but that they should be analysed critically.

The second reason is a reiteration of Locke's constant fear of the danger that when reason is subordinated to emotion and feeling, people can easily be manipulated by unscrupulous politicians and clergy. This is the basis of a recurring liberal criticism of populist appeals to the 'natural' emotions and feelings of 'ordinary' people, such as patriotism and identity with one's own kind rather than with liberal, cosmopolitanism view of the world based on rationality.[6]

The third reason is particularly important for the discussion over expertise and popular opinion because Locke warns against the dangers of both. In part his argument is against narrow expertise. A person may have detailed knowledge of a narrow subject area, and be able to apply that knowledge within the subject area very well, but fail to grasp the wider implications for people or events beyond the narrow domain of his or her expertise. So, for example, a person might have specialist knowledge of mathematics and economics which enable him or her to calculate the economically optimal choice between a range of educational policies but lack a broader social or political awareness to see that the consequences of implementing a particular policy would be detrimental to the children and families affected.

But Locke's argument also challenges populist assumptions that the people, rather than the experts, know what is best. In part, this follows on from the second reason, but more fundamentally, Locke's argument suggests that popular opinion suffers from the same narrowness of focus as the expert, as he explains in the following passage from *Conduct*.

> We are all short-sighted, and very often see but one side of a matter: our views are not extended to all that has a connexion with it. From this defect I think no man is free. We see but in part, and we know but in part, and therefore it is no wonder we conclude not right from our partial views. This might instruct the proudest esteemer of his own parts, how useful it is to talk and consult with others, even such as come short of him in capacity, quickness, and penetration: for, since no one sees all, and we generally have different prospects of the same thing, according to our different, as I may say, positions to it; it is not incongruous to think, nor beneath any man to try, whether another may not have notions of things, which have escaped him, and which his reason would make use of, if they came into his mind.
>
> (Locke 1824: *Conduct*, Section 3)

Locke's solution is to argue for a broader general understanding of issues and for open-minded and free-ranging debate, coupled with the need to maintain an attitude of indifference where there is insufficient information to make a rational choice. It is an idea which reflects his view in *Some Thoughts* that education should not aim to create specialists but well-rounded individuals who are able to understand and debate a wide range of issues. The key here is that education should prepare people to become engaged and active citizens. The expert (such as in Locke's own area of medicine to which he devoted much of his adult life) can be of great value, but the expert must temper his or her understanding with a wider social knowledge, which is why Locke argues that there is time once the child becomes an adult for him or her to specialise.

It might be appropriate, as Locke claims it is in a letter to the Countess of Peterborough, written in reply to her request for advice on the education of her son (Locke 1968: 396), to teach a child the basics of human anatomy, but clearly unwise to entrust the practice of surgery to a child, just as it would be equally absurd to entrust surgery to an adult who lacked the appropriate knowledge and expertise. Expertise in such cases is invaluable but even in the case of a skill-based expertise such as surgery the generally educated citizen has a right to argue for the laying down of certain boundaries. The strength of the debate over abortion in the contemporary United States, as elsewhere in the modern world, is indicative of this, where the argument is not primarily about the skills or medical knowledge of the surgeon but of the moral status of the foetus. If it is maintained that the moral status of the foetus changes at a certain stage in its development, appropriate technical expertise is clearly relevant. If, though, it is argued on religious grounds that the foetus is a person from conception, or on feminist grounds that the foetus has no moral status independent of the mother until it is born, the opinion of the medical expert has no greater intellectual status than that of any other person who has given serious thought to the matter. It is also important to emphasise that in Locke's view, neither being a priest nor being a woman would grant privileged understanding when considering the two arguments. The argument is to be decided, if it can be decided at all, on rational grounds that are open to all wish to engage with the debate. The proviso 'if it can be decided at all' is necessary because of Locke's view of the need to recognise that reason often does not supply a definitive answer and that indifference is the most appropriate response in many situations. One of the most important purposes of education, upon which Locke places considerable emphasis, is to recognise when one has reached the limits of what can be decided rationally and not pass over into unfounded dogmatic belief.

The duty of experts according to this argument is limited to offering judgments within their area of expertise. But even when they do make legitimate claims, they are still not immune from the criticism of those who lack their particular expertise. They also have to understand the broader social context in which their expertise is to be applied and as citizens to be engaged in society in such a way that they can contribute to the well-being of the community.

The opinions of experts then become something which can be subject to the serious, critical scrutiny of the well-educated active citizen. This is why a general education is so important. People who have been taught the basics of anatomy and human biology, for example, should be able to understand arguments about the physical development of a human foetus. Such understanding will help in following debates (such as those that take place in the United Kingdom from time to time) over at what point the foetus is sufficiently viable to make abortion morally unacceptable.

There is also a requirement for specialists to communicate their expert opinions as clearly as possible to the wider community, and not to hide behind jargon. Locke is scathing in the *Essay* about specialists who use obscure language as a means of mystifying the general population. In Book III he has in mind particularly the Scholastics, but his words might apply to many who claim specialist expertise and arcane knowledge from which the majority are excluded through their ignorance of the appropriate language:

> [t]his artificial ignorance, and learned gibberish, prevailed mightily in these last ages, by the interest and artifice of those who found no easier way to that pitch of authority and dominion they have attained, than by amusing the men of business and ignorant with hard words, or employing the ingenious and idle in intricate disputes about unintelligible terms, and holding them perpetually entangled in that endless labyrinth.
> (Locke 1824: *Essay*, Book III, Chapter 10)

Locke is not opposed to specialist knowledge, nor to expertise as such. His own interest and expertise in medicine throughout his adult life are clear evidence of this. What he is opposed to is the abuse of this knowledge as a form of social exclusion and control – an exercise of 'authority and dominion'. Again, the most effective way of preventing this abuse is to have a broadly educated citizenry who are able to probe and challenge the arguments of experts.

This has important implications for populism. On Locke's argument, all citizens have both a right and a duty to critically scrutinise the opinions of experts, but they also have a duty to be well-informed and open-minded: they should not allow others to do their thinking for them, even (perhaps especially) if those others are the leaders of a political party or social movement. Populist critics of liberal elitism have a duty also, to ensure if they take power that the education system is reformed to provide this more general education for all children.[7]

Education and the state

Locke's argument that education should promote critical thinking raises a new problem for a liberal philosophy of education. How far can a liberal state allow educational institutions to challenge the very intellectual and political foundations upon which the liberal state is built? Opponents of the educational policies of populist governments such as that of Viktor Orbán argue that they are deficient because they lack the capacity to build a principle of critical re-evaluation into their educational programmes. Populist governments, so this argument goes, cannot allow the state education system to encourage criticism of society's most important values. To this argument populists might reply that liberals are in the same position – for all their vaunted praise of critical thinking, liberals cannot permit their education system to allow searching questions which threaten the underlying values of the liberal state.

Posed this way the difference between liberal and populist visions of society is not caused by a conflict between a liberal championing of individual autonomy and a populist emphasis on social order and stability but by two different views of what is required for social order and stability. If that is so, it appears that questions about the scope of individual autonomy, and also of critical thinking, are subservient issues decidable only after the question of social order has been resolved. The question of expertise is also of secondary importance because the role of experts will be defined and limited by what society requires. Education, then, in a liberal state just as much as in one governed by populists, will have as one of its primary functions the teaching of these fundamental values.

The teaching of these values will often not be explicit in a liberal society but, from a populist perspective, they are no less restricting. The example of religion may serve to illustrate this. Populist governments which regard Roman Catholicism as part of the fabric of the nation, as do the Hungarian and Polish governments, specify that teaching about morality in schools should reflect Catholic moral teaching. Liberal governments, based on a belief in the separation of Church and State (*de jure* in the United States and France, *de facto* in England) respect the rights of people of all religious persuasions (and those of none) but discourage, in publicly funded schools, the teaching of any particular religion as being uniquely true. The apparently neutral approach of liberal education to religion in fact reflects, to many populists, an attitude to religious belief which, by making a commitment to a particular religion a matter of personal choice, relegates religion to the private sphere and refuses to accept that it has a right to a voice in the public debate.

How should a liberal like Locke reply to this? Nathan Tarcov draws attention to the fact that whereas many writers, starting with Plato, have understood the importance of the relationship between education and the state, and have treated them in the same work, Locke discusses them in separate works which do not refer to each other (Tarcov 1984: 1–4). One important reason for this is that whereas writers such as Plato argued that control of education by the state was essential if a just society with the right kinds of citizens were to be possible, Locke thought that education should be the responsibility of the parents not of the state. This difference reflects a fundamental disagreement at the heart of which is the contrast between Plato's view that one of the most important purposes of the state is the promotion of a particular idea of the 'Good' – of moral and religious values, the belief in which are essential to a person being a good person and also a good member of society – and Locke's view, spelt out in detail in the *Two Treatises* and his writings on toleration that the most important role for government is to provide security for a person's rights and property.

So for Locke, one very important way of ensuring that the state does not impose a uniform set of values on society which cannot be criticised is that the state does not have a monopoly on education. To clarify his argument further it will be helpful to briefly discuss Locke's criticism of the widely held view at the time he was writing that the state should allow a particular religious body to have a monopoly over the content and delivery of the curriculum. In the

England of Locke's day, the Church of England, as the established church, had this role, barring non-communicants from becoming either students or Fellows at the universities of Oxford and Cambridge.[8] It might be thought that that in the light of Locke's arguments about the general importance of thinking for oneself, about the specific, and sacred, duty of each person to think through their own religious beliefs, and of the dangers of relying on any authority, including priests, that he would have disapproved of such an arrangement. That is indeed the case. Although Locke remained a communicant member of the Church of England throughout his life he argues in *A Letter Concerning Toleration* for the separation of Church and State (Locke 1993: 397–402; see also Jolley 2016: 36, 44, 122, 139–41).

One of the most important practical applications of Locke's political principles was in the early United States where many of the liberal founders also believed in the separation of church and state. The argument is summed up memorably in a letter of Thomas Jefferson, while serving as the third President of the new Republic, to the Danbury Baptist Association:

> Believing with you that religion is a matter which lies solely between man and his God, that he owes account to none other for his faith or his worship, that the legislative powers of government reach actions only, and not opinions, I contemplate with sovereign reverence that act of the whole American people which declared that their legislature should 'make no law respecting an establishment of religion, or prohibiting the free exercise thereof,' thus building a wall of separation between Church and State....
> (Jefferson 1802)

Jefferson took the argument of the religious neutrality of the state and of education so seriously that when he later founded the University of Virginia he stipulated not only that it should have no religious tests for membership (unlike, for example, the universities of Oxford and Cambridge) but that there should be no teaching of theology.

This view of the importance of setting up institutional arrangements to ensure that people are free to choose their religious beliefs rather than have them imposed by a dominant religious body is central to the development of liberalism and so must play a large part in a liberal theory of education. But, as populists argue, this raises questions about the foundations of stability and order in a liberal society. Viktor Orbán, for example, argues that Roman Catholicism is an integral part of the cultural and moral fabric of Hungarian society and so its theological and ethical principles should form an important part of the education of Hungarian students.[9]

There is an important sense in which religious belief is not the central issue here. Rather, it is the importance of having a belief system which is sufficiently widely shared in society to provide a foundation for the values by which the members of that society can relate to each other. What is most required, as was suggested earlier (pp. 56–7), is a solid basis for creating and maintaining order and stability in society. There are echoes here of Plato's idea of the noble lie, but there is also a significant difference. Not just any set of beliefs will do, even if the education system seeks to reinforce them over a long period of time. Orbán, it will be recalled, was a fierce critic of communism, even though he had grown up in a Hungarian society and was educated in a Hungarian education system which taught the principles of Marxism-Leninism. One of the problems with the Hungarian Communist system, in this view, was that it was something artificially imposed on Hungarian society by outsiders. For Orbán, the liberal principles of the European Union and of the CEU are similarly at variance with Hungarian culture.

If the issue is the necessity of a shared belief system which can provide the basis of a stable community, what implications does this have for liberalism? What do, or should, liberals teach as the foundations of liberal society which can have the same emotional impact as the traditional culture and values of a society? Populists argue that abstract principles such as human rights or regarding oneself as a citizen of the world inspired by a cosmopolitan belief in the moral oneness of humanity can never have sufficient emotional appeal to the majority of people. These are beliefs for the wealthy educated elites who are graduates of institutions such as the CEU. Moreover, they contend, these are principles which, if widely adopted, will lead to a critical spirit which, far from leading to the liberal ideal of autonomous, critically-minded individuals living harmoniously in a stable society, will result in cynicism and social decay.

Education and civility

There is a sense in which Locke's argument side-steps the issue of foundations because he takes it for granted that almost everyone in his society accepts the basic principles of Christianity. In *A Letter Concerning Toleration* he argues that the freedom to worship following their own beliefs should be extended to Protestant Dissenters and to followers of other faiths. There are, though, a number of conditions attached, two of which are particularly relevant to our discussion. The first is that holding such beliefs must not commit a person to accepting an external religious authority as having precedence over the ruler (and the laws) of one's own country. For this reason he did not think it appropriate to extend toleration to Roman Catholics, because their first allegiance was to the Pope nor to those Moslems who '… yield blind obedience to the Mufti of Constantinople, who is himself entirely obedient to the Ottoman Emperor …' (Locke 1993: 426). There are some similarities here with contemporary populist arguments over migration, such as the refusal of the governments of Hungary and Poland to accept refugees from Moslem countries. For Locke, and perhaps to some extent for contemporary populists, the argument is primarily political rather than religious. The fundamental issue is allegiance to one's own state and Locke's readers would have realised that he was indirectly criticising the many prominent British Roman Catholics, including the King's brother, the Duke of York, who owed allegiance to the King of France as the political leader of European Catholicism.

The second condition is that in order to be tolerated people must believe in God on the grounds that '[p]romises, covenants, and oaths, which are the bonds of human society, can have no hold upon an atheist' (Locke 1993: 426). In the next sentence he reiterates the point in more metaphysical terms: 'The taking away of God, though but even in thought, dissolves all'. This argument is more directly about the importance of religious belief, and has echoes in the arguments of East Central European (and Russian Orthodox) populist arguments about the decadence of the liberal, secular West. But like the first argument it is primarily about who can be trusted to be a member of society.

These two arguments imply a background of shared political and religious values and it is against this background of a common culture that Locke's belief that the teaching of critical thinking is an important part of education must be understood. When this is done it seems to place limits on the curiosity and independence of mind which should be cultivated through education. How, if at all, can this be reconciled with the earlier claim that Locke's general epistemology contributed substantially to a recognition of the importance of critical thought and of the autonomy of the individual, and to the development of liberalism and to liberal theories of education? Locke's response to such criticisms is that an education which encourages critical thinking and the development of personal autonomy can only be effective in a community where there is recognition of the value and importance of a well-ordered society and, of crucial importance, one in which relationships are characterised by civility.

The importance of civility is widely discussed in contemporary society, where it is often feared that lack of civility towards those with whom one disagrees is contributing to the breakdown of tolerance and undermining social institutions.[10] These concerns are very much in evidence in Locke's account of society and of education. In an important passage in *Some Thoughts*, where Locke stresses the importance of civility in discussion, he defines civility as 'being, in truth, nothing but a care not to show any slighting, or contempt, of anyone in conversation' (Locke 1824: *Some Thoughts*, Section 145) and argues that civil discussion is best undertaken by people who are virtuous – virtue being more important, and more to be valued in a person, than even curiosity or critical thinking (Locke 1989: Section 147). This is in marked contrast to the Socratic Method, which involves persistent and insistent attempts to show the absurdity of the other person's point of view and which often led to exasperation with Socrates' relentless negative questioning. It is also relevant to Mill's discussion of debate and argument in *On Liberty*, which draws on the Socratic Method and which we will discuss later. Both Socrates and Mill regard incivility as desirable under some circumstances as a means of disrupting the status quo and bringing about change in society. This is particularly important with regard to the argument in the previous chapter that Socrates' constant questioning and debunking of other peoples' opinions (particularly those of the experts who Socrates says in the *Apology* (21b–4a) that he particularly sought out) has a populist edge which is potentially destructive of the basis of society.

Populist rhetoric, through being divisive and attacking an elite 'other' in society, has often seemed to its critics to lack civility. This is not incidental to populism because a key populist claim is that 'the people' have in the past been misled into accepting the economically and politically unjust system under which they live. This has been accomplished through a variety of methods, including a media owned and controlled by members of the elite. The most important means, though, is an education system designed to perpetuate the power of the elite by providing a superior education for their own children while simultaneously indoctrinating the great majority of children with a false understanding of the world, designed to keep them in subordination. Because these false beliefs have been internalised, and perhaps also because the deficient education has not provided any intellectual tools to properly challenge these beliefs, the only way the people and their true representatives can respond is by disputing the dominant narrative through aggressive rhetoric. This approach is, as we will see in the next chapter, much favoured by Rousseau who equated civility with social conventions intended to enhance the power of an elite and mystify the great majority of people who were overawed by it. Rousseau's writings abound with criticisms of polite society, both for its intellectual, as well as its economic, exclusiveness and for its lack of moral sincerity.

These populist criticisms have some force when applied to some aspects of particular liberal societies but how applicable are they to Locke? It is important to emphasise to begin with that Locke does not regard civility merely as a set of social conventions. He acknowledges that social customs are very different between different societies but distinguishes between these external expressions and the inner morality which is transcultural. The 'language', as he puts it, of these customs has to be learnt if we are to express the 'internal civility of the mind'. Civility, and the specific cultural language in which it is spoken, is only of value if it reflects a mind in which there is a '... general good-will and regard for all people ...' (Locke 1824: *Some Considerations*, Section 143).[11]

It was noted earlier that while Locke thinks that one purpose of education is to teach critical thinking, another is to prepare the child to become a responsible citizen. This second aim is, to use Locke's term, to enable the child to become a 'virtuous' member of society (Locke 1968: 241–5). To this end, it is not the purpose of a sound education to encourage the development of a specialist interest and expertise in some field of knowledge. As we have seen, Locke is dismissive of the need for most people to acquire detailed knowledge of a subject, beyond what can be useful to them in their adult lives.

Locke discusses these virtues at length. They include respect for others, exhibited in civility towards one's equals and inferiors (Locke 1989: Sections 109, 117) alongside other virtues such as courage and liberality.[12] The cultivation of these virtues is essential to the well-being and continuation of a liberal society and it is part of the duty of the educator to ensure that the child acquires them and learns to live in accordance with them. Education is not, therefore, essentially child-centred but has the well-being of the future adult, and the society in which he is expected to play a significant part, as its ultimate purpose.

This might be expressed by saying that while the *Two Treatises* is concerned with the role of the citizen in society, *Some Thoughts* is concerned (at least in significant part) with preparing young people to take their place in that society as good citizens. Yolton and Yolton express this succinctly when they write that while, 'civil society has the task of *protecting* the person, education has the task of *producing* persons' (Locke 1989: Introduction, 18). But this 'production' is not impersonal in the cold way in which Watson refers to his ability to turn the child into any kind of person he wishes. Rather, as we have seen, Locke considers the best type of education to be that which takes place within the caring environment of the family.

Yolton and Yolton go on to argue that this account of education lays particular stress on a person's moral development:

> It would only be a slight exaggeration to say that Locke's *Some Thoughts* is mainly a treatise on moral education.... While Locke writes about educating the son of a gentleman, his treatise is less about gentlemen than it is about developing a moral character.
>
> (Locke 1989: Introduction, 18)

This is an important point in the context of the populist criticism; that liberal societies have a tendency to encourage self-centred individuals who lack a sense of belonging to, and responsibility towards, a wider community.

Yolton and Yolton argue further that Locke's concern with moral education was not primarily a matter of preparing the child for the life of an English gentleman but of believing that 'virtue was the very fabric and basis for humanity. Man's humanity is achieved within civil society' (Locke 1989: Introduction, 39).[13]

Locke's defence of civility does not imply that one should agree to other peoples' opinions out of politeness, without demurring. Locke's own views on religion, for example, are far from orthodox and the idea of religious toleration, which will almost certainly involve disagreeing with people over matters of profound personal belief, is a central aspect of Locke's political thought. But Locke also believes that it is essential that these disagreements be expressed within the boundaries laid down by society for responsible discussion. For this reason, roughness of speech and manner ('the sure badge of a clown'), contempt, censoriousness and captiousness (Locke 1824: *Some Thoughts*, Section 143) are all dismissed by Locke as unacceptable.

Locke's view of education, therefore, requires a considerable emphasis on civility. But this does not mean teaching civility as a subject alongside of others, rather it requires that the teaching and learning of civility are (to use a modern phrase) embedded across the curriculum. Children learn to be civil through their daily interactions with teachers and others so that it becomes an integral part of their characters. If such an education is successful they grow up contributing to a society which is both stable and tolerant.

Attractive as such an education may seem, Teresa Bejan (2016, 2017) in *Mere Civility* argues that it can lead to a kind of intolerance. She argues that for many seventeenth century proponents of toleration (including Locke) the primary motivation for supporting toleration was a return to (or replacement for) the pre-Reformation ideal of *Concordia*: a harmonious peace based on shared Christian belief. This in turn lead Locke to latitudinarianism, a theological and ecclesiological doctrine in post-Restoration England which sought to encompass as many varieties of Christian belief and practice as possible within a national Church. The problem with this from a liberal perspective is that it necessarily excluded those who could not subscribe to the minimal creed.[14] Allowing education to take place outside the auspices of the state, particularly in the family, then, does not properly resolve the problem that it might promote certain shared values because many people in Restoration England shared the same broadly Christian values.[15]

This argument then sees Locke's theory of education as placing greater emphasis on stability than toleration. For Locke (as we have seen), such an education places positive duties on individuals, including the cultivation of virtues, and that these virtues are to be shared not merely as moral principles, but embodied in the individuals who are to live in that society. This argument can be extended further in that the capacity for inner civility is bound up with the much broader group of virtues which Locke discusses in *Some Thoughts* and which together contribute to the development of a person whose morality (and character) find expression in (among other things) civility. Education in the virtues as a whole is, therefore, essential for a sound education.

As Bejan points out, Locke's stress on the central importance of civility in *Some Thoughts* emphasises inner civility, rather than merely outward formalities. This civility is central to the functioning of a tolerant society which is based on trust in the integrity of one's fellow citizens. This is why, according to Locke, atheists, who cannot believe in ultimate moral principles, or Roman Catholics and Moslems who owe allegiance to authorities outside of their society, cannot be trusted and therefore should not be tolerated. The intolerance is not simply a disagreement about religious beliefs, or the absence of them, but of the kind of person who one is willing to accept as a member of one's society.

Bejan argues that Locke viewed religious communities, *from a political perspective*, as social organisations – (Bejan 2017: 129–31). From this perspective, the government should be indifferent to the views of church members, while they contented themselves with merely internal, religious matters. If, however, they engage in political activity, that becomes a matter of legitimate interest to the state. This is the case even where their political engagement (or even potential engagement) is based on their religious convictions – such as Roman Catholics or those Moslems who owed their spiritual allegiance to the Mufti of Constantinople.

This brings us back to the argument that because Locke's philosophy of education is based upon adherence to the liberal political philosophy which underpins his theory of education it will inevitably lead to an education system which, despite claims to moral, religious and political impartiality, privileges those who support liberal values. Although this would not have been thought of as problematic by those of Locke's contemporaries who shared his liberalism, it does seem difficult to reconcile with a more developed version of liberalism such as Mill's.

There is a further aspect to this argument which may also raise problems for liberalism. Locke, as we discussed earlier, and as Bejan's argument underlines, maintains that it is not merely a matter of teaching the principles of virtues such as civility but of ensuring that they are internalised so that they become part of a child's character. This is problematic because it suggests that it will be very difficult for the child, or the adult he or she will grow into, to challenge the belief in any of these virtues. Is it not the case, as populists argue, that liberals such as Locke are just as concerned to prevent critical thinking about their values as liberals accuse populists of doing about the fundamental values they espouse?

Critical thinking and autonomy

Joseph Carrig offers a variation on this argument in particularly strong terms, made all the more powerful, he maintains, because he is arguing from a liberal standpoint. He argues that Locke's prescription for a sound education in *Some Thoughts*, has a strong emphasis on the inculcation of appropriate habits and on fear of parental authority. If successful, such an education would lead to the indoctrination of children into liberal principles with the result that such children, and the adults they grew into, would be incapable of thinking critically about such principles (Carrig 2001). Carrig's argument is part of a larger discussion about Locke's philosophy of education which turns in part upon the question of whether Locke's account of education amounts to a process which encourages the uncritical internalisation of liberal values by children. Rita Koganzon has characterised the views of Carrig and others who argue in a similar vein as inspired by Foucault's arguments concerning 'internalized social discipline as a means of large scale social control' (Koganzon 2016: 547). Although Carrig's intent is very different, the conclusion of his argument has similarities to the populist view which characterises education in liberal societies, and in liberal institutions such as the CEU, as produced by the liberal elite for the reproduction of liberal values.

It is certainly true that Locke's theory of education is based upon the belief that a liberal society is superior to other forms of society. He has a particular illiberal society in mind, that which he believes Charles II and James II were committed to bringing about, based on the theory of the Divine Right of Kings, but Locke's particular form of liberalism, based on a belief in the universality of natural rights, is in principle opposed to all forms of illiberal society, including those, such as Plato's, which are based on very different political and religious ideas.

Yet at the same time, the liberal education envisaged by Locke aims to create individuals who are taught to be critical and so contains within itself the impetus for self-analysis and self-criticism. Koganzon argues that Locke is aware of the dangers of habituation but that he believes that the acquisition of *bad* habits is a widespread problem in society and that an education which develops *good* habits of critical analysis is a powerful defence against such bad habits. She also makes the very important point that for Locke education 'occurs in the context of the uneasiness of the mind, a condition of perpetual dissatisfaction from which it reflexively seeks relief wherever it can' (Koganzon 2016: 556).[16]

The argument that liberal education may create individuals who simply repeat the principles and values of liberalism without properly understanding or applying them is a reasonable one in so far as there is no guarantee that children will be sufficiently motivated to think for themselves, or that they will do so as adults. Yet examples of such outcomes in a liberal society would, in Locke's view, be the consequence of bad teaching, of a failure to simulate and encourage the uneasiness of mind in the pupil. If that were repeated in a recognisable and significant pattern across society that might indicate not merely the failure of individual teachers but of the education system as a whole. It might also reflect the inability of the liberal society to nurture a suitable education system which might, in turn, in the case of an advanced democracy, be evidence of political decay.

This point may be illustrated by reference to Locke's emphasis on the importance of active, rather than passive thinking in education. He makes this point very clearly in a discussion of reading in *Conduct*, referred to earlier (pp. 48–9), in which he emphasises the importance of an active engagement with what one reads: 'Reading furnishes the mind only with materials of knowledge, it is thinking makes what we read ours' (Locke 1824: *Conduct*, Section 20). Children should be taught to read in a critical way, so that they learn the habit of questioning what they read. The emphasis on the kinds of habits to be inculcated by education – reading critically and with a questioning mind, here – rather than being told what to think is central to Locke's understanding of education.

Critics such as Carrig err in neglecting the importance to Locke of education involving an understanding and application of virtues which are simultaneously individual and social. The education of the person and of the citizen take place simultaneously.[17] One learns to become a virtuous person, Locke argues, through social interactions. One reason why Locke is opposed to boarding schools is that a child will be in the wrong type of company. But it is equally important that if he is educated at home he will be able to socialise not only with his parent and siblings but also with the adult society of which his parents are a part. Socialising in such a positive way encourages the child to learn different perspectives and to recognise the need to weigh up competing arguments.

Locke does not assume that people are good by nature until they are corrupted by society. He does believe, as his warnings of the dangers of boarding schools make clear, that some elements of society can be corrupting (he no doubt has similar thoughts about the court of Charles II) but people have to be taught to be good and if sufficient pupils grow up to be virtuous members of society that will have a positive influence on the society in which they live, either to reinforce its goodness or to reform it to make it a better society. Naturally a young child does not understand all this and initially has to be told how to act and to be punished if he wilfully disobeys. But as the child matures so the relationship with the teacher changes, so that eventually child and teacher become friends and equals. What enables this change to take place is the child's gradual realisation of the need to take responsibility for his actions and opinions.

Locke's belief in the importance of education taking place within the family is significant for Carrig's argument that Locke's proposed method of education relies on fear, particularly fear of the father. Carrig's argument places considerable reliance on fear of the father because he believes that physical pain is one of the ways in which children are forced to internalise what they are being taught. His claim, though, is at odds both with an explicit argument in *Some Thoughts* and an important contemporary recollection of Locke by a close friend of Locke's own experience and practice.

The argument concerns Locke's disapproval (in almost all cases) of corporal punishment. The use of corporal punishment to force children to act in accordance with the teacher's wishes, and to apply themselves to learning out of fear of physical pain, would contribute to an education which discourages reflection – children acquire information and a semblance of learning because they afraid, not because they are engaged critically with the material they are supposed to be studying. Such a view of education has much more in common with Friere's banking model of education than one which seeks to prepare a child to be an active citizen in a liberal society. This argument is closely linked to the importance of civility, which is built on mutual respect, not fear. Locke does argue that 'fear and awe ought to give you the first power over their minds [that is, those of young children]', but immediately continues the sentence: 'and love and friendship in riper years to hold it' (Locke 1824: *Some Thoughts*, Section 42). Far from fear creating habits of thought, children who have been terrorised into repeating what their teachers have taught them are likely to reject what they have been taught once they have escaped the teacher's influence.

In her memoir of Locke, Damaris Masham writes that Locke always spoke of his father with respect and affection and expressed gratitude that while his father had treated him sternly as a young child, he had treated him increasingly as a friend as he grew into manhood (Woolhouse 2007: 6). The acceptance by the father of the son as a friend and an equal signifies that the child has grown into a mature, virtuous person capable of rational discussion and of the sociability which makes friendship possible. This goes hand in hand with the recognition that the final stage of his education has been successfully achieved and he is prepared to enter society as a mature and independent adult.

Growth or transformation

It is very important to emphasise at this point that for Locke the process of education is one of growth not transformation. Rousseau argues that it is only through a process of transformation that a child brought up in modern society can become liberated – it will always involve a radical break with the prevailing norms. Plato, too, believes that only a radical break with current society can lead to people becoming just. For Locke there is no need for such a radical transformation because he believes that the education he is advocating can take place in the relatively healthy society of late seventeenth century England which provides the environment in which the child can develop into a mature adult.

The 'relatively' in the last sentence of the previous paragraph is important. Locke thought that the society of Restoration England was far from perfect but for all the personal as well as political corruption of Charles II and his court, Locke did not believe that society as a whole was irredeemable. He played a major part through his own political activity, as a member of Shaftsbury's circle and as an active supporter of William and Mary, in helping to change that society in ways that he would have considered much for the better. But unlike Plato and Rousseau (or, indeed, the Quaker enthusiasts he is so critical of in the *Essay*), the change was to be one of reform rather than revolution, of growth rather than fundamental transformation. In this respect Locke helped lay the foundations of a liberal state based on law and gradual change.

Locke's view contrasts sharply with Rousseau's. For Rousseau, a child is born naturally good and becomes corrupted by society. That is why Emile has to be educated in isolation from society. This is not at all for the same reason that Locke has for discouraging parents from sending their children to boarding school. Locke wants children not only to be in the company of their parents and the wider household but also the company of family friends and acquaintances who will help the child learn how to live in society.

Although I shall be arguing in the next chapter that Rousseau's ideas have had a strong influence on populism, an argument can also be made that Locke's view of education, society and virtue addresses some of the concerns that underpin populist approaches to democracy. Among the criticisms that populists make of many governments in liberal democratic societies is the complaint that members of those governments form an elite who consider ordinary people to be too ignorant to understand the intricacies of economic and social policies and too selfish to act altruistically. Such arguments are not new – as we saw in Chapter 2, variations of this were often deployed, both by elites and their critics, in Ancient Greece. Locke's argument that his considerations on education were appropriate to the education of a gentleman, and not the majority of working men (let alone women), may reasonably be seen to have contributed to the preservation of an elitist view of education. But it is possible to suppose that a more developed version of Locke's theory would argue that everyone should receive a similar education and, as a consequence, the gulf between highly educated elites and the rest would shrink dramatically. This was the vision of nineteenth and twentieth century liberals and progressives, in both politics and education, such as Mill. This view would not entirely rule out specialists but, as Mill argues in *Considerations On Representative Government*, the specialists should be under the control of those who directly represent (and are answerable to) an electorate comprising the vast majority of the adult population.

Notes

1 Voltaire's enthusiastic discussion of Locke's philosophy in his *Letters on England*, first published in 1734, helped confirm Locke's reputation among the *philosophes* (Voltaire 1980: 62–7).
2 They did not think this of all governments. For Voltaire, the best form of government was that which could be guided by an enlightened absolutist, a ruler who was well educated in the natural sciences and the arts and who could use his or her power to bring about radical improvements. Voltaire believed, for a while at least, that Frederick the Great embodied this ideal (Blanning 2015: 329–35). This idea that well-educated rulers know best seems to critics to be perilously close to Plato's idea that the philosopher rulers cannot be challenged. Populists claim liberals are

particularly prone to this error which leads them to trust experts and to favour educational policies which are most likely to produce people with such expertise. Rousseau, as we will see in the next chapter, is particularly scathing of this belief in enlightened rulers. Jefferson and Madison, naturally, did not think that as Presidents they were corrupt but despite having strong claims to being the most learned and most liberal rulers of the age of Enlightenment, they did recognise the need to limit the power of all rulers.

3 Jefferson and Madison also had concerns about entrusting too much power to those without the education and leisure to make well-reasoned decisions but recognising this problem they thought that providing education was essential if the United States was to develop into a truly free society.

4 There are excellent modern editions of each of these works, which are indicated in the text, and I will refer to introductions and editorial notes from some of these during this chapter. All quotations from Locke's texts are taken from the 12th edition of his works (Locke 1824) unless otherwise indicated. *An Essay Concerning Human Understanding* is to be found in Volumes 1 and 2, *Of the Conduct of the Understanding* is also in Volume 2 and *Some Thoughts Concerning Education* in Volume 8.

5 Locke was particularly concerned to preserve the secrecy of his authorship of the *Two Treatises*. Arguably the principle reason for this was his fear that if the Revolution of 1688 were overturned and James II restored to the throne there would be reprisals against Locke for arguments in the *Two Treatises* which could be construed as critical of James. No such considerations applied to *Some Thoughts*.

6 This is not to say that patriotism and belief in the importance of national identity are necessarily based only on feelings and not at all on reason. Mill, for example, believes, as we will discuss in Chapters 5 and 6, that both can be defended on rational grounds. At the same time he also argues that the feelings stirred by identification with a nation can lead one astray unless kept under the control of reason.

7 Locke's criticisms of what he termed religious 'Enthusiasts' in his *Essay* (Locke 1975: Book IV, Chapter 19) are also relevant here. Such people, he argues, effectively give up their right to speak on matters which require them to have their own well-reasoned opinions, because they prefer to depend on the authority of others. Locke shows a general distrust of clericalism for similar reasons.

8 The place of an established Church was the subject of bitter debate during the Restoration period, with many Anglicans fearful that Charles II, and more especially James II, wished to disestablish the Church of England and establish the Roman Catholic Church in its place. Protestant Dissenters objected to any established national church.

9 The objection that the Hungarian government has to the teaching of Gender Studies at the CEU is based on its view that it undermines Roman Catholic teaching on topics such as the family, which it believes are essential to the well-being of Hungarian society.

10 Barack Obama, for example, frequently urged the need for greater civility during his presidency.

11 After Locke's death, Coste and Damaris Masham wrote memoirs of him and the portrait they draw of his character suggests how Locke envisages the practical outcome of his educational advice: a person of great civility, open minded and constantly open to learning new things (see Woolhouse 2007: 94–5). Both emphasise his eagerness to learn about practical, 'mechanical', matters and a desire to follow evidence rather than being guided by abstract theories, points which he emphasises in the education of a young man and which separates him sharply from Plato.

12 Nathan Tarcov provides a detailed account of the Lockean virtues (see Tarcov 1984: Chapter 3).

13 They also stress the importance of understanding this in the Christian tradition of moral thinking, but this does not mean that Locke thought that civility was only possible in European societies. As Teresa Bejan points out, he thought that Native Americans were better exemplars of civility than (many) Europeans (Bejan 2017).

14 See Bejan 2017: Chapter 1, especially 41–3 on the potential for exclusion.

15 It is arguable that the opposition to the Roman Catholic James II and the success of the so-called 'Glorious Revolution' of 1688 led to the preservation and entrenchment of Protestant culture in England. In doing so it narrowed the set of values which were to form an important part of most children's education until well into the nineteenth century.
16 This notion of uneasiness as a stimulus to critical – and creative – thinking is developed more fully in Mill's work – see Chapters 5 and 6 of this volume.
17 It might be tempting to say that they are so interconnected that they are indistinguishable, but this would be to misread Locke. The individual is not defined wholly in terms of citizenship – that is something which is only a part of what it is to be a person.

4 Jean-Jacques Rousseau
Education, *Emile* and remaking society

Rousseau and populism

Rousseau lived during a time that is often described as the Age of Reason. It was a period in which the arbitrary rule of absolutist monarchs was challenged by intellectuals who followed Locke (in many cases quite consciously and deliberately so) in asserting the importance of individual liberty and the need to test one's own beliefs and the policies of governments against the standard of empirically based reason. Many of these same intellectuals – artists and scientists as well as philosophers – considered themselves as citizens if not of the world at least of the cosmopolitan society of Europe.

Rousseau shares this dislike of arbitrary rule but he goes further and criticises almost all governments, including those whose leaders on occasion offered him financial and moral support, even Frederick the Great who offered safe sanctuary against those who wished him dead (Blanning 2015: 326–9). He believes that the societies of Europe, and the elites who rule them, are corrupt.

He detests cosmopolitanism, most especially the pan-European cosmopolitanism of men like Voltaire. There are no longer Frenchman, Germans or Spaniards – not even Englishmen – he writes near the end of his life, in *Considerations on the Government of Poland*, just Europeans who share 'the same tastes, the same passions, the same morals' (Rousseau 2019b: 187–8).[1] This anti-Europeanism is not new, as a younger man he pours scorn – of which he is a master – on the Abbe St Pierre's plan for a European Union with its own parliament, which the Abbe offered to the cultured men and women of Europe as a blueprint for perpetual peace on the continent (Rousseau 1991: 88–100).

He hates the intellectual elites whose clever, abstract thinking ignores the natural, unsophisticated wisdom of the ordinary people. In the work which first brought him international fame, and his first taste of notoriety, *Discourse on the Sciences and Arts*, he argues that highly educated intellectuals are too far removed by their rarefied education from the natural wisdom of the general populace who know in their hearts what is best for their society. Much elite education leads to empty speculation and it would be far better if educators ignored the frivolous pursuit of 'higher truths' such as are supposed to be found in abstract sciences like geometry and in the natural sciences such as physics, both of which are merely empty speculation. The same argument also applies to such apparently altruistic studies as moral philosophy which in fact is based on pride (clever people telling the rest of us how to live) (Rousseau 1992: 12). Rousseau, in other words, sounds rather like a modern-day populist.

Like modern populists, Rousseau believes that the society of his own day is corrupt and that the education system is an important element in maintaining and legitimising that corruption. Such education, he writes, 'adorns our minds and corrupts our judgements' (Rousseau 1992: 17). The belief that contemporary education is designed to adorn the mind, in the way that fashionable clothes are thought to adorn the man or woman in order to make them attractive in society, is a powerful image, expressing Rousseau's disdain for what he believes is its corrosive effect on the mind and morals of society. In pursuit of this end, children are taught dead languages and the ability to construct clever arguments but they are not taught those things which are conducive to true happiness and well-being. Education corrupts not only in a material, or even just a political, way but most fundamentally in a moral sense: it corrupts the heart of children, so that '... they will not know what the words magnanimity, equity, temperance, humanity, courage are; that sweet name Fatherland will never strike their ear ...' (Rousseau 1992: 17–18). He detests the selfishness, love of luxury and, most fundamentally, the artificiality which he believes this education has helped produce. People who have been subjected to such education have no true moral understanding and their lives are, to employ a widely used modern term which is much indebted to Rousseau, inauthentic.[2] Like actors in the theatre, they are merely playing a role over which they have no control and beyond which they have no fixed identity.[3] Society would be much better served if we listened to those who lead a simple life seeking only to serve their country, looking out for their friends and alleviating the suffering of their fellow countrymen.

This does not mean that Rousseau is opposed to education as such and in the *Preface to Narcissus*, written as a final response to the many criticisms which *Discourse on the Sciences and Arts* attracted, he firmly rejects the claim that he wishes 'to proscribe science and learning, to burn our libraries, to close our Academies, our Colleges, our Universities ...' (Rousseau 1992: 190). He does not want to destroy educational institutions, but he does wish to radically change them. Education can be of great benefit to both the individual and society, but only when it has been purged of wrong values and attitudes and is fit to prepare a child to become a responsible citizen, aware of his duties to others. Unlike an education which encourages a delight in wealth and luxury and a selfish pride which seeks to dominate others, it should produce an adult citizen who understands that his true interests can only be understood and brought to fruition in harmony with the rest of society. As one would expect from his criticism of the arts and sciences, the ideal education would be practical and general. He does not deny that some individuals can truly excel in the study of the sciences, and he refers approvingly to the accomplishments of Bacon, Descartes and Newton. But such geniuses would be hindered rather than helped by the limitations of their teachers and they have to work out their ideas by themselves (Rousseau 1992: 21).

Although Rousseau is critical of some aspects of *Discourse on the Sciences and Arts* in his later writings,[4] throughout his life he rejects all forms of what he regards as elitist politics and education. Like the other three writers discussed in the book, Rousseau thought that education and politics were linked at a deep level and, like Plato, he argues that a sound education is only possible in a just society. The only truly just society Rousseau argues, most fully in *The Social Contract* (Rousseau 2019b), is one in which sovereignty is not concentrated in one person or a small elite but in all the citizens of the state. It is not enough, though, for the sovereign to be comprised of all the citizens. It would be quite possible for such a sovereign citizen body to act unjustly, indeed, under the conditions existing in the European society of his own day, Rousseau would have expected such a sovereign body to behave in precisely this way. This is because the corruption of the society in which its members live clouds their understanding and their judgement to the extent that they often they do not know what is in the true interest of their state, or of themselves. What is required is a sovereign citizen body which expresses the general will, a concept which, as discussed in Chapter 1, features in many accounts of populism. To bring about such a citizen body requires a fundamental transformation of society, and of the education provision which will be vital to its continued well-being.

It is tempting to think that Rousseau envisages a utopian ideal society and it is possible on one reading to suppose that Rousseau is arguing that the society envisaged in *The Social Contract* will indeed be perfect, but this is not quite what he believes. He argues, rather, for the less ambitious view – which is also a major theme in populist political rhetoric – that it is possible to imagine a society which, although it may have flaws and potential weaknesses, is radically better than the corrupt societies of contemporary Europe.[5]

The purpose of education in the radically different society envisaged by Rousseau is to develop and maintain stability through instilling the values of the community into succeeding generations so that they may give expression to the general will. Does this mean that it is impossible to provide a child with a proper education when such a just society does not exist? Rousseau thinks that it is possible, but with significant limitations. This leads Rousseau to offer two views of how a sound education might be provided.

The first involves removing the child from a corrupt society and educating him in isolation. This is the solution he explores in *Emile*. The other is to seek to remove the corruption in society by bringing about a radical transformation of its political and cultural life; a process in which a purified and patriotic education system will play a central role. This latter alternative is explored at greatest length, though even then in far fewer words than he devotes to *Emile*, in *Considerations on the Government of Poland* (henceforth *Poland*; Rousseau 2019b). This second account of education is reflected to some extent in populist education policies such as those of Orbán's Hungary, but it seems to be in conflict with the ideas expressed in *Emile*. We will discuss both in turn, but I shall argue that Rousseau sees these as two possible solutions to the same problem: given that the elite culture which dominates European society is deeply corrupt how is it possible to educate a person so that they may escape the corruption? The echoes of this question in the education policies of European populist movements from the United Kingdom to Hungary and in the United States are unmistakable.

Emile

Emile (Rousseau 1979) is a rich and multi-layered work which defies easy categorisation: part novel, part treatise on education and part general speculation on a variety of philosophical, scientific and religious subjects. A long, theologically unorthodox, section on religion, 'Reflections of a Savoyard Priest', contributed to a hostile reception on its first publication, and led to the book being publicly burned by both the Calvinist authorities in Geneva and the Roman Catholic Church in Paris. The complexity of the book lends itself to different interpretations and it has been treated to a whole gamut of responses, ranging from the kind of fear and hatred which fuelled its burning in Geneva and Paris to extravagant praise as an essential guidebook for progressive educators.

The central theme of the book is the education of Emile, whose progress is followed from childhood to early manhood.[6] Emile's tutor, through whom Rousseau speaks, insists that the only conditions under which the child can be properly educated, given the corruption that pervades almost all European societies, is to be removed from his family and society to live alone with his tutor in the country. Once safely secluded in the countryside, the child is encouraged to learn things for himself, rather than be a passive recipient of what a teacher tells him. In this way, Rousseau explains, the child will have a much clearer understanding of what he is studying, and it will make a far deeper impression on him. Rousseau also lays great emphasis on a child's entitlement to happiness and pleasure. Education should be a joy rather than the relentless chore which he believes is true of the school education of his own day. In saying this he is partly being pragmatic, a child who enjoys his education is likely to learn much more than a child who dreads his lessons, but Rousseau is also motivated by a concern for the well-being of the child. One example of this is when he points out that because of the poor state of medical science at the time *Emile* was written, the likelihood of a child reaching maturity is quite low. It is unfair to burden the few years the child may have on earth with the miserable grind of a joyless education (Rousseau 1979: 78–9, 107).

At a more philosophical level, Rousseau is also concerned with the well-being of the individual and the importance of personal integrity. In that sense his theory of education is deeply moral, but his morality is not that of the orthodox Roman Catholics or Genevan Calvinists of his own day, which explains in large part their ferocious response to *Emile*, and particularly to the 'Reflections of a Savoyard Priest'. His emphasis is on the importance of being honest to oneself and to one's feelings, of being, in that sense, an authentic person, in contrast to the inauthentic people who inhabit sophisticated societies. The desirability of being removed from the pressures of the social life in a corrupt society in order to live a genuinely authentic life is explored at length in his novel *Julie, or the New Heloise*.

The words of Clare, early in the novel, reflect this.

> For myself, who am not a great reasoner, I want nothing to do with an honesty that betrays faith, trust, friendship; I imagine that every relationship, every age has its maxims, its duties, its virtues, that what would be prudence to others, would to me be perfidy, and that to lump everything together, rather than making us virtuous, makes us wicked.
> (Rousseau 1997: Letter VII Reply [Claire to Julie], 35)

In a similar vein, Julie writes in Letter IX that she was initially fearful of her own feelings as she was falling in love because she grew up being taught rules that made her feel guilty about her natural desires and emotions. This clash between doing what is honest to oneself and one's feelings rather than obeying the staid conventions of (a corrupt and stultifying) society is one of the central themes of the novel (Rousseau 1997: 40–2).

It is this emphasis on genuine feeling, of being true to oneself, rather than the artificial constraints of society, which Rousseau wants Emile to learn and embrace. This echoes Rousseau's own disdain for what he sees as the artificiality of European society and the need to escape its stifling conformity. It also reflects his argument in *Discourse on the Sciences and Arts* that European culture restricts rather than encourages natural goodness and undermines human happiness. This has seemed to many people to be one of the noblest elements in Rousseau's philosophy of education and its influence on subsequent educational thought has been immense.

Having set out the principle Rousseau has to explain how it might be applied in practice. To this end, he says frequently in the novel that Emile is encouraged to discover things for himself, rather than, as in the conventional education of his time, simply being told what he must believe. Among the many examples are Rousseau's suggestions that he would not teach Emile geometry but that Emile, through working out geometrical proofs for himself, would teach his teacher (Rousseau 1979: 145) and that Emile would naturally first embrace Ptolemaic astronomy because that is what accords with his initial experience, but later, through greater experience, accept Copernicanism (Rousseau 1979: Bloom's footnote 1, 486).

Educationally this might seem progressive, and in many respects it is. Students will usually learn more easily if they work things out for themselves: if, like Emile, they conduct their own experiments in mechanics or learn about botany by tending to plants. It is not surprising that many readers have seen in this approach to learning by discovery in *Emile* a passionate belief in the autonomy of the child as among the primary purposes of education. Nevertheless, such an interpretation, attractive as it is to minds accustomed to value education which promotes children's critical thinking and the development of autonomous individuals, underplays an essential element in Rousseau's understanding of what is involved here.

Because education is by its very nature a social activity, learning cannot be purely child-led. Encouraging the child to pursue a particular interest will certainly be easier if the student can be persuaded to think that he will enjoy learning about it, and even more if he thinks he has chosen it for himself, but in the philosophy of education set out in *Emile*, the child is always being educated to achieve a particular goal, even though for much of the time he is unaware of this. To this end, the tutor is always guiding the child, not only in what he should learn but also what he should avoid learning: those things which are harmful or simply not useful, the inappropriate acquiring of which may be detrimental to the good of the child. Rousseau puts the point very clearly to avoid any misunderstanding of what he is trying to achieve: '... the spirit of my education consists not in teaching the child many things, but in never letting anything but accurate and clear ideas enter his brain' (Rousseau 1979: 171).

There is certainly a positive element in Rousseau wanting the child to be preserved from inaccurate and unclear ideas, and he has in mind much of the education of his own day which forces false and confusing ideas upon children. This is true, he thinks, of the education offered by the fashionable elites which aim only to adorn the mind. It is also true of the different but equally pernicious kind of education provided by priests who, unlike the Savoyard priest, are neither liberally minded nor truly caring about those in their charge but seek to indoctrinate them with the teachings of their church. In each case the result of education is to close the mind.

Laudable as Rousseau's aspirations are, there are nevertheless significant limits on Emile's autonomy, as is indicated by the gate-keeper implication in the above quotation of 'never letting anything but accurate and clear ideas enter his brain'. The student may, for example, choose to conduct a scientific experiment to test a hypothesis he has arrived at by observation, but the context in which this choice is possible has already been established by the teacher. There is nothing particularly remarkable about such practice. School children or university undergraduates conducting scientific experiments in laboratories are doing so in tightly controlled artificial environments in which the experiments have been set up to demonstrate a particular theory. This arrangement is, from the widely accepted Kuhnian perspective, a standard part of the education of a scientist (Kuhn 1970: 45–7) and even if we substitute make-shift tools in a casual environment the context is still artificial. That is what is to be expected if we understand education to be a necessarily social activity. John Dewey's criticism in *Experience and Education* of progressive teachers who abdicate their responsibility to guide children (Dewey 1936: Chapter 1) is appropriate here.

This is not problematic if the context-setting is something that pupils are aware of, or, as Dewey, and also Locke, argue, they become aware of as they mature, and their critical skills are developed. There is, though, a potentially disturbing aspect to this precisely because of the very fact that education is a social activity. Social interactions often involve power relations, particularly teacher-pupil relationships, and this is certainly true of the relationship between Emile and his teacher. It is not putting it too strongly to say that Emile is not merely guided but manipulated at significant points in his education in order that he may become the man that his teacher believes he ought to be. This is exacerbated by the fact that Emile is, for much of his childhood, denied meaningful contact with anyone other than his tutor, including with children of his own age. Rousseau's claim that Emile would first learn Ptolemaic astronomy, because that is what accords with his initial experience and would later, through greater experience, embrace Copernicanism is an example of this. Rousseau's suggestion that he would not teach Emile geometry, but that Emile would teach him is reminiscent of Socrates and the slave boy in the *Meno*. In this dialogue a slave boy who has never studied geometry appears under close and leading questioning by Socrates to remember complex mathematics learnt in a previous life (*Meno* 80d–6b).

This is also evident in the tutor's treatment of Emile and his future wife Sophie in *Emile* Book V. Emile is led into thinking that his first meeting with Sophie is accidental, though the tutor has arranged the encounter with Sophie's parents beforehand, and their courtship is controlled by the tutor. He even takes it upon himself to advise them on their sexual relationship both on their wedding day and later.[7]

This criticism is not meant to suggest bad intent on the part of Emile's tutor, or of Rousseau. The tutor clearly wishes the young Emile to grow into an honest and confident man with a disdain for the artificiality of contemporary society and a desire to live a simple life. Yet for all the genuine emphasis on the well-being of the child, and of the importance of the child discovering for himself, there is also something rather controlling about Rousseau's theory of education in *Emile*. Part of this is due to the intense relationship between the tutor and pupil, but it also has to be seen in the context of Rousseau's general view of society and education. The child must be protected from the corruption of the society around him and the constant temptation to embrace its decadent attractions.

This stress on the removal from a corrupt society to be educated in a purer, safer one is fundamental to Rousseau's purpose in *Emile*. Despite Rousseau's unorthodox views of Christianity, there are similarities in the circumstances of Emile's education to parts of the Christian home-school movement whose proponents advocate withdrawing children from secular schools which, they argue, corrupt children through teaching subjects such as evolution and by promoting liberal ideas on sexuality and gender. Such measures would be unnecessary in a truly Christian society where education would promote Christian values rather than those of secularists, or those of other religions. It might appear to some of these parents that the attempt to reform the Hungarian education system to better reflect Roman Catholic values is a move towards such a society.

This last point is very much in the spirit of Rousseau, who believes that although the kind of education which Emile experiences is far superior to anything on offer in the schools of Europe, it also has significant limitations which are forced upon it by the circumstances of time and place. To fully understand why he thinks this is so, and as a bridge into his argument about what education would be like in a just society, requires a discussion of Rousseau's theories of the state of nature and the social contract.

From savage to citizen

The purpose of withdrawing the child from the influences of a corrupt society is not with a view to encouraging the child to become wholly autonomous, because Rousseau believes that such a condition is not possible. Rousseau certainly does want the child to be removed from the corrupting influence of the particular society into which he was born, but he does not think it either desirable or possible to live as a rational moral being without a society of some kind. This point is made more fully in *The Social Contract* when Rousseau argues that entering into society enhances personal liberty by opening up opportunities which the solitary life of the state of nature could not provide. Men become transformed (Rousseau 2019b: Book I, Chapter 8 and Book II, Chapter 7). In making this argument, Rousseau draws upon a theory of human nature developed in his *Discourse on Inequality* (henceforth, *Second Discourse*).

In the *Second Discourse* Rousseau argues that in the state of nature, the original condition of humanity, people (or savages as Rousseau calls them, though he means nothing pejorative by this term) lived solitary lives, rarely engaging with others and then only for fleeting encounters. Even if people met more than once they would probably not recognise each other and under such conditions, society would not be possible. Some in modern society might find this life of complete independence attractive, and even wish to live this way themselves, but Rousseau is not one of them. It is, he says, pointless comparing the lot of the asocial savages in the state of nature with that of people living in modern society because their lives, and their expectations of what life has to offer, are so utterly different (Rousseau 2019a: 146–8).

Leaving the state of nature and entering society is fraught with problems, among the chief of which is the introduction of private property and the economic inequality which it creates, but it also brings benefits, some potential, some actual. Among these benefits are the development of sophisticated languages to replace the bare grunts of the savage and through that the provision of education, neither of which would be possible without the transformation which living in society brings about. Emile has this society in the person of his teacher, who himself has lived within the wider society and is sufficiently mature and wise to be able to guide Emile through his educational development.

It is extremely important to emphasise that for Rousseau the process of becoming a member of society is in itself an educative experience. This is not meant in the sense that one might describe a significant event in at a particular point in their life as something from which they can learn because that would be to separate the event from the process of education. For Rousseau being educated into the society is one of the essential strands in becoming a member of that society. Education is an essential part of what transforms an asocial man into a citizen.

Part of this education is informal, learning through interaction with others, but there is a crucially important formal aspect as well in the role of the 'Lawgiver'. In *The Social Contract* Rousseau argues that social life becomes possible when people have left their asocial lives in the state of nature and come together to live in a society under a social contract. But how can people who are used to living in isolation become accustomed to living in a settled community? How can they have an understanding of a peaceful, harmonious community at all when they have no experience of the benevolent social institutions which develop and nurture such communal life? In many historical cases, says Rousseau, the transition was accompanied by force, but he rejects this as the basis for the just society which he envisages. In order to live harmoniously in society the people need a set of basic laws which will guide them. As they are not capable of creating these laws themselves, they need a Lawgiver who will be wise enough to develop appropriate laws for them. Rousseau argues that as a matter of fact it is better if the Lawgiver is not a member of that society, and gives examples of societies which have invited outsiders to write their basic laws for them.[8] This has the obvious advantage that as the Lawgiver will not be living under these laws he has no personal interest in advantaging any particular individuals or factions in drawing up the laws.

If the purpose of the Lawgiver were only to provide clear, rational, guidelines by which the citizens were expected to live, that would not be enough to ensure that the laws were obeyed – people might simply ignore those laws which they perceived to be against their particular self-interest. So Rousseau also emphasises the importance of the Lawgiver in reshaping individuals into a new community with shared values and a common sense of identity and purpose.[9] An additional role of the Lawgiver is to persuade the people to embrace the laws and obey them because they believe they give expression to something much more compelling than the mind of a man, however wise. The Lawgiver must have the ability to convince the people that the laws are of divine origin,[10] an aspect of the Lawgiver's function which is reminiscent of Plato's noble lie in the *Republic*. Rousseau's conceptions of the roles of the Lawgiver in society and of the teacher in education are strikingly close.

Poland: education for a just society

The solitary education of Emile, outside of society, is a second best, and it carries a heavy burden. Emile is told that it is his moral duty as an adult to return to the society from which he was withdrawn as a child and live as a just citizen as a model for others to follow. Such a task will inevitably be difficult, and his fate may be to suffer the misunderstanding and mockery encountered by Plato's enlightened philosopher descending back into the cave.[11] The situation would be very different if children could be educated within a just society, or at least one which is on the way to reforming itself. Doing so would greatly enrich their experience because they are being taught within a community of transformed people.

Geraint Parry captures this aspect of *Emile* in a powerful passage:

> Beneath the apparently idyllic concluding pages of *Emile* there is the clear sense that Rousseau is offering his reader only a second best. It is an education for a profoundly unsatisfactory world, and it largely consists in learning about it only to avoid it so far as is feasible.
>
> (Parry 2001: 260)

Parry also argues that when Rousseau did attempt to set out, albeit in sketchy form, something approaching a positive view of how education might be implemented in a reformed contemporary society, such as in the *Letter to M. d'Alembert on the Theatre*, or more substantially in *Poland*, his suggestions were far less radical and were anyway unworkable because they could only be applied in small societies (Parry 2001: 263–8). Whether the accounts of education in *Poland* are less radical, and whether they are indeed unworkable, is a question we now take up.

Poland was written many years after *Emile* so it might seem sensible to allow for Rousseau changing, or at least modifying, his views in the intervening years and not being too quick to assume that the educational philosophy which Rousseau expounds in *Poland* dovetails with that of *Emile*. Yet Rousseau refers in *Poland* to *The Social Contract*, saying quite explicitly the reader should refer to his earlier work (Rousseau 2019b: 260). *The Social Contract* was written in the same period as *Emile*, and as there are many points of overlap between them – for example, the political philosophy which *Emile* is introduced to towards the end of his education is, as Rousseau points out (Rousseau 1979: 462), a summary of the key ideas presented in *The Social Contract*. We may reasonably assume that Rousseau thought his discussion of education in *Poland* was compatible with the political philosophy developed in *The Social Contract*, and thus of *Emile*.

There is a further point to make here. Although *Poland* was written for a particular purpose it is also very helpful in seeing how Rousseau thought the ideas of *The Social Contract* could be applied. Some of these applications might strike the reader not so much as unworkable but as remarkably pragmatic. For example, while Rousseau argues that it is right that the Polish serfs should be liberated, he also warns against trying to accomplish this too quickly, arguing that it should be undertaken over a period of time, during which they can be educated to understand their responsibilities as citizens (Rousseau 2019b: 200–1). *Poland* can, in many respects, be read as a detailed attempt to apply the principles of *The Social Contract* to a concrete political situation as a practical exercise, or case study, of the general principles set out in the earlier work.

Both *Emile* and the discussion of education in *Poland* are embedded in the broader political philosophy of *The Social Contract* and indeed there are many detailed similarities. Perhaps the most important one comes towards the end of *Emile* during a discussion of the duties of citizenship (Rousseau 1979: 473–4) where Rousseau argues that Emile has a duty to his own homeland even though it is corrupt. Living in the country, away from the vices of the city, is one way of helping to minimise the effects of the corruption but it does not absolve the adult Emile from the duties of citizenship.

Education has a key role in *Poland* as a means of building and encouraging a strong identification with the community: 'It is education that must give souls the national form, and so direct their opinions and their tastes that they will be patriotic by inclination, passion, necessity' (Rousseau 2019b: 193). This is also true of the original contract, but the circumstances under which the Polish people enter a new social contract is different from the savages who have left the state of nature. The Poles are already living in a corrupt society so their transition to a new social contract requires a different kind of adjustment. There are parallels here with populist arguments in Hungary (and in the Law and Order Party government in contemporary Poland!) about the corruption in Western European Society (epitomised for many populists in the transnational policies of the European Union) and the need to ensure that Hungarian (and Polish) education should teach different, illiberal (and in these particular cases) conservative Roman Catholic values. This is one of the fundamental reasons behind Prime Minister Orbán's disagreement with the CEU.[12]

This education is intensely nationalistic – children by the age of ten years must know all the 'products' of the country, by the age of 12 its geography, become acquainted with its 'entire history' by the age of 15 and with 'all its laws' by 16 (Rousseau 2019b: 193). As in *Emile*, physical activity plays an important part in learning, helping to make it enjoyable rather than dull and boring. Significantly, and rather differently from Emile who is largely kept apart from other children (Rousseau 2019b: 195), all children in the reformed Poland which Rousseau envisages will spend much time together. He allows for the possibility of being schooled at home (Rousseau 2019b: 195)[13] but even these children must gather with the others for communal games. This is not simply to help make them physically strong and healthy but more importantly it is a means of 'accustoming them early on to rules, equality, fraternity and competition' and, it might be thought, rather disturbingly, 'to live beneath the gaze of their fellow citizens' and desire public approval (Rousseau 2019b: 195).

There is clearly an important connection between the inculcation of values and principles during the initial founding (or re-founding, in *Poland*'s case) of the republic and the reiteration of those values in the continuing education of people over generations. There are many echoes of Plato's emphasis on education as underpinning and sustaining the just state in his *Republic*, and those who have been critical of Plato's theory of education as a form of political and social control have been inclined to draw the same conclusions about Rousseau. But Rousseau's argument, both in *The Social Contract* and *Poland*, has an additional element which might help to mitigate the force of this criticism.

As we have seen, Rousseau argues that not all states are suitable for the form of self-government which he is advocating for Poland. Indeed, there have been very few in history – Sparta and Republican Rome being the two most prominent in Rousseau's mind – and of the countries of eighteenth century Europe, he only mentions – in addition to Poland and Corsica – Geneva and some of the cantons of Switzerland as being suitable. The reason is that the people must already share, or be very susceptible to, those values. The task of the Lawgiver, then, is to work with what is good in the current values and mould it into a coherent system of laws which the people will recognise as reflecting their deepest values. Rousseau believes that Plato accepted this principle himself, which is why he was unwilling to provide for the Arcadians and Cyrenians (Rousseau 2019b: 74).

In *The Social Contract* Rousseau suggests that at the time he was writing the only society in Europe which might be transformed along the lines he was setting out was Corsica. It is difficult to know how seriously Rousseau had considered the situation in Corsica, and whether he was using the example to contrast it with the more refined and cultured societies such as France which he affected to despise. When he was later invited to write a constitution for a future republic of Corsica he admitted that he had little detailed knowledge of the country, but he also applauded what he regarded the rather coarse and uncultivated lifestyle of the Corsicans.

In his *Constitutional Proposal for Corsica* (henceforth *Corsica*) Rousseau acknowledges the great difficulty in reforming any society, even Corsica itself (Rousseau 2012: 191). Democracy is best suited to small towns where citizens can easily gather together. For a larger island republic like Corsica a mixed government is more appropriate, composed of both democratic and representative elements (Rousseau 2012: 197–8).

Moreover, to have any chance of success, Corsica should aim to emphasise the abundance of its population rather than monetary wealth. It should seek an economy based on agriculture, which will help to make it self-sufficient but also allow for the simple, non-luxurious life style that is most conducive to a good society (Rousseau 2012: 194–5). He warns that towns are dangerous because they encourage idleness, and the vice that inevitably arises from it (Rousseau 2012: 201). Capital cities are even more problematic in this regard (Rousseau 2012: 202) and their function should be restricted to the administration of the republic. In this he is repeating his often-asserted dislike of towns and cities and his conviction that living in the country is more conducive to becoming and remaining a virtuous person. He was very adamant that Emile should be educated in the country to avoid temptations.

Rousseau, here as elsewhere, warns against the dangers of corruption and decline even in a virtuous republic and offers what he sees as the salutary warning of the decline of the Swiss cantons from robust, independent democracies to dependency on France (Rousseau 2012: 204–7). What is it, then, that makes members of some societies able to act virtuously? Or, to put it slightly differently, what is it about those societies of free men, such as Corsica and Poland, that allows them at least the possibility of developing just societies? The answer lies in the general will.

Sovereignty and the general will: the foundations of a stable and cohesive society

The idea of the general will is at the heart of what Rousseau thinks makes a society stable and cohesive. The purpose of education is to develop and maintain this stability and cohesiveness by inculcating the values of the community into succeeding generations so that they may be able to give expression to the general will. As such, the relationship between the education which Rousseau advocates and his understanding of both critical thinking and autonomy all differ radically from that offered by liberals such as Locke.

These arguments also distinguish his ideas on the social contract sharply from the absolutism of Thomas Hobbes. Unlike Hobbes' argument in *Leviathan*

(1996), Rousseau does not think that stability and cohesion – and the security which is of central importance for Hobbes – provide the real justification for the original social contract. Rather, he argues stability and cohesion – as well as genuine security – are only possible if the civil association to which the contract gives rise is based on certain fundamental values. In this he is closer to Locke than to Hobbes, but he also disagrees with Locke, both on what these values are and as to their underpinning foundations. This latter point, in which Rousseau stresses the importance of feeling, has, as we will see, far-reaching implications for his account of the general will as well as for his disagreement with Locke over the nature of education.

Despite the manner in which Rousseau is often read as a 'progressive' thinker who champions the freedom of the child, some of the arguments about education in *Poland* seem closer to aspects of populism which are seen by critics as opening the way to authoritarianism. This is particularly so of the argument that education should encourage children to accept the fundamental values of society uncritically. This is a controversial interpretation and one which is hotly debated, unsurprisingly so because the concept of the general will itself is notoriously controversial in studies of Rousseau. Political philosophers and historians of ideas have offered conflicting accounts of the theory, and of its implications, ranging from radical democracy to authoritarianism, and this divergence has been reflected in much of the popular discussion of the concept in relation to populism.

Many of the most important recent scholarly discussions of the general will are indebted to the work of Patrick Riley, whose book *The General Will before Rousseau: The Transformation of the Divine into the Civic* (1986), refocused attention on the concept and placed it, and Rousseau's development of the idea, in a larger historical context.[14] His influence is reflected in the work of scholars such as James Farr and David Lay Williams whose edited collection *The General Will: The Evolution of a Concept* (Farr and Williams 2015) provides an overview of the current work being done on the general will in the light of Riley's work.

Riley argues that the idea of the general will draws upon several previous ideas, one of which is the theological doctrine, central to the Calvinist theology which was officially[15] taught in Geneva when Rousseau was a child, of God's sovereign will. According to this doctrine, God's will is the basis of a universal morality which all people are obliged to follow. Although Rousseau rejects the main teachings of Calvinist theology he does accept the argument that all justice comes from God.[16] He significantly modifies this, though, when he further argues that the universal principles of this morality can only be understood when they are expressed through laws specific to particular communities. In practical terms, then, moral sovereignty is properly understood, and can only be expressed, in terms of a general will which is neither particular nor universal. It is general, as opposed to universal, in that it is generally applicable to all members of a specific community, but not universally to all members of humanity. It is general rather than particular because it is distinct from the particular wills of individual members of society: the general will is not the will of all or even the will of the majority (Rousseau 2019b: Book II, Chapter 3).

The general will is the expression of the sovereign, but Rousseau's concept of who, or what, the sovereign is, differs markedly from that of many of his contemporaries and most particularly from that of Hobbes. Hobbes argues that life in the state of nature is, in the most famous phrase in *Leviathan*, 'nasty brutish and short', a situation which he also characterises as a 'condition which is called war; and such a war, as is of every man, against every man' (Hobbes 1996: Book 1, Chapter 13). Under such circumstances, Hobbes argues, people would willingly give up much of their freedom to an individual or group who could guarantee their security. This individual or group of people would then rule as an absolute sovereign because only that way would they be able to control a naturally warlike and aggressive people.

Rousseau agrees with Hobbes that the sovereign should be absolute but differs radically on who comprises the sovereign, and the sovereign's relationship to the individuals who live under its authority. The sovereign, he argues is made up of all the people who are citizens of a particular community and the general will is the expression of the will of these citizens. Because all citizens are members of the sovereign, in collectively willing something they are each individually exercising their choice and so are bound by the decisions they themselves have made. This appears to be a very democratic position to hold and it has many echoes in populist ideas which emphasise the will of the people. Where it appears to differ from liberalism is in the lack of any restraint on what the general will may legitimately decide.

In making this claim Rousseau is in part following Montesquieu who emphasised the importance of understanding different societies in terms of their particular geographies, histories and cultures (Rousseau 2019b: 82), an idea which has significance for the nationalist strand in populism and its attendant implications for educational policies. The greatest significance of Rousseau's argument, though, lies in its contrast to the liberal idea of a universal will which reflects the good of humanity and which provides a rationale for the cosmopolitanism shared by many Enlightenment thinkers. Rousseau rejects this liberal idea emphatically in many places, such as his original second chapter of *The Social Contract* 'Of the General Society of Mankind' in the *Geneva Manuscript* (Rousseau 2019b: 156–65). Here he attacks Denis Diderot's argument in his article 'Natural Rights', written for the *Encyclopedia of Diderot and d'Alembert* (2009), where Diderot argues that there is a general will which all rational beings can come to understand and accept, and which should form the basis of laws in all just societies. In arguing to the contrary, that each community has its own general will and that the general wills of different communities will at times be different and potentially in conflict, Rousseau is placing himself against the prevailing values of the Enlightenment as profoundly and unapologetically as he had done in the *Discourse on the Sciences and Arts*.

We may conclude from this that education should not be based on cosmopolitan liberal ideas of global justice or universal human rights but on the need to teach the values of one's own community. In taking this position Rousseau's argument runs counter to the emphasis in many Western schools and universities on creating global citizens who able to work (and compete) in a global environment. Rousseau would have regarded education for global citizenship as a means to the creation of 'dead souls', Samuel Huntington's phrase to describe people who have more in common with an international elite who share their globalised values than they do with the great majority of members of their own country.[17] His position anticipates that of populists such as Viktor Orbán who emphasise the importance of a national education which promotes the particular values and interests of its own country as opposed to the cosmopolitan liberalism of the CEU. The autonomy of the individual is played down in order to strengthen the autonomy of the community.[18]

It might seem to follow from this that Rousseau cannot argue that values of one's own society are inherently superior to those of other societies: such a claim would not make sense because there is no possible neutral, global vantage point from which it might be possible to be able to assess such values – the claim that there can be is itself a liberal illusion. This is clearly linked to Rousseau's opposition to the idea that there can be a universal or cosmopolitan citizenship – citizenship is the product of particular histories and of values which can only be expressed through the general will. Our understanding – in an emotional as well as an intellectual sense – is shaped by the kind of community we live in and by the kind of education which it requires us to undertake, both formally and informally.

There is an apparent contradiction in Rousseau's thought, though; one mirrored in the contemporary populism. Rousseau is highly critical of the corruption that he detects in contemporary society, so much so that he believes that Emile has to be educated in isolation from French society in order not to become polluted by it. But if every society has its own general will, how is it possible to condemn various European societies as bad?

One possible way of defending Rousseau is to say that he, in contrast to the great majority of his fellow citizens, is giving expression to the general will of his society. Such a reading is not implausible, particularly given that Rousseau writes a good deal about his superior insight into moral truths, particularly in *The Confessions* (Rousseau 1995) and *Reveries of a Solitary Walker* (Rousseau 2011). This argument may also draw on the example of Emile, whose education is intended to make him understand and correctly express the general will in order that he too may act as a model of good citizenship.

A comparison might be drawn with Socrates, who while on trial for his life in the *Apology* tells the jury that he is a gift from the gods to Athens because he can see clearly what is wrong with the life of the city and how it ought to be put right (*Apology* 30d–31a). Rousseau would no doubt have thought it entirely reasonable to be compared with Socrates, but the comparison raises a particular difficulty. Socrates claimed to be able to offer guidance to the Athenians because of his knowledge (admittedly limited in the *Apology*) of moral principles that are true not just for Athens but for all human beings. In Plato's *Republic* this gives way to a full-blown theory of the universal Forms and the education system that is required if the wise are to rule. Rousseau does think that some things are morally wrong in all places and at all times, such as slavery, or significant economic inequality which can lead to corruption,[19] but is this reconcilable with what he says about the particularity of the general will?

This might be reformulated as the question of how universal principles can be applied in the different contexts of different societies. Many societies may be so corrupt that their members cannot understand clearly (if at all) what these principles are. Hence Rousseau's comment quoted earlier that only free men can live in, and sustain, free societies. But even when societies are just they will still have to apply the general principles in their own context.

Understanding Rousseau's argument more fully requires returning to his discussion of the state of nature. Rousseau argues in the *Discourse on the Origins of Inequality* that in the state of nature individuals were driven by two things: *amour de soi-même* and *pitié*. By *amour de soi-même* he means 'self-love, a natural feeling which reinforces the desire in all sentient beings for self preservation' and when 'guided in man by reason modified by pity produces humanity and virtue' (Rousseau 2019a: 224). By *pitié* he means pity in the sense of compassion, and gives examples drawn both from humans, such as a human mother's natural tenderness for her children, and from the behaviour of animals (Rousseau 2019a: 155). Neither the desire for preservation nor feelings of compassion are the result of reasoning. Both, we might say, are essentially pre-rational. This must be so because people in the original state of nature lack language and so could not reason. It is very important for Rousseau both that people did not need to be educated in the state of nature to develop self-love and pitié but also that, lacking language, they could not be. Education is possible only in society.

In his account of humans in the state of nature, Rousseau disagrees with Hobbes' view of human nature as being essentially violent and aggressive. Such traits, Rousseau argues, are not present in the state of nature but are the consequences of people living in society. Here education does have a role to play, though often a pernicious one. People in contemporary European societies, he argues, are taught to put aside these positive qualities and instead to cultivate *amour-propre*. This term is often translated as 'pride' or 'vanity' and indicates a belief that one is superior to others. Rousseau also associates it, in a highly critical manner, with codes of honour which are prevalent in highly stratified societies such as that of France in his day (Rousseau 2019a: 224). The practice of comparing oneself with others was unknown in the state of nature because of the solitary lives which individuals led and it becomes possible only when people have left the state of nature and live in settled societies.

Rousseau believes that this learning to be selfish, to be less compassionate and to regard oneself as superior to others are important features of education in contemporary Europe. It is one very important reason why Emile has to be educated in isolation. But this negative education is not the only possible consequence of living in society: both society and the education which sustains its propagation of these misguided and harmful attitudes are redeemable. Indeed, education has a major role to play in the process of redemption. This is why he says that when self-love is guided by 'reason and modified by pity' it 'produces humanity and virtue'. What is most striking in this claim is that humanity and virtue are the products of reason, as well as pity, which means that it is only after leaving the state of nature and entering into a well-ordered, just, society that these higher moral traits can be developed. This is not something which the individual can accomplish for himself, and even with the assistance of a virtuous and exceptional teacher it is extremely difficult. It is for this reason that the education in *Emile* is only a poor substitute for the education which would become possible in a just society.

This is so because the bringing about of a harmonious order in society through the general will and the development of virtue (and the suppression of the vices associated with *amour-propre*) within that society are mutually reinforcing. Consequently, when a society is reformed in such a way that it increasingly reflects the general will, its individual members become more virtuous. This helps to explain two things. First, it provides a reason for believing why, as Rousseau frequently claims, such a society will pose no threat to peoples' individual freedoms. Second, it explains the relationship between the laws established by the general will and universal moral principles.

Rousseau says on a number of occasions that individual freedoms are guaranteed by the general will because each member of society is a member of the sovereign and so would not agree to laws which threaten their own freedom. Liberals such as Locke are sceptical of this argument because of the constant danger that all governments, even legitimate ones, will try to manipulate public opinion to suit their own ends. Public education, in their view, is a powerful tool of government control and this is one reason why Locke and also Mill (as we will see in Chapter 5) are wary of allowing education to be brought under the control of the state. Rousseau agrees with the need to ensure that government does not act corruptly but argues that the best means of doing this is to ensure that the general will is functioning as it ought. A government acting under the guidance of the general will is much more likely to ensure that the freedoms of individual members are safeguarded while simultaneously promoting the good of the community as a whole. Under such circumstances, education carried out in the interests of the state will also be in the interests of the individuals who make it up.

There are echoes here of Plato's argument in the *Republic* that in a society ruled by the wise and virtuous philosophers, the rulers will be compelled to act in the interests of the community, and all its members, rather than in their own self-interest. Like Rousseau, Plato argues that education should be provided by the state and in one respect Plato does accept the importance of encouraging the individual to pursue his or her own interests in that everyone in the Republic is educated with a view to maximising their full potential and in keeping with their skills and aptitudes. Dewey's comment on the educational theory of the *Republic*, referred to earlier in Chapter 2, that '[i]t would be impossible to find a deeper sense of the function of education in discovering and developing personal capacities, and training them so that they would connect with the activities of others' (Dewey 1916: 56) identifies an important positive aspect of Plato's argument. In a similar way, the education in both *Emile* and *Poland* seeks to draw out the potential in the child. In *Emile* this may mean a difficult and often lonely life as a person of virtue in a corrupt society but in *Poland* it offers a far more positive hope of living a fulfilled life contributing to the well-being of a just society.

Yet there is still a problem here. Despite Dewey's broad approval of Plato's wish to ensure that each person receives the education most appropriate to him or her, he also criticises the limitations of Plato's theory of education. A major weakness, he argues, is that Plato is unable to see the wide range of possibilities open to each individual, a consequence, he claims, of living in a society which was insufficiently democratic. To which one might add Plato's own rejection of even the 'insufficient' democracy of Athens. Rousseau might be thought to be exempt from such a criticism because the general will is much closer to democracy than is the rule of the philosophers. But liberal critics such as Mill suggest that the implications of submitting to the general will lead to the same problems as submitting to philosopher rulers: in both cases they claim to know what is best for the individual and allow no right of appeal.

To see how Rousseau might be defended against this view, we must briefly discuss the relationship between the general will of a society and universal moral principles.

Plato's solution to the problem of the relationship between universal values and the values of the good society is to say that only a society based upon these universal values – the Forms of the Good, the Just and so on – can be a good society. David Lay Williams, in a wide-ranging work, *Rousseau's Platonic Enlightenment* (Williams 2007), argues that Rousseau is far more of a Platonist than is usually accepted and that understanding this enables a clearer view of the relationship between the particular and the universal. Rousseau, he argues, believes in universal, timeless truths, which place significant restrictions on the general will. If he is right this provides an answer to those who argue that the general will in particular societies can in principle lead to highly undesirable outcomes such as fascism or slavery. It also explains why Rousseau can argue that there are some things which can never be accepted even if the general will attempts to postulate them. This does not mean, though, that all general wills will come to the same conclusions on matters of detail because, as Williams argues, these fundamental principles are indeterminate.

An important part of Williams' argument is that there are, as Williams quotes Rousseau writing in *Rousseau, Judge of Jean-Jacques: Dialogues*, innate feelings of moral justice and truth which are 'engraved in all hearts', or in the *Reveries of a Solitary Walker* there are 'eternal truths' accepted in all times and places and 'indelibly engraved on the human heart' and in *Emile* where it is claimed that there are eternal laws of nature 'written in the depth of his heart by conscience and reason' (Williams 2007: 74).

Conscience is indeed of central importance in this discussion but as Williams acknowledges, 'conscience exists and operates only in the social sphere' (Williams 2007: 75). This being so, it is difficult to see how the values which are written into the heart by conscience (and reasoned argument in language, which is also a social phenomenon) can be universal.

It helps to resolve the problem if we recall Rousseau's argument that virtues are possible only in society. Conscience, grounded though it is in feelings of self-love and pity, has to be educated within society in order to respond to higher principles of justice.

A major difference between Plato and Rousseau is that while for Plato the universal morality is fundamentally based upon principles which can only be properly understood through many years of intensely abstract study and the application of a highly educated skill in reasoning, for Rousseau it is fundamentally based upon feeling. This is not to say that Rousseau thought reason was unimportant in morality, he did not, as we have seen. He thought the articulation of virtue in society was dependent on reason, but it is only when reason is properly grounded in the natural feeling of self-love and of pity that it can enable people to create 'humanity and virtue'.

The exercise of the general will, unfettered by *amour-propre*, will not permit slavery or significant economic equality because these are at variance both with natural human feelings of pity and the rational understanding of virtue which will have emerged in the society based upon these feelings. But feeling is not sufficient: a just society is needed in order not only to guarantee the application of these feelings in moral principles and moral actions but even to articulate them. It follows from this that the different contexts of different societies, even when their general wills are properly functioning, and so are grounded in self-love and pity, will develop different moral codes – different laws – to accommodate the specific needs of their society.

Education has a vital role to play in this articulation and the way it does so will be influenced by the context of the society in which it is situated.

Part of the role of education is obviously to pass these values on to the next generation. Doing so will ensure that young people will grow up understanding those values and being able to participate in the expression of the general will. This is one reason why Rousseau is adamant in *Poland* that teachers (unlike the original Lawgiver) must be members of the community. That does not mean, though, that the values of the community as they are taught in schools will be unchanging. Over time change will occur, perhaps because of the growth of empirical knowledge or advances in technology, both of which will require new ways of interpreting both particular moral principles and the deeper feelings of *amour de soi-même* and compassion upon which they are ultimately grounded. Rousseau makes this point explicitly in *Poland* when he writes of the need to constantly reassess the relevance of the laws of the state (2019b: 223–4). Rousseau is very clear, though, that these changes should not be entrusted to a group of skilled experts – all changes to the law are the sole prerogative of the sovereign as it expresses the general will. If this is so, education is not simply a matter of indoctrinating people into an unthinking acceptance of current beliefs and values because as citizens they must have the skills to assess evidence and analyse arguments to enable them to assess the laws. It must, therefore, include an element of critical thinking.

This points to an important difference between Rousseau's view of education and society and that of Plato. For Plato there is one set of truths which can only be known through long and arduous intellectual training. Once these truths have been learned there is no further need to question them: all that is required is obedience to the teaching and guidance of those who are in possession of these truths. Criticism will lead to the destruction of the ideal state. Whether it is an alternative based on a thymotic sense of honour, on wealth or democracy, all will lead in the end to the worst of all rules, that of the tyrant.

Rousseau does not share this idea of a perfect society and he does not believe that knowledge of the values that ought to guide society should be the prerogative of a highly educated elite. In a just society, the education which necessarily teaches people the values of patriotism and self-sacrifice must also provide future citizens with the skills to rethink and renew the laws for which they, as members of the sovereign body, are collectively responsible.

Put this way, Rousseau's arguments seem compatible with democracy and the education system which such societies require has a vital role in preparing people to participate in the democracy. Yet Rousseau also argues that most societies, including those of Poland and Corsica, are too large to be governed as democracies and that an elected aristocracy is more appropriate. How are these to views to be reconciled?

The answer is that Rousseau distinguishes between the sovereign and the government. Only the sovereign can make (or in the case of the original founding) endorse the laws of the state, but the execution of policies under these laws is the prerogative of the government. This explains in part Rousseau's claim in *The Social Contract* that the English (as he puts it) are only free when they vote in parliamentary elections (Rousseau 2019b: 17). The rest of the time Members of Parliament take on the role of lawmakers and so become the sovereign body. Rousseau claims that in a just society sovereignty must always remain with the people and that the role of government is to act in accordance with the laws laid down by them.

The implication for education is that in a just society people must be educated into the values of the general will because only through an understanding and, more fundamentally, a passionate identification with it can people be good citizens. Rousseau's argument marks a major difference from Locke at this crucial point. Locke places knowledge of the natural law as logically (though not practically) prior to knowledge of how to live in society, with the very important consequence that it is possible to appeal to the natural law against the will of the sovereign. For Rousseau this is quite wrong: without being educated into the values of the general will, people have no means of properly understanding how to think and act morally. The kind of people we are, including the kind of moral people, is a consequence of being the kinds of citizens our particular society moulds us into. Education plays a central role in this moulding because it shapes the minds of children and young people towards this social end.

As the general will is an indispensable guide to interpreting what is right and wrong, being a good citizen and being a good person become indistinguishable in this context. So, in a society in which the general will is sovereign, no appeal against the general will is possible and a properly functioning education system will have no space for the kind of radical critical thinking which Locke (and later Mill) argues is an essential part of education. Justified criticism of laws that no long function in the interests of the community can only be internal to the sovereign people and must rest on the particular values of the community rather than on the supposedly abstract reasoning of a hypothetical impartial observer.

This argument has similarities with the objections that the Orbán government have to the CEU's claim that by facilitating dialogue and debate among the members of a student population who are recruited from many different countries it is able to foster independent critical thinking largely shorn of local prejudices. Such an education, the Hungarian populist might argue, will result in replacing the natural, historically developed values of a nation with the unnatural, ahistorical values of a disconnected global elite. The students will be left feeling rootless, incapable of achieving a sense of belonging. As a result they will have no standpoint from which to judge the merits of suggested changes, or even whether such changes are necessary.

In light of this argument it will be useful to consider again Judith Shklar's argument, mentioned in Chapter 2 in connection with Plato (p. 43), that Rousseau should be read as a critic rather than as a constructive thinker. If that is so then we can see why Rousseau can be so critical of both politics and education in his own time. He can be as scathing and harsh (as uncivil, we might say) as he wishes because he believes, unlike Locke, that contemporary society is so corrupt that in most cases it is virtually impossible, short of some great disruptive event, to make people see the need to transform society. But this is only one aspect of his thinking and in the cases of Corsica and Poland, Rousseau does offer practical suggestions of how to build a more just society, and of the kind of education system it requires. Moreover, the suggestions in Poland are far more detailed than would be the case if it were, as Shklar suggests it is, intended only as a utopian ideal (Shklar 1985: 14–15).[20] Rousseau certainly thought that a successful radical transformation of Polish and Corsican societies was unlikely to happen, but if such a transformation were to happen this is how it must be.

Rousseau is certainly convinced that individuals can only become fully themselves when living in a harmonious society: only there can they fully understand the significance of their own life in the light of the values articulated through the general will. Yet he does frequently emphasise the importance of the individual. Despite the element of manipulation in *Emile*, there is also a genuine sense of wanting Emile to develop as an individual. At least in *Emile*, though more problematically in *Poland* and *Corsica*, the education of the individual is never lost sight of. Moreover, works such as *The Confessions* (Rousseau 1995) and *Reveries of a Solitary Walker* (Rousseau 2011), are focused very sharply on the life of an individual and the importance of conscience, and more generally of self-reflection, is central.[21]

It is also important to emphasise a strand in Rousseau's political thought to which liberal critics of Rousseau do not always give due prominence. In *The Social Contract* Rousseau distinguishes between the state as a 'public person' and the individuals or 'private persons' who are its members. The individuals, he argues, have 'a life and freedom' which are 'naturally independent' of the state. Because of this it is necessary to 'distinguish between the respective rights of the citizens and the sovereign ... and the natural rights they [that is, the citizens] must enjoy in their capacity as men' (Rousseau 2019b: 63). The just state and general will which underpins it do not subsume the whole of the individual into themselves, as modern totalitarian states have tried to do. The distinction between man and citizen is crucial to Rousseau's thought.

Does this mean that education, or the education which Rousseau writes about in *Poland* in particular, is just an education for citizenship? It need not exclude the study of literature, for example, but Emile's early reading – or virtual lack of it is – is highly restricted, and Rousseau's rejection of the idea of a theatre in Geneva is in line with this, as we will see later in this chapter (p. 96).

It follows from Rousseau's argument that a school, or a university such as the CEU, which aims to teach students from a liberal cosmopolitan perspective, is bound to act contrary to the interests of the community (any community) in which it is situated. He is explicit about this in *Poland* when he writes that if Poland is to become a just society based on its own general will all its teachers must be Poles. But it would seem that the implications go further than particular institutions and their control by the national government. If a society wishes to ensure that its students learn only those values which are conducive to the cultivation of the general will they ought not to permit its students to engage in educational activities outside its borders, and beyond its control. Such an approach would rule out progammes like the Bologna Process and the Higher European Education Area (HEEA) which exists in order, among other things, to facilitate ease of movement between institutions in different countries.[22] The following extract from the statement of the Fifth Bologna Policy Forum is wholly at variance with Rousseau's view of education and illustrates how far his position differs from a major contemporary European view of the importance of cross cultural exchanges and the sharing of values.

> Higher education has a long tradition of forging international links and there are many examples of productive partnerships between our countries. Higher education institutions and stakeholders are among the key drivers of international cooperation through the mobility of staff and students, international research partnerships, transnational education and collaboration on reaching solutions to global challenges. In this way higher education has provided a strong basis for the crossfertilisation of ideas and good practice that contribute to solving global issues.[23]

Rousseau would reject such proposals because they would expose students to the corrupting influence of bad teachers in decadent societies.

The emphasis on the general will as a moral will is important in Rousseau in another way that has significance for populist ideas and practice. If it were simply a method of deciding what is most efficient or even most financially advantageous, the general will would be a mere tool, a device for calculating the optimum outcome. It might still be possible to argue that the laws that are issued from such a sovereign should be obeyed because they are recognised to be in everyone's best interest. This becomes even more rational if one takes a Rawlsian perspective and argues that behind the veil of ignorance one would choose a system that minimises the dangers to oneself. But the general will in Rousseau is not at all like that. The general will imposes moral obligations on all citizens because they are citizens, not because they are men, and someone who is perceived to have acted against the general will has to be corrected – forced to be free – precisely because he is a citizen. The correction is fundamentally a moral correction – it is justified not only by being for the good of all but, perhaps even more fundamentally, by being for the moral good of the errant citizen.

It is also a matter in which education is central. To enable people to see the error of their ways a process of re-education may be required. Yet if that is so it suggests that, at least in the case of the erring individuals, the education which is provided by the state has been deficient. An objection to this might be that it is unreasonable to attribute the dissent of a few to a failure of education. This might be a feasible response if the individuals are few in number and have particular reasons, perhaps particular quirks of character or eccentricities, which have led them to dissent.[24] But where larger numbers dissent, and particularly when such dissent continues over a period of time, the education system, on Rousseau's understanding of how it needs to be if society is to be just, must be at fault.

Rousseau is aware in *The Social Contract* of the possibility that a just society might decay to the point where the general will ceases to function (Rousseau 2019b: Book III, Chapter 11) and this leads him in *Poland* particularly to emphasise the importance of education as a cohesive force. In doing so he places enormous power over education not in the hands of the sovereign but of the government.

Rousseau defines the government in *The Social Contract* as an intermediary body between the sovereign and its subjects (Rousseau 2019b: Book III, Chapter 1). This initially sounds odd because if the sovereign is composed of all the citizens and all the citizens are subjects why should there be a need for an intermediary body? The reason is two-fold. The first is that not every subject is a citizen – children, in particular, are subjects but only potential citizens (they are, we might say, in the process of being trained to be citizens). The other reason is a more philosophical one, that the citizens are sovereign only when they are engaged in law making or law changing. If the people at large were given the power of executing the laws they would be tempted to do so in their own interests which would clearly undermine the stability of the society. The power of executing the laws has to be entrusted to those who can be relied upon to carry out their duties impartially.

The role of the sovereign in society is the most important because it enacts laws; that of the government is merely to execute them. Yet in order to execute the laws the government must be clear about what the laws require. That is to say, it must also interpret them – and in doing so interpret what the general will requires in the enacting of any law. This means that given its privileged position as interpreter of the general will it can be very difficult to challenge acts of government when it claims that it is simply carrying out what the general will has required.

Here the relationship between government, the general will and education becomes crucial. The government in faithfully executing the laws, and thereby fulfilling the mandate of the general will, has to ensure the education system upholds, and passes on to the next generation, the values embodied in the general will. Rousseau argues in *Poland* that the government, in the persons of a group of particularly experienced and distinguished members, must take a close interest in what happens in the schools and have the right to dismiss a principal if the education in his school is not sufficiently patriotic (Rousseau 2019b: 196). What seemed to be a criticism of Rousseau, that where there is dissent that suggests a weakness in the education system, becomes instead, from his perspective, a strength – dissidents show there are problems in the system, or particular parts of it, and these must be addressed perhaps by dismissing the teachers in the schools which these dissidents attended.

This sounds disturbing enough, but what happens when the system is working properly is even more troubling from a liberal perspective. The children who are educated in the way that the government requires have very little option but to accept the interpretation of those values as laid down by the government. The government's claim to be interpreting the general will is extremely difficult to challenge and given the control of government over schools, this is the interpretation that is accepted by the children. This is the education about which Rousseau writes in the first paragraph of the section on education in *Poland*, stating that it directs the children's 'opinions and their tastes that they may be patriotic by inclination, passion, necessity' (Rousseau 2019b: 193). It is the government's interpretation of the general will which decides what it means to be Polish – or in the case of modern populism, Hungarian or American.

Authoritarianism and the general will

Rousseau's discussion of education in *Poland* helps to understand why, in Geraint Parry's phrase referred to above (pp. 78–9), the education plan set out in *Emile* is 'only second best'. The provision of a suitable education in the corrupt and artificial society of the European countries of his own day requires that the child is removed from society and educated in virtual isolation by his tutor. But such isolation deprives Emile of the benefits of being educated in a society which would nurture him and help to grow into a well-adjusted and sociable person. This is particularly important because much of the education in the values and *morés* of society does not come through reasoning but through directing the children's 'opinions and their tastes that they may be patriots by inclination, passion and necessity'. Although Emile's tutor seeks to instil these values, the society of one man, however wise and honourable, can only be second best. Moreover, Emile comes to realise as he grows older that the morality he has acquired is mocked by the larger society in which he will have to live. This is very different to being educated in a society where everyone shares this morality and reinforces it on a daily basis.

Rousseau stresses the importance of inclination and passions of the non-rational in education, in *Emile* during the course of a highly significant criticism of Locke in which he attacks what he describes as Locke's chief maxim: 'Reason with children'. The problem with reasoning with children from an early age is that the ability to reason is only learnt through the process of education – it is the goal of education and so cannot be a means to achieve the goal. But if this approach to education is taken the children will become arrogant, thinking themselves as clever as their teachers and, what is worst, 'become disputatious and rebellious'(Rousseau 1979: 89).

There is some sense in what Rousseau is saying here. It does seem counter-productive to use language which children will not understand, but Locke would not disagree with this (Locke 1989: Section 81). Where they do differ is that from a liberal perspective such as Locke's it is indeed desirable to encourage a child to be constantly questioning and to be argumentative, even 'disputatious and rebellious' on occasion. This will encourage children to grow into independently-minded adults, though any arrogance this might encourage should be tempered in a well-educated person by the requirements of civility. It is not difficult to see why Rousseau would reject this approach: it is not something which encourages the unity of the general will, and so not something which could contribute positively to the education of a member of Rousseau's society.

Does this emphasis on the importance of passions and emotions and the relative downplaying of reason in education, coupled with a belief in the need to continually reinforce the values of society and where necessary to purify it of those who dissent, imply that this type of education might lead to an authoritarian society?

It perhaps seems unfair to criticise Rousseau for the use which others have made of his work, though the temptation to do so is as old as Burke (Burke 1993: 269–74). When Rousseau's ideas were taken up and applied to practical politics during the French Revolution, it was his negative criticisms that were most often appropriated. But in the person of Robespierre, in particular, the negativity was compounded with a powerful conviction of the need to purify the corrupt society through what were effectively authoritarian methods (Scurr 2006). This is not to say that populists who share Rousseau's combination of disdain for the corruption that they see in the ruling elite and a desire for a simpler, purer life, wish to introduce a reign of terror, any more than did Rousseau, who loathed the idea of revolutionary change. The problem is that in rejecting the liberal emphasis on criticism and autonomous learners in the present political and educational system they are vulnerable to authoritarian arguments which claim to be offering a superior alternative to liberal democracy. That may be, in part, be why some right-wing populists such as the French Front National or the Hungarian Fidesz party express admiration for the government of Russia's Vladimir Putin, which claims to represent a purer society than that of the supposedly decadent West. It is also a reminder that Plato's response to the problems posed by the corruptions he saw in democratic society was to suggest rule by people who in serving the good of the republic would allow no dissent.

Is this an overly harsh criticism of Rousseau? Perhaps not. As we have seen,[25] education is at the heart of Rousseau's political thought because it is only through education (properly conducted) that people may over time become citizens who can express the general will. On this argument, the closer a society comes to the ideal which *The Social Contract* sets out, the more conservative it becomes. Emile has to be removed from the corrupt society into which he was born and taught a set of values radically different from those of eighteenth century France but a child in a reformed Poland would be educated in society and with the express purpose of finding within himself the values of that society and the ability to express the general will. Removing a Polish child from the public education and educating him in isolation in the way that Emile is (or even worse, educating him in another country) would be morally reprehensible.

If we read *Emile* as answering a question about the fundamental basis of what education should be, we can then see that the intensely individualistic element in *Emile* is not primarily to be understood as child centred. That might seem odd, because Rousseau constantly talks about the importance of a child learning for himself, and a good deal of more recent literature on *Emile* and education has emphasised a reading of Rousseau as the founder of progressive, child-centred education. Despite the ways in which Rousseau has often been interpreted in this way, it would seem that the education offered in Rousseau's ideal society, while it might encourage children to think they are discovering things for themselves, would in fact be geared to the promotion of a very particular set of values and, more fundamentally, to the production of a very particular kind of person. The child is still free to explore the world for himself and to learn through observation and experiment, but the limits set down by the tutor, or the government of a reformed society, place strict boundaries around the child's activities: boundaries which he cannot criticise because they are hidden from him. There is nothing in the account of education in *Poland* that is at variance with the essential message of *Emile*.

Applying these criticisms to the education in *Poland*, Rousseau's argument about social institutions and citizenship at the beginning of *Emile* go some way to undermine the liberalism that many have seen in his educational thought:

> Good social institutions are those best fitted to make a man unnatural, to exchange his independence for dependence, to merge the unit in the group, so that he no longer regards himself as one, but as a part of the whole, and is only conscious of the common life. A citizen of Rome was neither Caius nor Lucius, he was a Roman; he ever loved his country better than his life.
>
> (Rousseau 1979: 40)

This is not to say that Rousseau ignores the importance of reason altogether, far from it, but it is reason which is guided by the deeper underlying values of society. Emile is indeed educated in the country in an attempt to isolate him from the corruption of the city, but when he is sufficiently mature and properly prepared by the education his tutor has given him he can enter society with the clear-sighted reason which allows him to see through the illusions of the sophisticated. In some respects this might seem to have parallels with populist ideas of educating children away from the influences of elite values, and, in a further similarity with modern populism, particularly values which promote international or global as opposed to national identities. Rousseau's rejection of the Abbé St Pierre's plan for a European union, complete with its own parliament, would endear him to many twenty-first century European populists.

There is a particularly striking example of this in his *Letter to M. d'Alembert on the Theatre* where Rousseau argues (in a way that is clearly influenced by Plato's arguments about dramatic poetry in the *Republic*) that the theatre is dangerous because it appeals to the passions, not reason, and that consequently no theatre should be allowed to be built in Geneva (Rousseau 1960: 21).

It is also evident in Rousseau's highly rationalistic views on religion. In the *Letter to M. d'Alembert on the Theatre* he writes that although he believes that the Bible is 'the most sublime of all books' nevertheless 'of whatever authenticity the sacred text may be, it is still more believable that the Bible was altered than that God is unjust or malevolent' (Rousseau 1960: 13). Such a view would have appealed to the *philosophes* like d'Alembert himself but would have been profoundly disturbing to orthodox Roman Catholics and Protestants because it appeared to put human reason above Divine Revelation. These ideas are expressed more fully in *Emile* and *The Social Contract*. The 'Profession of a Savoyard Vicar' in Book IV of *Emile* is a detailed and closely argued defence of a rational, natural religion which, though theistic rather than deistic, rejects the supernatural, regards all religions as essentially equal and places reason above alleged divine inspiration (Rousseau 1979: especially 295–310). Book IV, Chapter VIII of *The Social Contract* is, if anything, even more controversial; not only does it argue for a minimal state religion (along lines very similar to that of the Savoyard Vicar) but it also claims that the true essence of Christianity is inimical to stable social life. A devout Christian whose life is given over to the hope of eternal life will have no great interest in or concern for the society in which he finds himself and will be a bad citizen (Rousseau 2019b: 146–55).

Both Rousseau's rejection of the theatre in Geneva and his emphasis on a rational religion turn fundamentally on his belief in the importance of deeply held values of society rather than on individual reason.

Plays in the theatre, he argues, manipulate the audience's feelings in ways which disrupt the relationship between the morality which underlies society and the reason which is built upon it. Rousseau criticises what he regards as the immorality of actors and actresses who through playing many different characters from many different times and places lose a sense of who they themselves are, and of the society which formed them. If, as Rousseau maintains, the theatre is a form of education, the greatest danger it poses to a healthy society is that by drawing people into the emotional life of the characters it dislocates them from the feelings which they have been taught through their formal education and which is daily reinforced by their fellow citizens. Theatres thrive, he says, in corrupt, cosmopolitan cities such as Paris but they ought to have no place in a society which seeks to remain uncontaminated.

Rousseau's account of religion is similarly based ultimately in the importance of feeling. Like many eighteenth century critics of the old order he attacks what he characterises as superstition in religion and thereby rejects much that is distinctive about Christianity. Most importantly, this means jettisoning much that appeals to the emotions of the believer, such as miracles. This explains the nub of his argument which relates to the place of religion in society. Devout Christians are incapable of being good citizens because their feelings are elsewhere. The value of religion to society is as a means of social cohesion.

This requirement of a state religion places him in opposition to those amongst the American Founders who shared his scepticism about many of the teachings of Christianity but who concluded that no established religion should be allowed in the new Republic. Thomas Jefferson, from his Ambassador's Residence in Paris, fully supported James Madison's arguments at the Constitutional Convention for a separation of church and state. He went further though when, in collaborating with Madison in the founding of the University of Virginia, he forbad the teaching of religion.[26] Like Rousseau, Jefferson recognised the power of emotions and feelings and the power of religion to control them. Unlike Rousseau, he rejected the opportunity to use religion as a means of manipulation in either the state or education.

Manipulation

There is another aspect to *A Letter to M. d'Alembert on the Theatre* which raises this concern about manipulation. For a significant part of the book Rousseau offers a detailed and highly critical attack on Molière and other playwrights yet he admits in a long footnote towards the end (Rousseau 1960: 131–2) that he actually enjoys the theatre and that he has 'never willingly missed a performance of Molière'. How does he justify this apparent contradiction, not to say hypocrisy? His answer is that he is writing not to express his own views but to safeguard the interest and well-being of his fellow citizens. After commending himself for his honesty and integrity, he writes:

> Never did personal views soil the desire to be useful to others which put the pen in my hand and I have almost always written against my own interests.... Readers, I may deceive myself, but I do not deceive you willingly; beware of my errors and not my bad faith. Love of the public good is the only passion which causes me to speak to the public....
> (Rousseau 1960: 132)

Bloom is sympathetic to Rousseau here, accepting his argument for the need to sometimes speak as a citizen rather than a philosopher (Rousseau 1960: xvii), an endorsement based on Bloom's Straussian understanding of the nature of philosophy and veiled knowledge. But the argument has implications for a populist reading of Rousseau, too. In speaking for what he takes to be true interests of the citizens of Geneva, Rousseau is claiming to represent (or articulate) the general will. He is also claiming that he is able to do this by putting aside his particular will and rising above it. But he does not think all Genevans will be able to do this, because if they did there would be no need for his concern about the possibility of a theatre in Geneva; if the Genevans were able to put aside their particular wills, or even just their confused opinions on the issue, and transparently consult the general will they would immediately veto the proposal. So Rousseau's whole argument here is that he has a deeper understanding of the true interests of the people of Geneva, and of the general will of the community, than they do themselves. Indeed, this 'love of the public good' is, he claims what morally obliges him to write the letter, and to show to the people of Geneva what is in their own true interest.

So is there a way of reconciling the manipulator and the lover of freedom? One way, suggested by R. D. Masters among others, is to argue that Rousseau was aware of the seeming contradictions in his work and that he was writing on two distinct levels. The first of these was the surface level at which what he writes is to be taken at face value. The second is an esoteric level at which he is writing for the few who can read between the lines and see what is only implicit. Masters and Kelly in their introduction to Volume II of the Collected Writings, argue that Rousseau consciously employed this technique from at least the *Discourse on the Sciences and Arts*, and that the esoteric teachings exhibit a fundamental coherence across all his mature writings on politics, education and society which other commentators have claimed is absent (Rousseau 1992: xviii–xxiii, see also 183–4).

Such a reading of Rousseau is by no means uncontroversial. Nevertheless, if we look at Rousseau's frequent acknowledgement that he does not mean what he says to apply equally to everyone, it is clear that Rousseau is advocating different levels of intellectual, and perhaps moral, understanding in society.

Such an approach has considerable implications for education. In such a view, the few who are truly wise and virtuous have, as Rousseau says in both *Emile* and *Poland*, a duty to protect those in their care. Teachers (and those magistrates those who guide them in what they should teach) have to ensure that children do not read the wrong books (or virtually any books in childhood, if Emile's education is to be a guide) or ask the wrong kinds of questions. The Platonic influence is pronounced.

This discussion brings us back to the fundamental point that society for Rousseau, even, indeed especially, the kind of just society envisaged in *The Social Contract* or *Poland*, is unnatural. Education, too, is unnatural, but more than that it is an essential factor in promoting and reinforcing the unnatural just society. A just society is one in which people have been transformed to make them virtuous citizens; education is the means of moulding each successive generation so that its members grow up as transformed individuals. This cannot be emphasised strongly enough, which is why for all the talk in *Emile* of the child coming to learn through his own curiosity and experimentation, the fundamental purpose of education is to form him into a particular kind of person. Patrick Riley makes this point very clearly by contrasting Rousseau's position with that of Kant.

> What moves us away from 'pathological' self-love for Kant is not a denaturing civil education ... but simply 'seeing' – at the 'age of reason' – a moral law which (as a 'fact of reason') is just *there*. It is no accident that education (domestic and civic) is everything in Rousseau ... and (nearly) nothing in Kant.
>
> (Riley 2008: 592)

Indeed, a lawgiver such as Moses (or Lycurgus) who Rousseau believes is essential to laying down the legal and moral basis of society would for Kant be not merely 'superfluous' but 'possibly autonomy-endangering'. The 'possibly' seems too mild here. From a Kantian perspective (and from that of other liberals), a society based upon a lawgiver who inculcates the values which are then internalised in the general will is the antithesis of a free society. It is a society of dependent children and the opposite of Kant's view in his essay 'An Answer to the Question: What is Enlightenment?' that becoming an enlightened person involves thinking for oneself (Kant 1991: 54).

Riley offers a possible way out of this dilemma, and one which, if correct, would have something in common with Kant. Kant argues at the end of 'An Answer to the Question: What is Enlightenment' that we are not yet living in an enlightened age but in one that is becoming enlightened (Kant 1991: 58). Riley's argument, though he does not refer to Kant's essay, follows a similar line. At the end of a long process through which people become fully formed members of society, perhaps over a number of generations, during which the education process will have fully moulded them, new citizens will emerge who freely embrace the general will. There is some plausibility in this interpretation which picks up on an important idea of timeliness and gradual rather than revolutionary change. Riley refers to Rousseau's discussion of this point in *The Social Contract* and we might also think of the way in which Rousseau writes of the slow changes that will need to be made before the Polish peasants can become free.

Nevertheless two problems persist. The first, and more philosophically acute, is that, as Riley points out, even if people wholly internalise the values which they have been taught and accept them as natural and normal their thinking has still been manipulated by those who established the society and the education system. There is a distinct echo of Socrates' admission when discussing the foundation myth in the *Republic* that it would only be after a few generations that the people would believe the myth (*Republic* 415c–d). That this is sometimes referred to as 'the noble lie' is telling: it is based on a deception, and it is hard to see how the same is not true of the society which Riley imagines emerging from Rousseau's scheme. In other words, the people are not freely arriving at their understanding of the general will – their 'choices' are, to borrow a Marxist term, the result of false consciousness. To a liberal such as Locke or Mill, such an education system would be a travesty because it must, by its very nature, forbid thinking which is critical of the general will. As we saw in the discussion of the government control of the curriculum, where such thinking occurs it has to be corrected and the deficiencies in the education which led to it rectified.

The second problem is a more practical one, though it too has philosophical implications. This is that it is hard to see how this could be implemented in a particular society without sealing that society off as far as possible from other, 'corrupt', societies. This is something which would not necessarily worry those populists who are opposed to migration from other places, particularly by people from other civilisations whose values are very different. From a liberal perspective, though, it suggests a closed society which bars its borders to ideas as well as people. Although the Orbán government does not wish to break ties with all other countries – it has no plans to follow the United Kingdom out of the European Union, for example – its dispute with the CEU is coloured by the fear that such a cosmopolitan institution will cause confusion and uncertainty, particularly in the minds of those young men and women who might one day become leaders of the country.

We have seen in Chapter 3 that for liberals like Locke uncertainty is not something to be fearful of. In the next chapter we will see that from the perspective of Mill's more radical liberalism, uncertainty, and the challenges it brings to the settled order, is to be welcomed.

Notes

1 A note on editions of Rousseau's works. The standard French edition of Rousseau's works is the five-volume *Oeuvres Complète* edited by B. Gagnebin and M. Raymond (Pléiade, Paris, 1959–1995). Two major scholarly editions of Rousseau's works are available in English translation which provide volume and page references to the Pléiade edition. The first of these, two volumes edited and translated by Victor Gourevitch in the 'Cambridge Texts in the History of Political Thought' series was first published in 1997, and a new edition (to which I refer) was published in 2019 (Rousseau 2019a, 2019b). The second is the *Collected Writings of Rousseau*, various editors (Hanover, N.H.: University of New England Press 1990–2012): I refer to individual volumes in the text and Bibliography. In addition I refer to standard editions of *Emile* and the *Letter to M. d'Alembert on the Theatre* translated with introduction and notes by Alan Bloom (Rousseau 1960, Rousseau 1979) and also to two other useful collections on international relations (Rousseau 1991) and Bertram's edition of *The Social Contract and Other Writings* (Rousseau 2012) which complements his excellent study of *The Social Contract* (Bertram 2004).
2 For an influential modern discussion of authenticity which recognises Rousseau's importance in the history of the idea, which is also critical of his use of the concept, see Charles Taylor's *The Ethics of Authenticity* (1991).
3 An argument he makes at length in his *A Letter to M. d'Alembert on the Theatre* (Rousseau 1960: 79–81)
4 *Discourse on the Sciences and Arts* was first published in 1750 and in a new Foreword published in 1763 Rousseau refers to 'the unfortunate work' as being 'at best mediocre' (Rousseau 1992: 3), though as Masters and Kelly point out in their editorial notes, he was willing to see it republished as part of an edition of his collected works (Rousseau 1992: 203).
5 This does not necessarily mean that the aspiration to create a truly radically better society avoids all the problems attributed by liberals to utopian ideas. Karl Popper criticises utopian plans for society – which he attributes to Plato among others – because they are inflexible and permit coercion of the population in order to bring them about. It may be that in practical terms plans to bring about fundamental changes in society to make it radically better may carry the same problems. Popper's criticisms are echoed in some of the CEU's criticisms of the Orbán government.

6 *Emile* is explicitly about the education of a male student – females are regarded as less capable and, therefore, require a different education. In this Rousseau differs sharply from Plato and Mill who both believe that certain women are more intelligent and deserve a higher and more demanding level of education than do the majority of men. For a further discussion of Rousseau's attitude to women in his writings see Wokler 1993: Chapter 5 and Shklar 1985: 144–5.
7 Locke, by contrast, argues that a tutor's involvement with the child's education and his moral welfare ends at the time when he becomes 'within view of matrimony' (Locke 1824: *Some Thoughts*, Section 216).
8 The examples he gives are 'most Greek cities' of antiquity, the Republics of modern Italy and Geneva (Rousseau 2019b: 72).
9 Rousseau discusses the role of the Lawgiver in some detail in *The Social Contract* Book II, Chapters 7–12 (2019b). There is also an excellent discussion in Bertram 2004: Chapter 7.
10 For this reason I follow Gourevitch (Rousseau 2019b), Bertram (2004: Chapter 7) and Williams (2014: 89–96) in preferring 'Lawgiver' to 'Lawmaker' though the latter term is preferred by some older translators.
11 See *Republic* 516e–517b. Rousseau seems to have come to think of his own fate in similar terms.
12 Rousseau and these Central European populists also share a similar self-confidence (or, depending on one's point of view, self-righteousness). Such education, Rousseau maintains, is not for everyone, it is 'only suitable for free men ...' (Rousseau 2019b: 193). Hungarians and Poles (and not only the populists among them) might well feel that they have earned the right to be called free having shaken off the tyranny of the Soviet empire.
13 Unsurprisingly so, as Rousseau often writes approvingly of his own private education. He was taught at first by his father and then by a private tutor – see Cranston 1982: 23–5.
14 In turn Riley expresses his indebtedness to the work of Judith Shklar, to whom the book is dedicated (Riley 1986: v).
15 The extent to which the Calvinist theologian of Geneva in the eighteenth century had modified the theology of Calvin's *Institutes of the Christian Religion* was a controversial issue at the time. D'Alembert's article on Geneva in the *Encyclopedia* (d'Alembert 2003), argued that they had departed from most of Calvin's teachings. Rousseau, who took considerable exception to the article on a variety of grounds, the most important of which will be discussed below, argued that it was unhelpful to the theologians to say this in public, but he did not disagree with the underlying claim.
16 On this see Rousseau 2019b: *Social Contract*, Book II, Chapter 6.
17 Huntington borrowed the phrase from Sir Walter Scott. The section entitled 'Dead Souls: the denationalization of elites' in *Who Are We* (Huntington 2004: 264–73) captures very powerfully the reasons for nationalist rejection of global elites.
18 Rousseau's claim that the individual remains free because he is not subordinated to an external sovereign has similarities in nationalist thinkers who claim that the leader gives expression to the will of the national community – an idea which many nationalists (and some of their critics) trace back to Rousseau.
19 He does think that time may be needed to correct historical wrongs but of course that implies that there is a goal to be achieved which transcends the particular historical circumstances of any particular society.
20 Even if it were only a utopian ideal that would still imply a belief in universal values: a model to be aimed at, even if never achieved – as some have understood Plato's *Republic* to be.
21 This element in Rousseau's thought fed into Romanticism.
22 The aims and principles are set out in detail on the EHEA website, see European Higher Education Area (date unknown) 'European Higher Education Area and Bologna Process', www.ehea.info/.
23 This quotation is taken from European Higher Education Area (2018) 'Statement of the Fifth Bologna Policy Forum Paris, 25th May 2018', www.ehea.info/media.ehea. info/file/2018_Paris/36/8/BPFStatement_with_Annex_958368.pdf.

24 Mill argues in *On Liberty* that toleration and even encouragement of dissenting eccentrics is one of the signs of a free society. We will see in the Chapter 5 of this volume that this is indicative of a fundamental disagreement on his part with Rousseau and of the complex relationship between education and liberty.
25 A point made forcefully by Riley (2001: 133–4).
26 Madison, in defending the foundation of the University of Virginia as a secular university which refused to appoint professors of theology, acknowledged that this might lead to public disapproval: 'Without any such professorships, it may incur for a time at least, the imputation of irreligious tendencies, if not design'. But he thought it was outweighed by the benefits for students of not being subjected to religious teaching. Letter to Edward Everett, 19th March 1823 (Madison 1999: 795).

5 John Stuart Mill
Education and liberty

Education and the *Autobiography*

John Stuart Mill's education was in many respects as curious as that which Rousseau suggested for Emile. Mill was taught at home by his father James who was a close confidante and colleague of the philosopher and social reformer Jeremy Bentham. Between them they devised an education for the young Mill which was intended to prepare him to be the pre-eminent thinker and spokesman for Utilitarianism, and for the radical branch of liberalism which Bentham and James Mill championed.

'Nobody,' Locke writes, confident of being unchallenged, 'can think a boy of three or seven years old, should be argued with as a grown man. Long discourses, and philosophical reasonings, at best, amaze and confound, but do no instruct, children' (Locke 1824: *Some Thoughts*, Section 81). James Mill did not agree.

In his *Autobiography* Mill writes that before he was eight years old he had, under his father's guidance, read

> a number of Greek prose authors, among whom I remember the whole of Herodotus, and of Xenophon's Cyropædia and Memorials of Socrates; some of the lives of the philosophers by Diogenes Laertius; part of Lucian, and Isocrates Ad Demonicum and Ad Nicoclem.
>
> (1873: 5; CW, I: 8)[1]

He also, at the age of seven, read six of Plato's dialogues, 'from the *Euthyphron* to the *Thecetetus*': though in a passage which goes at least some way to redeem Locke's claim, he writes that the last of these dialogues 'had been better omitted, as it was utterly impossible I should understand it' (Mill 1873: 5; CW, I: 8). But his father 'demanded of me not only the utmost that I could do, but much that I could by no possibility have done' (Mill 1873: 5–6; CW, I: 8).

What is probably remarkable to most readers of the *Autobiography* is not that a child of seven would find the *Theatetus* impenetrable but that he could understand the other five Platonic dialogues he had been set to read. Mill claims that he was not a particularly gifted child (Mill 1981: 32), an assertion that is patently false, but his experience does add force to the claim that teaching abstract subjects such as philosophy to children can be inherently beneficial even at primary school age. One of the claimed benefits is that it helps to develop at a young age the type of critical and enquiring mind which is conducive to active citizenship, and this view Mill, and his father, would strongly endorse. Mill emphasises the importance in his own education of learning to think critically, rather than simply acquiring facts (Mill 1873: 31; CW, I: 35).

James Mill's policy of making demands upon his son which he could not possibly achieve is one that many twenty-first century teachers would reject as counterproductive and harmful to the self-esteem of the student. His approach to teaching also involved other unpleasant practices, such as the use of harsh, sometimes contemptuous language (CW, I: 48) which would undoubtedly have raised the concerns of modern school inspectors. Despite this, Mill argues that when the desire of the teacher is for the ultimate good of the pupils, the ill effects that might arise through the desire to stretch them and push them to achieve their best is better than an education in which they never achieve their full potential.

James Mill had read *Emile* and Nicholas Capaldi suggests that this influenced his belief in the need to control the environment in which a child is educated and exclude bad influences (Capaldi 2004: 21). Collini takes the reference to *Emile* further when he suggests that the *Autobiography* is more akin to *Emile* than it is to Rousseau's *Confessions* (Collini 1984: xlix). We might add that it is closer to how a highly intelligent and independently minded Emile might come to reflect on the way in which he was guided by his tutor. The great difference between the two models of education might seem to be that James Mill, as Mill himself recognises, taught his son to think for himself. On a generous reading of *Emile*, that is Rousseau's aim as well (though such a reading is more difficult to maintain in Rousseau's discussion of education in *Poland*), but it is hard to see how the manipulation of Emile's environment and the acts of deception could lead to the kind of independent individual that Mill, in large parts became. That said, James Mill clearly was a controlling person – and his son's fear of him is an indication of this, as he relates at various places in his *Autobiography* (for example CW, I: 52–4) – but this seems to have been more a matter of personal temperament than of pedagogic theory. In some important respects James Mill's approach to education has similarities with Locke's. There is a common stress on the need to avoid too much interaction with other boys, because of the potential for bad influence (CW, I: 38–9) but also – in contrast to Rousseau – a willingness to encourage the child to engage in serious discussion with older people. Mill himself refers to what he recalls as his sometimes (unintentionally) rude manner in discussion with adults but many of these adults seem to have taken little umbrage at the precocious young man (CW, I: 37). Some, like the economist David Ricardo, became close friends (CW, I: 55). Mill also spent a year in France at the age of 14 with Samuel Bentham and his family whose outlook and way of life were rather different to Samuel's brother Jeremy. In addition to the experience of a very different family life, the stay in France provided the very English Mill with a lasting love of France and French liberalism (CW, I: 56–62), an openness to the culture of another society of which Emile's tutor would have strongly disapproved, especially in one so young.

The differences between James Mill and Rousseau are further widened when we consider that James Mill's view of education, and the experience of it by his son, was far from Rousseau's ideal of an education in which the child is not hindered from pursuing his natural inclinations by the need to read books. Emile was denied access to books until well into his teens while, as we have seen, Mill was reading Plato in Greek by the age of seven.

Democracy and the need for an education in critical thinking

As a young man Mill had been taught by his father and by Jeremy Bentham to be an ardent advocate of democracy. He remained a democrat all his life, but through the influence particularly of Harriet Taylor,[2] his companion and later wife, and of Alexis de Tocqueville,[3] his concept of democracy evolves as Mill realises the complexity involved in creating the kind of democratic society which liberals like himself were trying to bring about in nineteenth century Britain.

This underlines two important reasons why Mill's writing on education and democracy are particularly relevant to today. The first is that he is grappling with problems of how to nurture and embed democratic practices which are still very real in those parts of the world where democracy is relatively new and where it may be fragile. The second, which is especially germane to our purposes, is how to respond to challenges to the liberal values which Mill takes to be essential by people who feel that they are disadvantaged by the political and economic circumstances. The two are connected in Mill's approach by the fear that if people are enfranchised too soon – or in the wrong way – they may pose a threat to social order, but the equally strong belief that extension of the franchise and the encouragement of civic engagement are morally imperative.

In both cases a major part of dealing with the problem lies in ensuring the right kind of education and part of the reason for this concern about stability and order has to do with what Mill refers to as the serious imperfection of education in England. In a phrase that will strike many modern readers, liberals as well as populists, as offensively elitist he writes that he and Harriet Taylor 'dreaded the ignorance and especially the selfishness and brutality of the mass ...' (Mill 1873: 231; CW, I: 239). Yet such an attitude was, as we discussed in Chapter 1, widespread among liberals in the nineteenth century and only began to disappear as the newly enfranchised working men were seen to take their responsibilities seriously. Linked to this fear of the uneducated masses is also a concern about what Mill, in *On Liberty*, following Tocqueville, refers to as 'the tyranny of the majority' (CW, XVIII: 217–20) and he argues that the great problem for the future will be how to reconcile individual liberty with the need for radical changes in the economic and social conditions of society. In what is to more recent eyes another equally unfortunate turn of phrase in the *Autobiography*, he argues that for such a far-reaching change to happen it will require that 'an equivalent change of character must take place both in the uncultivated herd who now compose the labouring masses, and in the immense majority of their employers'. 'Education, habit and the cultivation of the sentiments ...' (Mill 1873: 232; CW, I: 239) will be central to accomplishing this, but it will be a slow process: 'it is only by slow degrees, and a system of culture prolonged through successive generations, that men in general can be brought up to this point' (Mill 1873: 233; CW, I: 239–41). There are echoes here of Plato's fears about the potential for democratic societies to be driven by irrational, confused and self-centred individuals, and for a demagogue to usurp the place of rational, selfless rulers. Mill's view of Plato will be discussed later in this chapter (pp. 113ff.).

In this respect, Mill's political thought seems to be the antithesis of populism. It is distrustful of the mass of the people and, in *On Representative Government*, he does not even trust their elected representatives to write laws (CW, XIX: Chapter V). This said, there are other aspects to Mill's thought which contribute to a more complex picture. One of these is his emphasis (which he also shares with Tocqueville) on the need for greater political participation to help maintain freedom from over weaning governments. These might include local school boards, local government, churches (the Unitarian Church produced many radical thinkers and activists, including Harriet Taylor) and, particularly later in life, as part of a growing sympathy with aspects of socialism and workers' cooperatives 'as the intermediate institutions between the individual and the large industrial enterprise' (Capaldi 2004: 127). This reference to intermediate institutions is a particularly important one in Mill, as it is in Tocqueville, but it directly challenges the idea of a single, united general will. In this, again, Mill is at odds with populism (and with Rousseau) but it reflects a very important aspect of Mill's version of liberalism and helps to offer a significant alternative to populism. Most importantly, perhaps, it recognises the danger not only of the tyranny of the majority in terms of social pressure but also the way in which governments can manipulate the views of the majority either for its own malign purposes or because it genuinely believes that in doing so it is truly expressing the will of the people. This latter problem is one which, it was argued in the last chapter, Rousseau is unable to satisfactorily deal with in *Considerations on the Government of Poland* because, in part, of the government's very tight control of the educational institutions of the state. Among the most important roles of intermediate institutions is to provide bulwarks against government power, both through creating countervailing centres of power and by providing people with the skills and confidence to defend their interests and the interests of others. This latter role may potentially contribute significantly to an education which encourages critical thinking and personal autonomy is indispensable.

It might be thought, particularly in the light of Mill's ill-measured references to the majority of people in the earlier quotations from his *Autobiography* that he is, at least in some moods, too pessimistic about the ability of ordinary people to take a serious and informed interest in political affairs. But Mill responds positively to what he sees as the responsible and measured behaviour of the newly enfranchised, in a manner similar to the that of Gladstone and other Liberal Party politicians who become increasingly optimistic about the capacity of working-class men to participate seriously in political life following the extension of the franchise.[4]

Mill recognises the importance of institutional reform – in addition to matters of broad principles such as his advocacy of the widening of the franchise to include women, he also engages in detailed discussion on issues such as proportional representation[5] – but the most important change it is necessary to bring about is in ideas.

Mill argues that in times of social change and upheaval (such as he is living through) new ideas are more likely to be given serious attention. In such circumstances it is possible that by a wide and thoughtful acceptance of those ideas which are progressive significant improvements may be achieved. He is also aware, though, that this 'necessarily transitory' period of flux will come to an end and that in the emerging period of a new stability these erstwhile critical ideas and values will become embraced as the norms and that 'education impresses this new creed upon the new generations without the mental processes that have led to it ...' (Mill 1873: 254; CW, I: 259–60). Mill believes that the use of education to inculcate values in this way, as if they could not be challenged – which is what new periods of stability have always done hitherto – is 'obnoxious' and he hopes that his writings will help to prevent this happening again. Among the reasons for this cautious optimism is the belief that a widespread use of the Socratic Method will help prevent this.

Another point emerges from this argument, which is closely tied to the need for critical thinking. If all ideas are open for discussion, this ought to include liberalism and democracy. Indeed, Mill's own views on democracy are modified over time as he comes, partly, as we have seen, under the influence of Tocqueville, to fear the tyranny of the majority but also as he is increasingly influenced towards the end of his life by socialist ideas (CW, I: 241). Perhaps Mill would say the same of our current time when liberal democracy is being challenged by populists from within as well as authoritarians from without. He might well view with a measure of sympathy at least some aspects of the policies of a populist government which takes power following a period of economic, political and intellectual upheaval when many different ideas have been widely discussed. The emergence of populist governments in Eastern Europe may be partially explained in terms of the long period of change which followed the collapse of communism including both the harmful consequences of an abrupt introduction of free market economics and the exposure of the populations of countries such as Poland, Hungary and Czechoslovakia, as it then was, to liberal political and moral values from Western liberal democracies. The educational policies such as that of the Hungarian government of Viktor Orbán, with its emphasis on Roman Catholic moral values and its dislike of subjects such as gender studies, which it regards as in conflict with those values, might then be seen as a reaction to the period of flux and an attempt to assert the values it regards as essential to the health and well-being of its society.

Mill would undoubtedly be critical of many of the educational policies which have been embraced as a result of these changes, particularly those rooted in

Roman Catholic moral teaching, against which he would repeat his warning against the 'obnoxious power' which a misuse of education could wield over successive generations. But while this may be true, he would also agree that it is equally possible that ideas of liberalism and liberal democracy might become oppressive if taught uncritically. Mill himself is critical of many liberals of his own day who, for example, frequently reject the idea of votes for women in parliamentary elections (and of women standing for parliament).[6]

Mill's point is that any set of values, even the most liberal, is in danger of becoming a means of social control (perhaps as part of the tyranny of the majority, but not necessarily so, or not exclusively so) if not subjected to constant criticisms and development. This is not necessarily because people consciously set out to be oppressive: it may result from the best of intentions. But unless ideas are subject to constant analysis and critical reflection – a process in which education has a crucial and continuing role – the danger is there. Indeed, the danger is a constant one, which is why one of the most important roles of education is to provide the tools for critical analysis to enable active, educated citizens to meet it head on.

Developing the self

This criticism that education based on liberal values may teach in such a way that liberal principles may be accepted uncritically has already been encountered during the discussion of Locke's theory of education in Chapter 3 (pp. 64ff.). I argued there that Locke had strong arguments against this criticism, but Mill offers an additional strand to the augment through his analysis of self-development.

This is an important theme in *On Liberty* (CW, XVIII), its central significance being alluded to in the epigraph from Wilhelm von Humboldt which Mill places at the front of the book.

> The grand, leading principle, towards which every argument unfolded in these pages directly converges, is the absolute and essential importance of human development in its richest diversity.

It is also evident in the justification he offers in the *Autobiography* for publishing a detailed account of his own education:

> ... in an age of transition in opinions, there may be somewhat both of interest and of benefit in noting the successive phases of any mind which was always pressing forward, equally ready to learn and to unlearn either from its own thoughts or from those of others.
>
> (Mill 1873: 1–2; CW, I: 5)

Some commentators have argued that Mill's concept of the evolving self is primarily rooted in the Romantic notion of *Bildung* (Capaldi 2004: 70), but while it is generally accepted that Mill was influenced by Romantic writers such as Coleridge and Wordsworth at the time of his mental crisis, and later, the lasting effect of their influence, and its depth, are matters of greater conjecture. At the very least, it is important to emphasise that Mill's notion of a developing self, of openness to new ideas and the willingness to both 'learn and unlearn' owes a great deal his acceptance of an empiricist epistemology. The comparison with Locke here is important. Locke's claim that we can, in the physical world at least, at best arrive at an understanding of the truth, 'for the time being' is one which Mill strongly endorses.

Philip and Rosen link this idea of the developing self to the nurturing of a good character and they draw out some of the key implications of very helpfully: 'Active, independent character requires a capacity for reflection, questioning, and self-examination on the part of individuals. It is the ability to make one's beliefs and commitments one's own, rather than merely inheriting or passively accepting them' (Mill 2015: xix). Mill's view, as it is characterised here, is again reminiscent of Locke's views, both in *Some Thoughts Concerning Education* and *On the Correct Use of the Understanding*. It also draws on Mill's interpretation of the Socratic Method.

One of the implications for education is that this emphasis on self-development might seem to be in conflict with the idea of educating people to be active citizens concerned for the well-being of the community as a whole. Mill does not see this as a problem. An education which encourages self-development through constant reflection and critical analysis is not narcissistic: it is constantly open to new ideas and to challenging one's own convictions. Very importantly, it will aim to develop a person who has is self-confident enough to articulate his or her criticisms of society and to put forward well thought out alternatives.

It must be said, though, that the way in which Mill sometimes presents this confident self, notably in *On Liberty*, can at times appear overly acerbic, such as when he argues that there may be a justification for aggressive use of language which goes beyond what is conventionally acceptable (CW, XVIII: 258–9). This, and his enthusiastic endorsement of the Socratic Method, invites comparison with the way in which Socrates was regarded as an irritant by many Athenians. There is need on occasion to temper the image which Mill sometimes employs of the brave, honourable, but also eccentric, individual pitted against society with arguments drawn from Locke's account of civility. Locke's argument that a primary purpose of education is to nurture a sense of civility in a person's character is something which can help to clarify and deepen Mill's account of education as a social as well as an individual process.

This problem of overemphasising the isolation of the individual, can be further alleviated by recognising that this ideal of development and self-reflection is not limited to the individual. Mill does recognise that communities of people can also grow and develop in a way analogous with the growth and development of the individual. Personal development is not something that occurs in isolation, as it does for the young Emile, but as part of a community, though in a way that is significantly different from Rousseau's ideas in *Considerations on the Government of Poland*.[7] One of the important ways in which Mill address this is through his discussion of nationality.

Nationality

In the initial definition of populism in Chapter 1 I suggested that one concern some liberals have expressed over the growth of populism during the past few years has been the use by populist politicians of rhetoric that incorporates the language of nationalism. This fear of the negative aspects of nationalism is reflected in the liberal support for avowedly internationalist programmes of educational institutions such as the CEU. Such cosmopolitan liberals see the nationalism of the nineteenth century as a phase through which Western society should have passed but which metamorphosed into anti-liberal integral nationalism in the first half of the twentieth century. From such a perspective, current populist expressions of nationalism are highly suspect because it is impossible to return to the earlier liberal nationalism which reflected a particular time in the evolution of Western society.

There is, though, a different strand of liberal thought which maintains that certain forms of nationalism are compatible with liberalism, and may even contribute to the success of liberal states. This defence of liberal nationalism owes a great debt to Mill's writing about nationality, whose account in *Considerations on Representative Government* recognises the power of national sentiment and argues that in many cases it provides a strong basis for a peaceful and stable political society. Mill couches this in democratic terms, of people being able to choose their own governments and the arrangements for their political association. He begins the chapter entitled 'Of Nationality, as Connected with Representative Government' by defining the term 'nationality':

> A portion of mankind may be said to constitute a nationality if they are united among themselves by common sympathies which do not exist between them and any others – which make them co-operate with each other more willingly than with other people, desire to be under the same government, and desire that it should be government by themselves, or a portion of themselves, exclusively.
>
> (Mill 1865: 120; CW, XIX: 547)

These common sympathies might arise from a shared language or religion, but it will most often, and most successfully, be based on a strong sense of a shared history. The basis of national identity, in this view, is partly emotional, a sense of belonging and sharing which necessarily includes some and excludes others. The exclusion need not involve dislike or disapproval, nor should it lead to violence. Moreover, the relationship between nationality and representative government can be defended as an eminently rational and liberal arrangement. 'Where the sentiment of nationality exists in any force, there is a *primâ facie* case for uniting all the members of the nationality under the same government, and a government to themselves apart', he writes a little further on, adding a very important consideration: 'This is merely saying that the question of government ought to be decided by the governed' (Mill 1865: 120; CW, XIX: 547). This seems to be giving priority to democratic decision making over national sentiment, as if the more fundamental principle is the importance of free choice and nationality is a secondary matter. This reading is, at least partially, correct; Mill does argue that the justification for people being able to choose to live in the same nation is that they are exercising their democratic freedom. But there is an additional point which adds a further complexity to the argument. 'Free institutions', he writes, a little further on in the same paragraph, 'are next to impossible in a country made up of different nationalities' (Mill 1865: 120; CW, XIX: 547). This seems to suggest a particular importance for national identity and its necessity for a liberal society to flourish which is very different from those later versions of liberalism which see national identity as both transitory and a hindrance to the acceptance of cosmopolitan values.

Such an argument has been seen by liberal critics such as Kymlicka (1995a, 1995b) and Parekh (1994) as illiberal and betraying an imperialist outlook and a disregard for the interests of small nations. They point, for example, to what they take to be Mill's claim that small and less advanced nations may be absorbed into larger ones to the advantage of both. It is beneficial, he claims for Bretons and Basques to be part of the 'highly civilized and cultured' French nation, 'admitted on equal terms to all the privileges of French citizenship .. than to sulk on his own rocks, the half-savage relic of past times, revolving in his own little mental orbit...' (Mill 1865: 122; CW, XIX: 549). He claims that this applies also to 'the Welshman, the Scottish Highlander' and, a little further on in the chapter, to Irish people, as members of the British nation.

There are, though, problems with this view of Mill as an English imperialist. Georgios Varouxakis points out, in the course of a detailed and critical discussion of the views of Kymlicka and Parekh, that Mill's contention that the Bretons and Basques should be admitted on equal terms to all the privileges of French citizenship suggests a coming together of equals rather than a domination of one by the other (Varouxakis 2002: 14).

Moreover, Mill has a further argument, in the next paragraph, which underlines this point further, and undermines the suggestion of an ethnic superiority. This mixing of different nationalities is effective because '[t]he united people, like a crossed breed of animals (but in a still greater degree, because the influences in operation are moral as well as physical), inherits the special aptitudes and excellences of all its progenitors ...'. In other words, mixing of different national cultures reinvigorates and strengths both.

Mill's emphasis on the importance of members of the minority culture being admitted on equal terms, and the consequent intermingling of the identities, is indicative of his belief that nations are not fixed and immutable but grow and develop through new influences. Nevertheless, this raises questions about how such incorporation is dealt with in the education system of the merged nation. If a genuinely new culture is to emerge, the education system will have to reflect that, but this is very difficult to do particularly if, as in the cases to which Mill refers, the languages of the merging cultures are different. In Wales during the nineteenth century, to take one of his examples, children in Welsh schools were sometimes forbidden to speak Welsh while at school, even though it was their first language, and were punished for doing so.[8]

Mill is clearly very concerned by the lack of 'fellow-feeling', as he terms it, and his arguments have a broader application to the significance of identity in politics.

> Among a people without fellow-feeling, especially if they read and speak different languages, the united public opinion necessary to the working of representative government cannot exist. The influences which form opinions and decide political acts are different in the different sections of the country. An altogether different set of leaders have the confidence of one part of the country and of another. The same books, newspapers, pamphlets, speeches, do not reach them. One section does not know what opinions or what instigations are circulating in another. The same incidents, the same acts, the same system of government, affect them in different ways, and each fears more injury to itself from the other nationalities than from the common arbiter, the state. Their mutual antipathies are generally much stronger than jealousy of the government.
> (Mill 1865: 120–1; CW, XIX: 547)

This is very relevant to the situation in liberal democracies where even though people may speak the same linguistic language they read different newspapers, watch different television channels (Fox News and CNN, for example, speak very different political languages) and follow like-minded people on social media.

Mill's belief in the importance of nationality would not lead him to support the forms of aggressive nationalism that were such a blight on the twentieth century. Mill's position does, though, suggest a view of nationalism which might be all the more valuable precisely because he did not know the ways in which it would come to be misused and is able to view the significance of national sentiment more dispassionately. This is particularly so with regard to understanding nationalism in the context of populism. An increasing number of liberal writers such as Francis Fukuyama (Fukuyama 2018b) and John B. Judis (Judis 2018) argue the need for a more nuanced account of nationalism which addresses at least some of the concerns which populists and their supporters have.[9] Recognising the importance of nationalist sentiment does not require accepting all the negative qualities which weigh so heavily on the mind of someone who has learned of the horrors of Nazism but nor need it be seen as a passing phase on the road to a more rational and enlightened political order. In this respect it may be an important counter balance to the cosmopolitan dismissal of national sentiment as reactionary and illiberal. It also has extremely important implications for education.

Clearly one way in which national identity is reinforced is through education, and it is at least plausible to argue that agreement on a basic national curriculum is necessary to ensure the growth and sustainability of a national identity. This might seem close to populist education policies such as those of the Hungarian government of Viktor Orbán. But there is an important difference. Mill, as we discussed earlier, fears the danger of an education system which is controlled by the state as a threat to liberty. This suggests a variety of different interpretations of the shared sense of identity – reflected currently in the United Kingdom, for example, by the different national curricula established following the devolved settlements in England, Wales, Scotland and Northern Ireland. Mill does not see this as the problem that populists do because he believes that the freedom to challenge particular interpretations – perhaps especially official government interpretations – is central to a free society, and that education should prepare children to become confident, questioning adults. But he differs from the CEU too, because he sees the importance of belonging, of engaging in discussion and criticism as a member of a community, not as a detached outsider.

The tension in Mill's thought between the autonomy of the individual and the responsibilities as a citizen to promote and sustain a stable, cohesive society has significant implications for his view of education.

The first is that for Mill education ought not to be merely vocational, although practical skills are important and are part of the key to developing the individual both personally and politically. One aim, perhaps in some ways its most significant, ought to be to allow the individual to be able to develop his or her own potential, the principle he emphasises so strongly in his account of self-development in *On Liberty*. In seeking to achieve this aim Mill explicitly invokes the Socratic Method in *On Liberty*. Later in life he came to see universities as having a particular role in promoting such education, an idea spelled out in detail in his address on being elected by the students as Rector of St Andrews University (CW, XXI: 217–20, 253–5).

The second implication is that such an education equips citizens to actively participate as free-thinking individuals in the political life of their society. One of the ways in which Mill's position is different to populism is his rejection of the populist appeal to the will of the people as an undivided whole, which Mill believes very often means the will of the people as interpreted by their leaders (CW, XVIII: 218–19).[10] For Mill, every citizen has a duty to critically assess the policies of government and opposition, and division and debate within society is a sign of its political health.[11] The Socratic Method is again of central importance here.

Mill and Plato

The Socratic Method

These references to Mill's advocacy of the Socratic Method and mention of them elsewhere in this chapter requires further discussion, as does his relationship to Plato more generally. Mill's view of Plato was complex and reflected a wider Victorian ambiguity about Plato's political philosophy and the Platonic theory of education (Jenkyns 1984: Chapter X).

In his *Autobiography*, Mill says that studying Plato was one of the greatest influences on his intellectual development and in *On Liberty*, he writes approvingly of the Socratic Method, arguing that the clash of ideas which it encourages is the best way to achieve understanding and to show up the faults in one's own (as well as other peoples') reasoning. It is, he thinks, an essential tool of education in a liberal society, and modern education has nothing that can improve upon it (CW, XVIII: 251).

Mill provides an extended discussion of Plato is in his long review of George Grote's three volume study *Plato and Other Companions of Sokrates*. Grote's book was published in 1865 and Mill's review appeared in *The Edinburgh Review* of April 1866. Both the book and review shared the leisurely Victorian length of such works, with the review occupying pages 275–379 of the journal. Grote and Mill were friends and they shared a common sympathy for Utilitarianism, though Mill's version was more flexible and sophisticated. Mill's discussion of the book was positive and laudatory, and Grote professed himself delighted with it, but the article is much more than a review. Although Mill had clearly read Grote's book closely, as he had also read, and separately reviewed, Grote's *History of Greece*, the review of *Plato and Other Contemporaries of Sokrates* is at least as much about Mill's view of Plato as it is about Grote's. In the following paragraphs I will discuss Mill's ideas in the article without reference to Grote (as, it must be said, Mill himself does of Plato's ideas for much of the review).

Central to Mill's view of Plato is Mill's attempt, which was discussed in Chapter 2, to draw a sharp distinction between the Socratic Method and what he regards as Plato's speculative philosophy. Mill is dismissive of the metaphysical foundations of the theory of Forms, a position he makes clear on the second page of the review. Mill's argument here is motivated on part by a rejection of Neoplatonism, which he considers to be a later mixture of decadent Greek thought and Oriental speculation but most significantly, he claims that what little connection it has with Plato 'belongs chiefly to the decadence of Plato's own mind' (CW, XI: 378). This last phrase is important because it illustrates at the very beginning of Mill's discussion his view that Plato's thought deteriorated from a position where he was open minded with no fixed opinions on anything and to which the Socratic Method was central, to a late stage at which he abandoned a critical approach altogether and became, in one of Mill's favoured terms of abuse, a 'dogmatist' (CW, XI: 413).

Mill is highly critical of the metaphysical speculations of the pre-Socratic philosophers, whose views he regards as obscure and sometimes unintelligible. Socrates, he argues, challenged these ideas and what is valuable in Plato arises from the interpretation and continuation of the Socratic Method (CW, XI: 381–2). But the Socratic Plato's most important enemy was, in Mill's view, not the Pre-Socratics, nor the Sophists, to whom Mill, in common with Grote and other mid-nineteenth century liberal thinkers, is very sympathetic because of their willingness to engage in critical debate and challenge received opinion. The real target of Socrates' criticisms was what Mill refers to as the 'commonplace',

> ... the acceptance of traditional opinions and current sentiment as an ultimate fact; and bandying of the abstract terms which express approbation and disapprobation, desire and aversion, admiration and disgust, as if they had a meaning thoroughly understood and universally assented to. The

men of his day (like those of ours) thought that they knew what Good and Evil, Just and Unjust, Honourable and Shameful, were because they could use the words glibly, and affirm them of this and that, in agreement with existing custom.

(CW, XI: 403)

Here Mill is taking up an argument which he returns to in the *Autobiography*, and which was discussed in the previous section. For much of the time, societies simply reinforce unthinkingly established ideas and beliefs. In his inaugural address as Rector of the University of St. Andrews he links this glibness and unquestioning reliance on existing custom to a bad education:

Whatever helps to shape the human being, to make the individual what he is, or to hinder him from what he is not – is part of his education. And a very bad education it often is; requiring all that can be done by cultivated intelligence and will, to counteract its tendencies.

(CW, XXI: 217)

A central purpose of education in a liberal society is to develop in future citizens the capacity to be critically minded so that they may challenge these confused ideas. They will be taught how to apply negative reasoning (the Socratic Method) to demonstrate the inconsistencies in many commonplace beliefs and also how to develop the positive skills of uncovering and clarifying the common elements of concepts such as justice (CW, XI: 229–30).

Mill's insistence on the importance of challenging commonly held beliefs is developed most powerfully in *On Liberty* where he argues that the liberty of adult individuals, in what they think and say, and in how they act, should be sacrosanct and restricted only in cases where their speech or their actions would deliberately harm others (CW, XVIII: 223). He refers admiringly to Socrates as someone who shared, and was indeed a martyr for, this view (CW, XVIII: 235). For Mill, Socrates and the Socratic Method represented what was best in Plato (CW, I: 25).

Critics of Mill have sometimes argued that the idea of unrestricted freespeech is problematic, an argument which brings us back to a criticism in Chapter 2 of undemocratic aspects of the Socrates Method. Jason Stanley raises the question directly in the context of current debates about threats to liberal democracy. Why, he asks, do conspiracy theories gain so much traction in modern literate societies when they are so obviously irrational? Should not the airing of public debate quickly show them to be absurd? He refers to Mill's argument in *On Liberty*, that it is wrong to silence any opinion, however outlandish, because knowledge arises, in Mill's striking phrase, 'from the collision [of truth] with error' (Stanley 2018: 67).

Stanley makes two important points in criticism of this view, which he refers to as 'the motif of "a marketplace of ideas"'. His first criticism is that on this reading of Mill's view such conversations are always carried out by rational people offering reasoned views which can be countered by other reasoned arguments. In practice, as Stanley argues, language is used for many purposes, including, in the context of debate, 'to shut out perspectives, raise fears, and heighten prejudice' (Stanley 2018: 67–8). He quotes an eloquent passage from Ernst Cassirer's *The Myth of the State*, on how the corruption of the German language caused by Nazi politics, propaganda and education meant that 'words which formerly were used in a descriptive, logical, or semantic sense are now used as magic words that are destined to produce certain effects and to stir up certain emotions' (quoted in Stanley 2018: 68).

Stanley's second criticism is that Mill fails to realise that in order to engage in a meaningful debate the participants must share 'a set of assumptions about the world' (Stanley 2018: 68). He appears to be thinking here of shared understandings of good reasoning, but the argument also returns us to the notion of civility. I have already argued that Mill, like Socrates, risks undermining civility by his championing of aggressive debate. What would provide the basis of a shared set of assumptions about the world is a common education which promotes a particular understanding of what it is to be a citizen of that society and of how to conduct oneself as a member of society. Education, therefore, as Locke argues, must involve an element of cultivating moral virtues, one of which is the virtue of civility.

The problem with this is, as we have already discussed in Chapter 3, how can an education in civility be achieved without stifling a critical, enquiring spirit? There clearly is a great danger here. Stanley discusses at several places in his book the way in which education can, if brought under the control of authoritarian governments, be used as a means of control[12] (Stanley 2018: 36, 48–52). If Locke is right to argue that there is a need for an education which induces a sense of civility, how are we to avoid the danger raised by Bejan (2017) and others that it will be intolerant of other views?

As discussed in Chapter 3, Locke argues that a certain kind of intolerance is acceptable, and even desirable, in a liberal society. He does so by distinguishing between those who criticise the liberal values which are widely held within that society and those wish to undermine the most fundamental values of the society, which he thinks are distinct from liberalism. Locke uses this distinction when he argues that toleration should not be extended to atheists because, lacking belief in a divine enforcer of morality, they cannot be trusted to act morally. Here the liberal principle of freedom of thought is trumped by a religious principle which is foundational to the societal values of seventeenth century England, and which was widely shared among Christians of different traditions. Decline in religious belief, particularly theistic belief, means that finding what such foundation principles are in a secular Western democracy is no easy matter, and may be one reason why many populists embrace a religious foundation to society.

This last point is not meant to deny the significance of the deeply held religious convictions of many devout Europeans and Americans. Rather, it recognises a point made by Charles Taylor in *A Secular Age* that '... faith, even for the staunchest believer is one human possibility among others'. 'I may find it inconceivable that I would abandon my belief', he continues, 'but there are others ... whose way of living I cannot in all honesty just dismiss as depraved, or blind, or unworthy, who have no faith (at least not in God, or the transcendent)'

(Taylor 2007: 3). Taylor depicts a condition that would be recognisable to many Europeans or North Americans since the nineteenth century, and one which Mill would have no difficulty in endorsing.[13] For most of Locke's contemporaries, by contrast, such a situation would have been unimaginable.

Yet, as Taylor points out later in the paragraph from which I have quoted, recognising the reality of non-religious views and practices has sometimes led religious believers to question their own faith and on occasion to abandon it entirely. If this is coupled with a rigorous application of the Socratic Method, as advocated by Mill, it becomes very difficult to find a consensus about any principles, moral and political as well as religious. Mill's discussion of nationality is intended to address this problem in a pragmatic fashion. I will return to some of the implications of this in the next chapter.

Experts

Despite his disdain for the 'dogmatic' Plato, Mill shares with the Plato of the *Republic* a belief in the indispensability of highly skilled experts. Indeed, in his review of Grote's Plato he attributes to Socrates as well as Plato, the belief that 'morals and politics are an affair of science, to be understood only after severe study and special training ...' (CW, XI: 382). This was one reason why, although he certainly does not agree with Plato's outright rejection of democracy, he does have reservations about aspects of democratic government. The best form of government in a democracy, he argues, is one in which the citizens do not make decisions about policy directly but elect representatives who, being well-educated and of high moral purpose, would make wise decisions on their behalf. Aware that this picture of Members of Parliament might seem idealistic to his British readership, Mill also argues, in another clear difference with Plato, for the importance of promoting universal education so that citizens would become increasingly able to choose their representatives wisely and judge whether they should be re-elected (CW, XIX: 470–1).

Like Plato, Mill sees the extension of the franchise to people who are poorly educated as a serious problem, but this reflects only part of Mill's position. Mill believes that education can help to develop everyone's potential far more than either Plato or many of Mill's own nineteenth century contemporaries were willing to accept. So important was the dissemination of this idea to Mill that he says it is one of the purposes which motivated his writing of the *Autobiography*. This is introduced in the opening paragraph:

> ... I have thought that in an age in which education, and its improvement, are the subject of more, if not of profounder study than at any former period of English history, it may be useful that there should be some record of an education which was unusual and remarkable, and which, whatever else it may have done, has proved how much more than is commonly supposed may be taught, and well taught, in those early years which, in the common modes of what is called instruction, are little better than wasted.
>
> (Mill 1873: 1; CW, I: 5)

He grapples in *On Liberty* and *Considerations on Representative Government* with the problem of how to promote democratic government at a time of poor education but a major part of his solution to resolving this is to improve education. Some of the limits which he seeks to impose on democracy in *Considerations on Representative Government* may be seen as temporary expedients until the general population has benefited from the introduction of universal education. His argument, mentioned earlier, that an expert committee, not Members of Parliament, should draft laws is not an argument that some people are more intelligent than others but that they have acquired a different level of expertise. To use one of Mill's favourite example, that of the surgeon, one would not wish to be operated upon in hospital by an expert in drafting parliamentary legislation, but equally one would not expect a surgeon to be able to draft legislation (not even, perhaps on matters directly related to surgery, though the draftsmen or draftswomen might seek the surgeon's specialist advice).

As liberals like Mill came to accept that a serious electorate could be trusted to act responsibly, the opposition to the extension of the franchise lessened. But the belief that extension of the franchise was morally and politically required went hand in hand with a belief that there was a duty to improve education so that the newly enfranchised could exercise their votes in a serious and measured fashion.

This should not be understood in paternalistic terms, as if Mill were advocating a system whereby people were taught what to think and how to act. Here again it is important to emphasise that he differs strongly with Plato's argument, and that of Rousseau in *Poland*, that education should be centrally controlled by the state. This approach to education has been much utilised by religiously orientated governments in the past, a practice to which Mill is adamantly opposed, and also by authoritarian governments in the twentieth and twenty-first centuries with their emphasis both on sound education and the need to 're-educate' dissenters. It is also seen by liberal critics as a policy which populists in power are tempted to pursue. On this last point Mill would sympathise with the policy of the CEU to promote critical thinking, and with its aim to educate students to become autonomous individuals, rather than with the Orbán government's wish to develop a state education system based on its interpretation of Hungarian values and Roman Catholic moral teaching.

Educating adults

One obvious objection to the various movements to extend the franchise in nineteenth century Britain was that even if, as Mill strongly advocates, universal education for children would eventually produce adults capable of exercising the vote in a responsible manner, that would not help current adults. Might it not be better to wait until after the education reforms could be put into practice and eventually bear fruit? Mill himself puts forward a similar line of argument when warning against what he saw as the danger of too hasty a transfer of power in India (CW, XIX: 567–8). One response to this is to stress the importance of adult education, both formal and informal.

Collini, writing in the Introduction to the volume devoted in part to education in Mill's *Collected Works*, argues that, 'Mill's conception of society is an exceptionally and pervasively educative one ... one could without strain regard his whole notion of political activity itself as an extended and strenuous adult-education course' (CW, XXI: xlviii). Mill argues in typically Victorian fashion that one role of parliament is to provide, through its moral leadership and the quality of its debates, a significant contribution to the informal education of the electorate. In *Considerations on Representative Government* Mill links the respect in England for seeing two sides of an argument (limited though he believes this often is) to the practice both of parliament and the law courts, but thinks the Athenians were much better practised at it because of their greater participation in the government and the courts (CW, XIX: 411). Listening to the debates in parliament and serving on juries, particularly when combined with an improved and enlarged formal education system, would, as mentioned earlier, enable people to participate as active citizens not only through voting but also through participation in activities such as local government and membership of political parties (CW, XIX: Chapters VI–VIII).

The nineteenth century witnessed a rapid growth in adult education, which was often met with resistance from conservative forces in both education and politics. In the 1820s there was considerable activity in this area, in part due to the political debates which led to the Reform Act of 1832 (Ashton 2012: 59). This included the establishment of the London Mechanics' Institution (Ashton 2012: 58) and the establishment of University College London, which was intended to offer open university education to middle class and professional people and with which James Mill had been closely involved (Ashton 2012: Chapter 1). As the century wore on The London Mechanics' Institute developed into Birkbeck Literary and Scientific Institution and eventually Birkbeck College and, university extension departments were established, in Oxford and Cambridge as well as in the new universities such as Manchester. A major aim of these institutions was to broaden access to higher education and, as part of this, to provide the intellectual space for older people to reflect upon and discuss political issues as well as broader cultural matters.

For Mill, these two linked ideas of education as both an exercise in practical civic participation and as lifelong, is fundamental to an understanding of education in a liberal democracy.[14]

Conclusion

Mill represents a significant modern liberal response to the challenge posed by Plato to an education based on principles of individual freedom and development. Like Plato he accepts the importance of reason and, therefore, again like him, he stresses the importance of education for those who are to rule society. Unlike Plato he believes that ultimately the basis of power should rest in the consent of the people as a whole rather than in the unchallengeable wisdom of a few. In the case of earlier liberals such as Locke, the consent is, by and large, tacit rather than explicit but in the historical development of the concept of representative government the percentage of the adult population who are called upon to exercise influence through various means, including elections, grew steadily. By the middle of the nineteenth century, in Mill's version of the theory, this encompasses a large proportion of the adult population, women as well as men. With such an increase in the number who were expected to play a responsible role in the political system the need for a corresponding widening of education provision was recognised as being imperative.

One of the reasons for the emphasis on the need to provide an appropriate education for the mass of the people was to help meet a potential difficulty with a system of representative government. What happens when the majority vote in ways that might harm the well-being of society, or some part of it, or indeed undermine the democratic system entirely? This is thrown into sharp relief not only by populist arguments which equate the will of the people with the votes of the majority but also by authoritarian systems which seek to validate their policies through plebiscites. In grappling with this problem in the Constitutional Convention at Philadelphia, James Madison sought to prevent this from happening by an elaborate system of checks and balances. Mill, following Tocqueville, is much exercised by what he sees as the danger of the tyranny of the majority in the American Republic and argues for a gradual expansion of the franchise in order to allow time for the education system to be embedded and to do its work (CW, XIX: 219–20). Both Mill and Madison though, see education as a key factor in enabling people to make wise decisions and so be well prepared to participate in the political process. This does not mean that either of them treat education as a means of social control, in the way in which authoritarian governments have often done in the twentieth century, but that they think education would nurture and develop people's natural reason and help them to see the intrinsic values of acting in the interests of society a whole.

This of course raises the further question of what these values are, or indeed whether they are intrinsic at all or perhaps simply reflect the values of the educated elite. One might go a step further and ask, as Rousseau does, whether current societies are so corrupt that it is impossible for its institutions to reflect, and its education system to nurture and develop, any sound values. The only alternative might be to rethink these values and rebuild society from the ground up. In which case, revolution, not reform, is the answer.

Mill, for all his later growing sympathy for socialism, is not in favour of revolution. He does, however, argue that in times of social change and upheaval (such as he is living through) new ideas are more likely to be given proper attention and it is possible for the acceptance of those which are progressive to bring about significant improvements. He acknowledges that regressive ideas may also be entertained and argues that it is very important for these to be challenged before this 'necessarily transitory' period of flux comes to an end and in the emerging period of stability new ideas and values become embraced as the norms and education impresses this new creed upon succeeding generations.

Notes

1. A note on referencing. Most references to Mill are to the *Collected Works* and are given in the format CW, volume number: page number. I have taken quotations from Mill's *Autobiography* and *Considerations on Representative Government* from Mill 1873 and 1865 respectively and also indicated where they may be found in the *Collected Works*.
2. Much has been written and speculated about the relationship which Mill and Taylor enjoyed before the death of her first husband and their subsequent marriage. Mill is clear that she was both his closest friend and his intellectual equal and collaborator (CW, I: 251–61). For Mill's estimation of her influence on his thinking about democracy see (CW, I: 259).
3. Particularly in his two reviews of Tocqueville's *Democracy in America* (CW, XVIII: 47–90, 153–204).
4. This is discussed further in Chapter 6 of this volume.
5. For Mill's views on proportional representation and more generally of the technical issues involved in extension of the franchise see *On Representative Government*, CW, XIX, Chapter VIII.
6. Mill argues this at greatest length in *On the Subjection of Women* (CW, XXI).
7. Mill argues that this notion of the development of communities is true both of the working class of his own day and also of people of other cultures and other races. It is particularly important to emphasise in this context that Mill was firmly opposed to any suggestion that people of particular races were inherently inferior to those of any other. This is evident in many places in Mill's writings, two of which are particularly striking. The first is in his highly critical view of Carlyle's overtly racist defence of slavery and the supposed inferiority of people of African origin and Mill's own rejection of racism in 'On the Negro Question' (CW, XXI: 85–96). The second, and related, is Mill's denunciation of American slavery and his passionate defence of the Union and complete opposition to the Confederacy 'In the Contest in America' (CW, XXI: 125–42) and 'The Slave Power' (CW, XXI: 143–64).
8. John Davies argues in *A History of Wales* that the practice was not as widely followed as is sometimes suggested and points out that it was never official government policy (2006: 443). Yet even though there was no law forbidding the use of Welsh in schools, the fact that was it not given any government support or recognition had a significant impact on the subsequent history of the language.
9. See also Eatwell and Godwin (2018) and Tamir (2019). All these writers emphasise the importance of recognising positive aspects of nationalism as a way of confronting the challenges which populism raises for liberal democratic societies, though they differ over their particular responses. Some of these writers, notably Tamir, draw on earlier writing on nationalism and liberalism by Isaiah Berlin (Berlin 1979; 1990a).
10. In this passage, Mill criticises the view '… that the rulers should be identified with the people; that their interest and will should be the interest and will of the nation'. Although he does not refer to Rousseau here the argument appears to be directed against Rousseau's theory of the general will. Mill's position here is also the antithesis of populist appeals to the will of the people.
11. He would have approved of the late nineteenth century American populist Farmer's Alliance who argued that rural farmers needed an appropriate form of adult education to equip them to make use of scientific developments and to help them negotiate with government agents and representatives of large corporations. Because universities were reluctant to change their curricula to serve the interests of the farming community, the Farmer's Alliance established their own educational facilities. This would serve as a good illustration of Mill's argument that education should not be controlled by government and that private organisations should be free to provide education suited to those they teach because in doing so they act as a restraint on government power. See Postel 2007: Chapter 2, 'Knowledge and Power: Machinery of Modern Education'.

12 Stanley offers the education policy of the Orbán government, including its attack on the CEU, as an example of what he refers to as a fascist education policy (Stanley 2018: 50–1). Stanley's use of the term 'fascist' is discussed in more detail in Chapter 1 of this volume.
13 Mill's education was entirely secular. 'I am thus', he writes in the *Autobiography*,

> one of the very few examples, in this country, of one who has, not thrown off religious belief, but never had it. I grew up in a negative state with relation to it. I looked upon the modern exactly as I did upon the Greek religion, as something which in no way concerned me.
>
> (Mill, 1873: 43; CW, I: 45)

14 Mill contributed to the encouragement of the wide dissemination of political ideas to working-class men and women by agreeing for some of his books to be published in 'People's Editions' at greatly reduced prices and with a subsequent loss of royalties (Reeves 2007: 323).

6 Education in democratic societies

The primary purpose of the central chapters has been to explore how some of the key ideas in liberal democracy and populism have deep roots in Western philosophy, and to consider the implications of these ideas for educational thought and practice. Although during the course of the preceding discussion I have criticised various arguments of all four philosophers, it has not been my intention to defend either populist democracy or liberal democracy per se. I have tried instead to take stock of the arguments as they have developed in the works of Plato, Locke, Rousseau and Mill and by doing so lay bare some of the underlying assumptions, both political and educational, that lie at least semi-concealed beneath contemporary arguments. Doing this might, with sufficient good will on both sides, and assuming a reasonable level of civility, help to make discussion between adherents of the two views more productive and lessen some of the tendency to talk past each other. This first part of this final chapter uses the four themes outlined in the Introduction, and to which I have referred throughout the intervening chapters, to draw out some important differences and similarities between the different approaches. The second part suggests some specific conclusions that are relevant to the place of education in the current crisis of democracy.

Four themes

Education and a stable society

All societies require a measure of stability and consensus in order to function. This is as true of liberal societies as those populists wish to bring about. Stability and consensus are not more important than critical thinking or individual autonomy in liberal thought, but they are a requirement for these to flourish. In some societies, stability and consensus are enforced by fear or through the imposition of religious or ideological beliefs, an imposition in which control of the education system frequently plays a vital part. Liberal democratic societies claim to be different in that the stability is based on a consensus which is both voluntary and open to internal revision.

Plato argues that democratic societies are inherently unstable. Democracy, in his view, creates citizens who are inevitably motivated by a confused and misinformed sense of self-interest, which renders impossible any form of consensus.

For this reason, he argues that the best form of society, and the one which has the greatest stability, is that in which the majority of people are educated to have no interest in political affairs, and to put their trust in the wise few highly educated men and women who alone are suited to govern because of a blend of wisdom, virtue and skill in ruling.

Plato's criticism is particularly important because it cuts directly across an argument frequently made in contemporary democratic societies by political theorists, politicians and journalists that stability is possible in democratic society provided that (among other things) it is accompanied by a measure of civility. On this view, Plato's criticism of democracy is applicable not, as he thought, to all possible democracies but only to those errant ones which lack the means of peaceful and rational resolution of disagreement. If this is the case, it casts a new light on the current discussion of civility in contemporary democratic societies and the perception of its increasing absence from public political debate in countries such as the United States and the United Kingdom where freedom of speech and tolerance of the views of others have traditionally been regarded as given. Perhaps these democracies are showing signs of what Francis Fukuyama, drawing on the work of Samuel Huntington, characterises as political decay, a situation where political institutions are no longer capable of fulfilling the functions they were designed for and political order becomes unstable (Fukuyama 2014).

'Civility', Keith Thomas has written in his wide-ranging survey of the history of the concept,

> was (and is) a slippery and unstable word. Yet although it was employed in the early modern period in a variety of senses, they all related in one way or another to the existence of a well-ordered political community and the appropriate qualities and conduct required of its citizens.
>
> (Thomas 2018: 6)

It is out of such well-ordered societies that modern democratic government grew.

This is certainly the case with Locke's use of 'civility'. It suggests a powerful role for education in preserving social order and stability through transferring the value and practice of civility, and the broader notion of social responsibility of which it is a part, across generations. It also implies that a very important purpose of education is to equip young people to navigate their way through society as they mature and enter into the duties and obligations of citizenship.

One criticism of civility is that it is exclusionary: that advocates of civility effectively discount those who do not accept the rules for polite discourse which they have laid down. Keith Thomas refers to those who claim that 'civility' is linked to 'civilised' and that the 'civilised' European societies which dominated the world from the seventeenth to the twentieth centuries were able to ignore the claims of those they conquered and ruled because, being 'uncivilised', they could not enter into the kind of political debate which required 'civility' (Thomas 2018: 2). Theresa Bejan offers a specific criticism of Locke along broadly similar lines, as was discussed in Chapter 3. Education is of great importance here because if the critics are right, the teaching of civility which ought, according to the liberal argument of Locke, to promote critical thinking and toleration, is wrapped up in a programme which is exclusionary and so, whether implicitly or explicitly, encourages intolerance. This would bring it into direct conflict with the argument that a very important part of education in a liberal society is to emphasise the importance of toleration and inclusivity.

Populists sometimes argue along similar lines when they claim that at least some calls for civility are an attempt to defend the privileges of an elite who wish to remain immune to criticism. Education, they argue, seeks to support this attempted immunity in two ways. The first is by indoctrinating children with ideas such as the need to maintain order and harmony in society through respect for those in positions of authority. At times of social upheaval, such as Western democracies are experiencing at present, these ideas have less power over people (cabinet ministers in Britain or senior members of Congress in the United States, for example, are no longer granted the respect they might think is their due). But liberal education also has a more subtle agenda. It provides a two-level education; a more sophisticated education for the children and young adults of the elite (and those it wishes to co-opt) and a more basic education for the remainder. What makes this particularly effective is that those receiving the more sophisticated education acquire skills in reasoning and argument which place them in a position to dominate the less articulate graduates of the lower level education.

This criticism of education in liberal societies as being exclusive and elitist is not new: it bears a strong resemblance to Pierre Bourdieu's concept of education as 'reproductive' (Bourdieu and Passeron 1990; Bourdieu 1998). Bourdieu's account is similar to that of populists in so far as it sees education as having a primarily ideological function in society. By inculcating the dominant values of the wealthy and powerful it reinforces and perpetuates their privileged positions while for the rest, 'persuading each social subject to stay in the place which falls to him by nature, to know his place and hold to it ... as Plato put it' (Bourdieu and Passeron 1990: 210).[1] Mill's own highly unusual education at the hands of his father and his subsequent career working with his father in the East India Company, eventually rising to the highly lucrative post of Chief Examiner (Reeves 2007: 256), might seem to fit this picture.

Populists argue that the lack of access to quality education deprives the majority of people of the skills needed to rationally debate with the highly educated members of the elite; uncivil language which is aggressive or mocking may be among the few tools available for disrupting the status quo. This is an argument which we encountered in Rousseau and it is apparent in populist rhetoric such as the chants to imprison Hilary Clinton at Trump rallies during the 2016 presidential election and the daily abuse of political opponents on social media.

Yet populists also require a form of civility for their arguments to be heard, and for the democratic process to function and to allow them to take power – or, as they might argue, to reclaim it. This suggests that, despite some appearances to the contrary in Rousseau's thought and the rhetoric of some contemporary populists, civility is very important but it can only function properly in a society conscious of its national identity and values. (Populism appeals, after all, to a pre-existing sense of national identity, even if it is largely based on nostalgia, as in the case of much of the rhetoric over Brexit.) Cosmopolitanism, in this view, dilutes the possible range of shared values by enlarging the number and variety to the point where they cease to provide a coherent basis for a social consensus. This is certainly Rousseau's view, particularly in *Poland* where he argues that in order for a national community to flourish, teaching ideas of civil responsibility and a sense of commitment to the well-being of all through a well-ordered (or, perhaps more aptly, 'tightly controlled') education system, is essential. Rousseau would not approve of the CEU any more than he approves of the Abbe St Pierre's project for a union of European states.

Elements of this argument can be traced back to Plato. While he agrees that people within the same community should be treated as deserving of respect and dignity, his view of an ordered society excludes the need for the element of toleration which is a key part of liberal ideas of civility. There is no need for political civility because there is no scope in the ideal republic for political disagreement. Civility amongst the philosopher rulers, who are by their very nature virtuous people, is unnecessary. A due measure of politeness and respect between members within classes, and between classes, is desirable, but that is a product of the social harmony that comes from wise government, not a cause of it. This is one reason why education is so important in the *Republic*. It prepares people for membership in this harmonious society, by recognising their distinctive abilities and providing them with the education best suited to develop those abilities, both for themselves and for the good of the community. If this is so, education may easily become a form of social control or, more charitably, social guidance. The charitable interpretation requires not only a belief that the philosopher rulers are most skilled at ruling but also that they are virtuous. This is why the question of nationalism is so important to the debate between populists and liberals, and why education is at the heart of the alternative visions they have for society.

Nationality and national education

One response from within one strand of contemporary liberalism to the criticism that civility is exclusionary is to argue for a form of cosmopolitan civility – a sense of global inclusion and respect which transcends national boundaries. The most successful practical, though limited, attempt to do this is the European Union, which has promoted transnational educational programmes as an important part of its aims. It is not surprising that the European Commission has been a staunch defender of the CEU in its dispute with the Hungarian government.

In seeking to define contemporary populism in Chapter 1, I argued that nationalism is one of its distinguishing features. Contemporary populists frequently promote national identity as a means of ensuring stability and argue that education should teach the importance of patriotism and encourage acceptance of one's own community. In this they reflect Rousseau who, particularly in *Poland*, emphasises the importance of belonging to a specific community and argues that only patriotically-minded citizens should be allowed to teach in its schools. Foreigners should not be allowed to teach Polish children because, not having been educated themselves since childhood to think and feel like Poles, they cannot possibly nurture the necessary Polish ways of thinking and feeling in their pupils.

Those liberals who are especially critical of nationalism fear that it contains, at the very least, the potential for intolerance, and quite likely the use of violence towards those who may be regarded as not being true members of the national community. This is one of the elements that fuels the antagonism of many liberals towards contemporary populism, not least because it often leads to resistance to immigration, except in strictly controlled ways. Yet many theories of nationalism in the nineteenth century were based on liberal values and political movements based on aspirations for the creation of states based on national communities were widely supported by prominent liberal thinkers and politicians. Mazzini's defence of liberal nationalism in works such as *The Duties of Man* (Mazzini 1907) provided a powerful intellectual justification for Italian unification and was much admired by liberals throughout Europe and North America,[2] including Mill.[3]

We can see the difference between populist and liberal views of nationalism by referring to Rousseau and Mill. Both defend forms of national identity as the basis of a stable society, but the kinds of society they envisage are very different, a difference reflected very clearly in their contrasting views of education.

Rousseau argues that a society should protect its distinctive culture and values, which are the expression of its identity. This is especially true for the kind of society he envisages in *The Social Contract* and recommends in *Poland*, because sharing in this culture and these values is essential if citizens are to properly express the general will.

Because formal education is the most powerful force in shaping the thinking and character of a society's young people, its primary aim should be to nurture this culture and these values. As such there are limits to what critical views and values students should be exposed. He is sceptical of any kind of cosmopolitanism, and wary of the influence of outsiders, who he fears will corrupt the purity of the nation, which is a further reason why he argues that only citizens of the nation should be allowed to teach in its schools.

The need to preserve the values of society and to protect its people from malign foreign influences also permeates his account of informal education, most notably in his *Letter to M. d'Alembert on the Theatre*, where he objects to the building of a theatre in Geneva. Such an action, he fears, will corrupt the older members of society through being exposed to the decadent values of foreign dramatists such as Moliere.

This argument is seen in current populist arguments on the need to restrict migration. This is based on the contention that a large of influx of people from other communities, particularly those that have a different culture, would undermine the consensus, and the possibility of civil agreement that arises from it, which members of the host society currently share. This argument is powerfully expressed in a book I referred to in Chapter 1 as a rare defence of what are currently regarded as populist themes by a major political theorist, Samuel Huntington's *Who Are We: The Challenges to America's National Identity*. Huntington offers a more fundamental argument, though, in his best-known work *The Clash of Civilizations and the Remaking of World Order* (1996) and the article on which it is based 'The Clash of Civilizations?' (1993) where he contends that members of different civilisations often have irreconcilable differences over their most fundamental beliefs and practices.

> The people of different civilizations have different views on the relations between God and man, the individual and the group, the citizen and the state, parents and children, husband and wife, as well as differing views of the relative importance of rights and responsibilities, liberty and authority, equality and hierarchy These differences are the product of centuries. They will not soon disappear.
>
> (Huntington 1993: 25)

In such cases a unifying education system becomes impossible because there can be no agreement on fundamental principles. This argument provides a clear articulation of a set of opinions and values that underpin claims by the populist governments of Hungary and Poland against accepting non-Christian migrants from the Middle East and North Africa and the desire of populists in the United States to build a wall against the threat of migrants from Mexico.[4] With such migrants, as with the cosmopolitan elites who champion them, civility is impossible because the differences which make civilised discussion and interaction possible is absent.

Mill's defence of nationality in *Considerations on Representative Government*, coupled with his concerns about the dangers of an illiberal state-run education system, offers a very different account of nationalism. In particular it recognises the potential of the democratic nation as a focus of civic engagement and of the liberal nation state as a safeguard of liberty and equality. But it also recognises the dangers of the tyranny of the majority and the need for genuine, ongoing, critical debate and argument as a safeguard against that. Most importantly for our present purposes, it warns against the danger of an education system which is controlled by the state, with all the potential for stifling the views of minorities. It also, despite Mill's respect for highly educated specialists with appropriate skills, raises concerns about the abuse of expertise which has something in common with populist distrust of experts. We will return to Mill's discussion of nationalism in the last section of this chapter.

Expertise in education and politics

One difficulty with the argument about the need for stability in society is how to ensure that rulers can be trusted to promote order. In the early modern period in Europe one influential argument was that rulers could be trusted because they ruled by divine right and were given special grace to rule wisely. Locke's attack on this view in *Two Treatises of Government* offers a powerful rejection which deeply influenced Enlightenment thinkers like Voltaire and, perhaps most importantly, Thomas Jefferson, James Madison and other liberals among the founders of the American Republic. But if the Divine Right of Kings is rejected, as in Jefferson's more radical development of Locke's argument, and all claims to religious authority must be excluded from government, what is the basis for a belief that rulers are capable of ruling wisely? For liberals such as Jefferson and Madison, this is linked to the broader worry that no one can be entirely trusted with the exercise of power. Unlike populist arguments about the purity of the people, though, they are wary of giving too much power to governments *and* to their fellow citizens. Madison's celebrated argument in 'Federalist 51' draws out the dilemma very powerfully:

> But what is government itself, but the greatest of all reflections on human nature? If men were angels, no government would be necessary. If angels were to govern men, neither external nor internal controls on government would be necessary. In framing a government which is to be administered by men over men, the great difficulty lies in this: you must first enable the government to control the governed; and in the next place oblige it to control itself.
>
> (Madison, Hamilton and Jay 1987: 319–20)

Jefferson echoes the imagery of angels in his first inaugural address, in a passage (delivered, it is worth stressing, on the day he ascended to the presidency of the United States) which rejects the divine right of kings:

> Sometimes it is said that man cannot be trusted with the government of himself. Can he, then, be trusted with the government of others? Or have we found angels in the form of kings to govern him? Let history answer this question.
>
> (Jefferson 1801)

One response is in part to return to a modified version of Plato's idea that potential rulers have to be educated to a level at which they will know how to act wisely and in the best interests of the people as a whole. Jefferson's founding of the University of Virginia was based in part on this ideal. This argument is linked in the liberal democratic mind to a key idea in modern discussions of education which is that of bringing out the best in the student – often expressed in such terms as intellectually stretching the student to encourage their full potential. This does not mean that every student is expected to become an expert in what they study but there is the conviction that in seeking to achieve that potential children should not be discouraged from acquiring depth of knowledge and insight. To do this one needs to have a teacher who has a high level of expertise in what he or she is teaching. This idea underpins traditional ideas of the apprentice where a master would instruct and guide the student.

130 *Education in democratic societies*

The purpose of this, of course, was not to keep apprentices in perpetual subordination to a master but to prepare them to become autonomous masters who would in turn themselves take on future apprentices.

An important element of the master-apprentice relationship and its function as a means of enabling knowledge and skills to be passed from the more experienced to the novice may also be seen in Mill's argument for the educative value in serving in local government, on school boards and the like. New members learn from the more experienced how the system works and they also acquire broader skills in the process, such as those of negotiation and leadership. The way in which the successful outcome of the master-apprentice relationship leads to the apprentice becoming independent of the master also reflects the important emphasis in Locke and Mill of education being intended to allow the mature individual to be autonomous.

Contemporary populists are often highly critical of claims to expertise because of their argument that the claims of the elite to possess expertise in the form of unquestionable knowledge and insight are a means of demanding unquestioning obedience on the part of the people at large.[5] But populists are not opposed to all specialist knowledge, only knowledge which is restricted to a small elite. They argue that such restrictions undermine the principle that the will of the people, however that is variously defined, should take precedence over the inevitably partial opinions of a small elite whose understanding and application of their specialised knowledge is infected by their distance from the people as a whole.

This distance is due in large part to the education of the elites. Populists argue that education should reflect the values of society, but elites are often perceived as being educated in values that are transnational or global. This is so even when their education has been in their own country as elite educational institutions, particularly the most prestigious Western universities, are held to reflect the values of global liberalism rather than those of the society in which they are based.[6] It is also reflected, some argue, in elite support for multi-culturalist education which undermines attempts to integrate newcomers into the host society. Agreeing with this analysis, Huntington argues that in the past it was seen as the responsibility both of public education and private corporations to ensure that migrants were integrated and that large industrial corporations 'established schools at their factories to train immigrants in the English language and American culture' (Huntington 2004: 132). By contrast, he argues, multiculturalism in the 1970s, 1980s and 1990s was greatly aided by educational practices in the United States, sponsored by academics and politicians committed to cosmopolitan liberalism (Huntington 2004: 171–7).

This belief in the importance of the rulers sharing the values of society as a whole is central to Plato's vision of education in the *Republic*.[7] Plato argues that the purpose of education is to discover children's abilities and then to educate them accordingly. This has often been taken as an elitist position – a claim that most people should only be educated to a low level so that they will be content with a life of work which requires only manual or technical skills. But, as was argued in Chapter 2, this is to misread the argument of the *Republic*. One purpose of Plato's system of education is to ensure that everyone leads a life that is best suited to their skills and abilities and is employed in a form of work which will best satisfy them. Moreover, the life of the soldiers and the philosopher rulers is a frugal one, living in barracks with no personal wealth and no family life, whereas the artisans have a life based around family and a modest amount of private property.

The learning and practise of skills is central to Plato's understanding of society and he argues that ruling is a skill which can be learnt like any other. Indeed, a society can only be governed well, and justly, if its rulers have the skills needed for the task and have been educated to the point where they can use those skills wisely. This is at the heart of Plato's rejection of democracy and particularly of populist ideas of democracy as reliant on the will of the people as a whole. Asking the general population to decide on complex economic and geopolitical issues as was the case with the British referendum on membership of the European Union would be regarded by Plato as the height of folly.

This view of education is challenged directly by John Locke's argument that education should be general to enable a gentleman to take his place in society, not to make experts. Locke restricts this broad education to a relatively few members of society though, as was argued in Chapter 3, his view of education does not rule out it being extended much more widely. John Stuart Mill expands this generalist, Lockean, view of education to include many more people but Mill, like Locke, still maintains a role for the teaching and training of experts. Both emphasise the need to ensure that expertise does not isolate experts from the interests and needs of the community at large.

Education, politics and critical thinking

Benignly intentioned anti-democrats like Plato offer stability through order and view education as a means of reproducing the values and beliefs which sustain that order. For them, belief in the value of experts goes hand in hand with a belief in the importance of reason as the only reliable guide to right thinking and acting. Those who are experts have a right, even a duty, to guide the rest of us. That is at the heart of Plato's argument for the philosopher rulers in the *Republic*, and it is an idea which has resonated with many intellectuals and leaders, of various kinds, ever since.

Liberals oppose this view but the populist argument that liberals do the same things, merely more obliquely, is a powerful one. One problem with views such as Locke's on the importance of teaching civility as a means of preserving stability and providing an entrée for young citizens into society is that it can appear to undermine the ability to think critically and stifle their autonomy. A liberal philosophy of education must find a way of resolving what can appear to be a threat to its coherence. One liberal response, following Locke, is to argue that if critical thinking is part of the culture to which people are being introduced, it will play a significant part in education and so deter any attempts at indoctrination.

This helps make clear a tension between two aspects of the defence of rational thought; that which acknowledges the importance of expertise and that which values critical thinking. They are not necessarily in conflict; indeed they ought not be, but they often are. Immanuel Kant sums the problem up in a famous passage in 'An Answer to the Question: What is Enlightenment?':

> It is because of laziness and cowardice that so great a part of humankind, after nature has long since emancipated them from other people's direction ... nevertheless gladly remains minors for life.... If I have a book that understands for me, a spiritual advisor who has a conscience for me, a doctor who decides upon a regimen for me, and so forth, I need not trouble myself at all.
>
> (Kant: 1991: 54)

Kant's choice of experts here mirrors the anger of many populists. Those who claim to have knowledge treat us like children, telling us what to think, even what to eat and drink to live a healthy life. All choice is denied us: we are treated, as Kant says a little further on in the same paragraph, as if were 'domesticated animals dumb and ... placid'.

How is this immaturity to be overcome? It is, says Kant, by learning to think for oneself, to be a free, autonomous person. Moreover, that is something more easily done as part of a community than as an isolated individual (Kant 1991: 55). There are echoes here of Rousseau, whom Kant greatly admired. Where Kant appears to differ from Rousseau is in his view that individuals are not to be treated merely as members of a community, a means to the end of the general will, for example, but as ends in themselves.

On one level it is not true to say that Rousseau did not think that individuals should be treated merely as means to the ends of the greater good of the community. Because, in Rousseau's view, the good of the individual and the good of the community as expressed in the general will are the same; the community cannot ignore the interest of the individual and treat him or her as merely a means of achieving the greater good. A problem arises, though, because Rousseau claims that individuals will on at least some occasions be confused about what is in their true interests and have to be forced to act in accordance with the general will – to be forced to be free, in the famous phrase. But coercing people to act in their own true best interest is not to treat them as means to an end but ends in themselves – the community is enabling them to act in their own true best interests. It is very important not to lose sight of respect for the integrity of the individual in Rousseau's thought.

This has important implications for education because while the students are guided by the teacher they are being led towards a clearer understanding of what is good not only for the community but also for themselves as members of the community. The echoes of the education system of the *Republic* are clear here. In both cases the intention is a laudable one, to draw out the best in the individual and to help him or her lead a fulfilling life.

This is not to deny that there are practical issues in trying to ensure that individuals are not coerced against their true interest. Part of the difficulty here lies in treating the general will as if it were a metaphysical entity distinct from the individuals who make up the community. Another problem, not unconnected, is the way in which Rousseau's arguments have been interpreted (or twisted) by avowed followers such as Robespierre (Kloppenberg 2016a: 533, 541). But perhaps the problem is intractable; once one believes that there is a guiding power that has revealed the right way to live, those who endanger themselves and the community by ignoring it must be corrected. It is only a step away from that to conclude that it is better to arrange the education of the people that they are prevented from considering such heretical questions in the first place, a view which Plato explicitly advocates in the *Republic*. It is apparent also in Rousseau's argument in *The Social Contract* that the Lawgiver has to convince the people for whom he has prepared the laws that he is acting as a transmitter of divine wisdom and in his view of the necessity for government control over what is to be taught in Polish schools.

Populist politicians frequently berate liberal politicians for their failure to be transparent, arguing that their belief in the importance of liberal ideals, and the policies which flow from them, causes them to ignore the views of those who are less enlightened. Such claims, made frequently during the Brexit campaign in Britain and during Donald Trump's election campaign in the United States, often link this with the charge that elite politicians from privileged backgrounds, who have been educated at exclusive institutions, consider the general mass of the less well educated to be too ignorant to make suitably informed decisions. Yet there is also a potential problem here for populism.

Rousseau's Lawgiver, it was argued in Chapter 4, fits rather awkwardly into the structure of the argument of *The Social Contract* but more easily into that of *Poland*. The problem in *The Social Contract* is that although the general will is held to be the only legitimate source of law in a community, the people who leave the state of nature to create that community need an external Lawgiver to tell them what their laws should be. In *Poland* the situation is different because the Polish people are already living in a settled community but one which needs to be reformed because of the corruption within it. In the latter situation, the Lawgiver is needed because of the way people have been misled by their former rulers, not least through the education system, and are still too confused to adequately express the general will. The role of the Lawgiver in *Poland* is to provide a re-education so that the people will eventually be able to properly express the general will. But this will inevitably involve people being asked to take some things on trust – such as an interpretation of Polish history that reinforces the values which the Lawgiver is providing for the new society.[8]

There is clearly a danger of censorship here in that any alternative narrative will be castigated as unacceptable and banned from the education system, both the formal education that will take place under the auspices of the teachers who must themselves be loyal Poles, and the informal education that takes place in the media. Attempts by populists such as Donald Trump and some of the leaders of the Brexit campaign to delegitimise mainstream media as promoters of fake news is a dangerously illiberal ploy that is one of the most serious threats to the democratic culture of both these societies. Further down the line of illiberal threats to democracy is the simultaneous decision of the Orbán government to allocate considerable resources to state-run primary schools while undermining the position of the CEU in Hungary.

An adequate theory of the role of education in a liberal democratic society must recognise that democracy is by its nature invariably subject to change – or to put in more positive terms, that it can adapt to new circumstances and challenges. It must also recognise that democracy has no single essence and that there will inevitably be tensions between different groups and values in a democratic society. Part of the purpose of education is to help provide an understanding of the ground rules for discussion of these various alternatives while acknowledging that the ground rules will change over time and stressing the need to adapt to them. This need to adapt shows that while education may have a crucial role to play in a democratic society it does not occupy a uniquely privileged position which is in some manner 'outside' of or above that society as a whole.

This brings us back to conflicting views of the Socratic Method and of its significance for the importance of critical thinking in education.

A liberal view of the Socratic Method would lay emphasis on the idea that Socrates was concerned to challenge the views of the experts of his day not because he thought there was no truth in what they said but rather in order to make the truth clearer and fuller. The proper use of the Socratic Method, on this view, is not to cynically debunk the views of those who claim to have expert knowledge but to enter into dialogue in order to learn and to further the truth. Of course, as Socrates often found, subjecting other people's opinions to sustained criticism can often lead to acrimony and it is sometimes difficult to concede a point in the heat of the debate. Mill, who strongly approved of the Socratic Method and its encouragement of robust debate, argued that it would often be the case that those looking on or listening might learn more than the direct participants. Following the cut and thrust of the debate in a more detached manner, and being able to reflect at their leisure upon what they had heard, would enable the onlookers to take a more dispassionate view of the strengths and weaknesses of the various arguments (CW, XVIII: 251-2).

This last point leads to a further consideration. Encouraging people to think critically means that they should be more willing to question their own beliefs as well as those of others. Socrates was not advocating, as Rousseau did on some occasions, the subordination of reason to feelings or emotions, but a more acute use of reason to question one's own views as well as those of others. In Plato's *Apology* (20e-22e) Plato reports Socrates as claiming at his trial that his constant questioning of the opinions of others was motivated by a pronouncement of the Oracle at Delphi who, when asked who the wisest man in the world was, replied that it was Socrates. Socrates claimed to have been baffled by this and went about initially trying to find people who through their greater knowledge and deeper understanding were wiser than he was. His conclusion was that he was wiser than any of the people he had spoken to only in the sense that he was aware of the state of his own ignorance.

It is this modesty about what one can claim to know that Mill is particularly attracted to in the Socratic Method and it is reflected in a key part of a liberal theory of education. This is, to make one aware that one's own knowledge is bounded by many types of ignorance and lack of skills, and, through recognizing one's own limitations, to be sympathetic and tolerant of the limitations of one's fellow citizens. In place of the certainties of Plato and Rousseau, Locke emphasises the provisional nature of all claims to knowledge and Mill stresses the fundamental role of debate in allowing alternative and competing claims to be heard and assessed.

By contrast, at the heart of contemporary populist ideas of education, and of those of Rousseau, is the aim of drawing out the truth that is implicit in all those who are truly members of the renewed and purified society. The Socratic Method then becomes a means of undermining claims to expertise and skill by the current elite. Doing so prepares the way for dismantling the corrupt social and political order and replacing it with something superior. For Rousseau, this willingness to be honest to the truth which Emile finds within himself is the means by which he can retain his purity within a corrupt society. But it is only when a whole society is transformed, and, in the strongest sense of the term, re-educated, that people can truly be free to understand and express the truth within. This echoes Plato's rejection of the corruption of his own society and his belief that only through being guided by rulers with a complete understanding of the Forms can society be remade, and its members be enabled to lead just and fulfilling lives. For both Rousseau and Plato, the most important idea is that only those who are guided by a knowledge of the truth can be good people. It is not surprising, then, that those who do not understand the truth have to be re-educated (again), exiled from the community or, in the case of those who wilfully and persistently reject the minimal state religion envisaged in *The Social Contract*, executed.

Autonomy in education and politics

The implication of the argument of the last paragraph is that populists have to set boundaries outside of which critical thinking is unacceptable. This is in sharp contrast to liberals like Mill who believe that one of the benefits of teaching critical thinking is that it breaks down boundaries and in doing so promotes autonomy. Autonomy has been particularly associated with liberalism, and understandably so as liberal political theorists, including Locke and Mill, have developed versions of the concept into a central theme in liberal thought. Yet liberals do not have exclusive claims on the concept. If we define autonomy as 'self-rule' or 'self-direction', populists may also be understood as advocating a certain kind of autonomy. Indeed, much of their political discourse is couched in terms of the need to free people from various types of oppressive rule, whether from the tyranny of expert guidance, from the rule of unresponsive internal elites such as politicians and bankers or by external powers such as the European Union and the United Nations and international agreements such as the Paris Climate Treaty. In view of this the role of education in promoting autonomy is, of great importance but also problematic.

This can be seen in the different views of Locke and Rousseau. For Locke, autonomy is an essential aim in the education of the individual both as a person and as a citizen. Rousseau, particularly in *Poland*, gives greater weight to the view that the primary aim of education is not the autonomy of the individual but of the community.

Rousseau is often written about, quite rightly, as an advocate of authenticity and it is sometimes argued that this explains his different account of autonomy. Arguments of this kind are also used to suggest that populists have a greater commitment to authenticity than to autonomy, particularly where autonomy is understood in the liberal sense of individual freedom (or as populists like Orbán argue, licence). In part this argument turns on the role of reason in autonomy, which liberals such as Locke and Mill argue is central and which, on some interpretations, Rousseau thinks is less important. But it would be wrong to draw too sharp a division between autonomy and authenticity. Claims to the primacy of authenticity arising from natural feelings such as patriotism may provide a rationale for asserting national autonomy for a populist, but liberal versions of identity politics, which appeal to notions of personal autonomy, with regard to choosing sexual preferences, for example, are also frequently based on powerful appeals to peoples' emotional sense of who they are. What is significant is the manner in which different views of autonomy, one based fundamentally on communal identity and the authenticity of the society to which a person belongs, the other on individual identity and the right to create one's own identity, both appeal to authenticity but lead to different views of autonomy. In doing so they also imply very different views of the aims and purposes of education and some of the tension in Rousseau's thought arises because he is drawn to both views.

Locke's argument against patriarchalism in the *Two Treatises* is relevant to his discussion on education at this point. As Kelly (2007) argues, Locke did not believe that children had a natural right to be treated as the equal of adults and they were legitimately under the authority of their fathers (though it is also important to add that Locke places duties on parents regarding the way they should treat their children). As they grow older their education should equip them to be responsible adults and so become equal members of society, alongside their parents. Kelly points out that Locke distinguishes between parental authority which is patriarchal and political authority which is not. The authority of parents over their children is of a different nature to political authority (Kelly 2007: 81–90).

While this is true, and Locke has good philosophical reasons for differentiating between the authority of the father and that of the sovereign, one important feature of this distinction is that education in a liberal society is understood as a process of enabling children to grow into citizens who will be independent and critically minded. The authority of the father should be gradually replaced, Locke argues in *Some Thoughts*, by increasing friendship and eventual treatment of the son (and daughter?) as an equal. Politically that has significant implications because the king in a patriarchal society can never allow his subjects to become mature and so be considered his equals; they must always remain subservient to their royal father. An education which prepares one to be an independent adult and a responsible citizen is central to liberal thought because it emphasises the autonomy of the individual growing up, so to speak, to recognise, in Mill's later phrase, that '[o]ver himself, over his own body and mind, the individual is sovereign' (CW, XVIII: 224). Moreover, in order to do this successfully it must provide the educated citizens with powerful intellectual and moral tools to challenge the authority of the sovereign. The consent given to the on-going social contract by free and equal adults in a liberal society is always conditional on the sovereign abiding by his side of the contract. The workability of the liberal contract assumes the ability of the governed to understand and challenge the actions of the sovereign. This is fundamentally and irrevocably a two-way process for a liberal society.

This throws Locke's position into direct contrast with Rousseau, for whom the citizen and the sovereign should, ideally, be identical, one of the key differences that distinguishes liberal democracy from populist democracy. Rousseau's view of education in *Poland*, as well as in *The Social Contract*, assumes that the education is not intended to create autonomous, critically minded individuals who will constantly call the sovereign to account but people who are at one with the sovereign because they are part of the it.

This is not to suggest that the power of the sovereign for Rousseau is patriarchal. Quite the opposite is the case. The opening section of *Political Economy* is a sustained attack on the attempt to equate the sovereign with the father in which Rousseau refers to 'the odious system' of Robert Filmer's *Patriacha* (Rousseau 2019b: 6). The sovereign does not stand against the individual as any kind of other, fatherly or otherwise. But that is also why, ultimately, the sovereign cannot be challenged. Locke's insistence on the right of rebellion would not make sense in Rousseau's ideal society – how can one rebel against oneself? Populist appeals to the will of the people being more fundamental and insightful (because it is somehow purer, less corrupt) than politicians or judges clearly has affinities with this.

As Riley argues (2001: 132) when Rousseau writes about being forced to be free he means that that the education system will have brought the individual to realise that he can only become fully free when he is at one with the general will.[9] On such a view the education system seeks to internalise values which cannot then be challenged, because there are no independent grounds upon which the challenge can be made. This is in considerable part because Rousseau rejects the idea, which is central to Locke's liberalism, of a universal, cosmopolitan natural law. It also means that Rousseau believes, like Plato, that once created the just society cannot be improved in its essence, though for Rousseau, as for Plato, it can deteriorate. For Locke this idea is fundamentally wrong – there can be no ideal society because our understanding of politics, just as much as of the natural world, is always subject to development and improvement as our knowledge increases. This is why education for Locke should include enough science and history, among other subjects, to provide the educated adult with an awareness of the provisional nature of knowledge.

There are two important points to make about this. The first is that even if liberal democratic societies function in this way it does not mean that all social and economic inequalities, or even serious injustices, will disappear. But second, it does mean that liberal and civic-minded members of such a society will recognise many of the injustices and seek to remedy them. Locke did this through his writing and through his political activism as a member of the opposition to James II and his defence of the Revolution of 1689 (Woolhouse 2009: Chapters 6 and 7). Mill also campaigned for greater justice through his writing and by his political activism, including as a Liberal Member of Parliament (Reeves 2007: Chapter 13).

Plato and Rousseau, by contrast, see education as an important aspect of the need to purify society and remake it to reflect the needs of all members, not just the few. In this respect they are, as Rousseau acknowledges both about himself and Plato, radical innovators. Their views of education may be termed, following Mezirow 'transformative' (Mezirow 1991, 2000).

Plato and Rousseau reject the idea that there are any values in the societies in which they lived that could be accepted and defended without question. Instead they claim that a radical purification, of both society and the individual heart, is necessary. Contemporary education cannot help – it will only perpetuate the corruption into the next generation. The Socratic Method, as we have already seen, becomes in such a view a means of attacking the very foundations of society with a view to undermining it in preparation for the transformation to a qualitatively different society. From this perspective, representative government is far less attractive, particularly when the representatives are drawn from what is regarded as an elite whose values and opinions and interests are removed from those who have elected them. Liberal constraints such as the rule of law and written constitutions are often dismissed as defending the interests of the elite.

It is important to emphasise the point that for Rousseau, education is transformative – it liberates Emile both from his own childish ignorance and from the dangers of becoming corrupted by society. In the term that Rousseau uses to describe Plato's *Republic*, it purifies. For Locke, by contrast, education is not about transformation, either of the individual or society. It is about enabling the child to grow into both a good citizen and a good person. This can be best achieved by drawing out the critical and rational faculties of the individual but in the context of enabling the person to become virtuous. For Locke there is no need for the child to be transformed because, unlike Plato and Rousseau, Locke believes that for all its weaknesses and failings, English society in the late seventeenth century is reformable and that one means of that reform is a sound education which emphasises and builds upon the positive aspects of society.

Plato and Rousseau believe that in an ideal society people would indeed be educated in the values of society. But the difference for them is that in the ideal society there would be very little room for dissent. Citizens would have to submit to the greater wisdom of the philosopher rulers or the general will. What appears to be the liberal, child-centred education of *Emile* turns into the illiberal forcing to be free. What appears to be the illiberal, virtue imbuing character building of *Some Thoughts* is tempered and transmuted by the liberal individualism of *Two Treatises* and the critical, scientific temper of the *Essay*.

In Rousseau's view, when a truly just society is established following a revolutionary transformation (or purification) of both society and the individual heart, there would be no need for further fundamental change or improvement. All that would be left would be the need to ensure that the general will was sufficiently well understood and its wishes carried out. In such a society education would become entirely reproductive because any deviation from the fundamental values would be potentially dangerous to the stability and security of society. The education system would play its part in ensuring that people learnt what it is to be truly free with the aim of minimising the occasions when they would have to be forced to be free as citizens.

The authoritarian threats attendant on such a view are perhaps even clearer to people in the twenty-first century than they would have been to Rousseau. By contrast, the liberal democratic view espoused by Mill argues that there is no single, ultimate concept of democracy, or liberty, against which the various manifestations of theory and practice can be measured. It also explains how it has developed over a long period, from the undemocratic liberalism of Locke through the development of a strong version of representative liberal democracy in the later Enlightenment to a more fully developed, but still far from complete, version in Mill. In that respect Plato's view of democracy as a reaction to, or even a protest against, other types of government, has an element of truth in it. Plato was also right, from his own perspective, to be wary of democracy because by its very nature it involves change and adaptation rather than seeking perfection: the very antithesis of his account of politics in the *Republic*. In that sense too, it is opposed to ideologies which claim to have found the truth about political order, whether secular such as fascism and communism or religious such as the theory of the Divine Right of Kings or contemporary Islamism. To many of its defenders, that is one of the great strengths of liberal democracy and a reason why, despite some recent setbacks, it remains such a powerful force in the modern world.

Part of the tension between liberal and populist accounts of democracy is that between individual autonomy and responsibility as members of a community, but the tension is also particularly evident within the writings of both Mill and Rousseau. Mill's emphasis on individual freedom, particularly in *On Liberty*, has to be put beside his comments on the generally positive aspects of nationalism in *Considerations on Representative Government* and his broader defence, in the latter work in particular, of the importance of decision making by specialists working for the greater good of society. Rousseau's comments on the general will and his emphasis on the importance of communal moral renewal as a necessary precondition of a more just society have to be balanced by the greater stress on individual development in *Emile* or the keen sense of his own individualism (and loneliness) which are to be found in his *Confessions* (1995) and *Reveries of a Solitary Walker* (2011).

This tension is also reflected in the education systems of mature liberal democracies and may explain why people in such societies grow up with an awareness, and usually acceptance, of the differences among members of a democratic society. It may also help to explain why democracy is hard to introduce and sustain in societies where education is more rigorously ideological or religious, such as the old Soviet Union or in some conservative religious societies.[10] The growth of populism might seem to reflect a wish to suppress one aspect of the tension, or it may reflect a confused attempt to keep them in an unstable balance: if either is the case that would suggest a failure of education, as well as failures elsewhere in society.

Education and the crisis of democracy

> We have it not in our power to choose between democracy and aristocracy; necessity and Providence have decided that for us. But the choice we are still called upon to make is between a well and an ill-regulated democracy; and on that depends the future well-being of the human race.
>
> (Mill CW, XVIII: 56)

It is difficult to imagine any serious disagreement with the initial part of Mill's claim here, written in 1835, during the course of his first review of Alexis de Tocqueville's *Democracy in America*, that aristocracy is no longer a serious alternative to democracy. Unfortunately, as the current debate between liberal democrats and populists demonstrates, it is equally difficult to disagree with the second part about the serious conflict between rival accounts of democracy.

This may suggest a gloomy view of the viability of democracy. If we are still facing a crisis between a well- and an ill-regulated democracy almost two centuries after these words were written, what reasons could there be for optimism about resolving democracy's current crisis and about its long-term future? How can we even decide which is the ill-regulated democracy – liberal democracy or populism, or even both? But a longer view may also help to dispel the gloom, or at least offer some clarity.

Democracy's current crisis is part of a wider problem in Western society, caused in part by globalisation – the phenomenon which has contributed so much to what populists regard as the malaise of cosmopolitanism. One of populists' most frequent criticisms is that the elites in this society, particularly politicians and financiers, have more in common with their international colleagues in a global elite than with the great majority of people in their own society. Taking a position of which Rousseau would wholly approve, they argue that the existence of such people should be dealt with by suitably robust action, chief among which involves ensuring the next generation is educated in institutions which reflect national values and priorities. But the particular features of our crisis should not blind us to the fact that comparable crises have occurred in the past and have, in some cases, been followed by the emergence of new and more stable institutions and ways of life. Each of the four thinkers we have discussed in the previous chapters lived through periods of intense change and social upheaval.

Plato writes against the background of what he sees as the corruption and decay of Athenian society and the part which he thinks democracy has played in this. Locke living during the period of the Restoration and the Revolution of 1688, sees, more than any of the other three, the ideas which he champions becoming accepted and established as the new, more liberal, norm. Rousseau, both visionary and pessimist, is acutely aware of the radical changes taking place in the political and cultural life of eighteenth century Europe, but his own ambiguity about how best to deal with them perhaps explains why the kind of just and fair society he argues for so eloquently, has not been realised. Mill, like Locke, is optimistic, though without the assurance that came to Locke in later life, after the accession of William and Mary.

Mill speaks in a manner directly relevant to the present crisis when he argues that in times of social change and upheaval, such as he is living through in Victorian England, there is much greater opportunity for new ideas to be seriously considered. When such ideas are subjected to proper critical analysis it is possible that, through the acceptance of those which are progressive, significant improvements can be brought about. Mill believes that education has an essential role to play in this, arguing, like Locke, that it should equip people with the critical skills and a wide-ranging knowledge to be able to make sense of the changes and evaluate possible outcomes. This is an important way in which a liberal philosophy of education both acknowledges the need to preserve some values whilst also recognising the importance of preparing the way for change and improvement.

Mill's optimism is tempered, though, by his warning that change may be for the worse rather than the better and his warning against the 'obnoxious power' which a misuse of education could wield over successive generations is a salutary one. One might assume that he thinks this applies only to alleged misuses of education by the illiberal governments of his own day or by contemporary populist governments such as that of Hungary. But Mill's argument is more nuanced than that. It is equally possible that ideas of liberalism and liberal democracy might become oppressive if taught uncritically. Mill, borrowing from Tocqueville, warns that a majority composed of liberals may become tyrannical. Mill's concern is that any set of values, even the most liberal, is in danger of becoming a means of social control if not subjected to persistent criticisms and development. This is not necessarily because people consciously set out to be oppressive: it may result from the best of intentions. But unless ideas are subject to frequent analysis and critical reflection the danger is there. Indeed, the danger is a constant one, which is why one of the most important roles of education is to provide the tools for critical analysis to enable active, educated citizens to meet it head on.

Mill's argument that times of social change might also be times of great opportunity for progressive-minded thinkers and politicians is echoed by some writers today who caution against a defeatist, even apocalyptic, view of the current crisis of democracy. One of the most perceptive of these, Walter Russell Mead,[11] draws a comparison between the current situation and that of the period between Reconstruction and the emergence of the Progressive Movement in late nineteenth century America (2018).[12] Then, as now, average Americans were disillusioned with the remoteness of members of the elite, a remoteness exacerbated by great inequalities in wealth. There was also a general sense of chaos and confusion, and of the fear of violence, along with the perception that politicians were generally inept and unable to exercise any significant control over events. Yet out of this period came the Progressive Movement which, led by powerful, competent politicians radically improved society.

Two of Mead's arguments are of particular relevance to our present concerns. The first is that, like Mill (whom he does not mention), Mead maintains that we cannot at present know what new ideas and institutions will emerge to enable us to adjust to the great changes currently taking place (2018: 17). This can be a source of optimism but, as Mill makes clear, the ability on the part of a society to meet such challenges requires the provision of an education which is flexible and creative and which values critical analysis.

This leads to Mead's second argument, that the education system which was developed for the age of industrialisation is no longer appropriate for the new post-industrial information society. Mead's description of the older education echoes some of the analysis of populists when he writes that 'it provided basic literacy for the whole work force, offered more advanced schooling to a percentage of it, and socialized children into the unique working environment of the industrial age...'. But his main point is that 'today's educational system socializes young people into a world that no longer exists' (Mead 2018: 18).

Mead's argument about the relevance of contemporary education in the United States and other Western societies to future patterns of employment is timely. Education needs to adapt to the challenges such as those of new technology and the major disruption that they will bring to the way people work, and to more adequately prepare students for the new kinds of employment that will be available. But it is also important to point out that the education system which is being superseded is one which Mill defended – and in part helped to bring about through his writing and his work as a Member of Parliament – as a means of providing people with the requisite levels of literacy and numeracy to be able to participate meaningfully in political debate and to make informed choices when voting. While Mead is right to emphasise the need to rethink and redevelop current education provision it is also important that a strong humanistic element is retained in order to provide the knowledge and understanding which can be drawn upon to engage as an active citizen.[13]

The current wave of populism is the expression of a far more pessimistic response to the unsettling effects of rapid social change than that embraced by Mill. Its emphasis on the importance of national identity and of the need for an education system which unequivocally defines, and then defends, that identity is one response to this. Paradoxically, though, the speed at which Western societies are currently undergoing change undermines populist arguments for preserving national culture and preventing external influences from influencing it. However much people in the old industrial heartlands of England and the American mid-west or the old coal mining communities of South Wales or West Virginia lament the passing of industries and the way of life that went with them they are gone and cannot be recreated. That is why an education based primarily on the conservation of traditional national values is bound to be inadequate in the current time of crisis and rapid change, just as would be an education based on the needs of an industrial society that no longer exists.

This is not to say that an education which disparages national identity and gives greater importance to cosmopolitanism has no problems of its own. The emphasis on national identity and a sense of belonging is still important. This is why education which includes serious and non-pejorative discussion of nationality, to use Mill's term, should provide an understanding of the historical context within which the national community has developed (including where necessary debunking myths about the past) and also as a basis from which to interpret and where possible (and desirable) help to control and direct the change.

It is entirely understandable how the inclusion of such a discussion of nationality is important in the education system of a country like Hungary which has experienced so much trauma over such a long period of time. But it is not enough to rely on government sponsored guidance. Internal critics, such as Mill in Victorian Britain or Locke in Restoration England, or indeed Rousseau in eighteenth century France, are necessary. So too are more detached institutions such as the CEU who can offer the tools for a more dispassionate analysis. From that perspective, the move of the CEU from Budapest is a greater loss for Hungary, and especially the stated desire of the Hungarian government to meet the challenges of a globalising world, than it is for the CEU.

Mill's concept of nationality which was discussed in Chapter 5 offers one idea of how discussion of nationality might feature in a liberal philosophy of education. Mill shares with many of his liberal compatriots an idea of British nationality, but it is not based on the superior understanding of highly educated rulers nor on a belief in the unsullied wisdom of ordinary people giving expression to an unchallengeable general will. It is a pragmatic nationalism which seeks to map the shifting boundaries of what is considered part of the nation rather than seeking a fixed and timeless definition which it then teaches people to accept uncritically. Mill's account of nationality allows the incorporation of other nationalities into the existing nation as equal partners, and accepts that both national values and national institutions change. In doing so it allows for and even encourages the liberal civility which Locke argues is such an important part of the education of a responsible citizen. A major challenge for liberal philosophies of education is to design curricula which recognise the importance of national identity while also encouraging genuinely critical thinking and openness to constant change.

Mill as we have seen recognises that acknowledging that a democratic nation will change does not mean that one can accurately predict what these changes will be. In his *Autobiography* he writes that from the outbreak of the American Civil War he was convinced that, despite the horrors of the war, a northern victory would have a positive effect, not only through the abolition of slavery but more generally in the ability of American democracy to expand and develop away from what he takes to be the narrow confines of the Constitution (CW, I: 266–7). Yet Mill was in many important respects wrong in what he thought the consequences would be, particularly with respect to the Constitution, which was modified but not fundamentally changed.

This brings us back to Mead's first point that it is impossible to know at present how democratic societies will evolve to meet the crisis they currently face. New insights, and consequent changes in practice, inevitably emerge as society develops, perhaps especially as it is forced to define itself against newly emerging alternatives. The liberal interpretation of the Socratic Method, to which Mill is firmly committed, becomes, in this view, an essential component of education. It provides a means of drawing out and clarifying opinions and beliefs which, particularly in rational discourse among adults, will sometimes lead to significant amendments to the understanding and application of liberal values. Such a view sees liberal democracy as the best form of government because it enables the population at large to vote and thereby not only appoint their representatives but also to reject them if they are deemed to have acted in an unsuitable manner. Just as importantly, it emphasises the importance of an educated population being able to enter into a rational analysis and discussion of political and economic policies.

This does, though, raise a problem which has been discussed at several places in the preceding chapters. While Mill is willing to accept radical change he does also claim that the fundamental principles and structures of a society based on liberal values should be preserved and protected. This commitment is partially obscured by his argument of the need to extend freedoms and to uproot oppressive forces in society. Nevertheless, it is clearly apparent in *On Liberty* where he criticises the threats to the principle of liberty posed by intolerance and the social opprobrium which he believes both encourages and feeds off the tyranny of the majority, but defends the inviolability of the principle of liberty.

This might be seen as a particularly acute problem for Mill because if there are some non-contestable values at the core of liberal democracy such that an education ought to ensure their transmission to the next generation, would that not fall under Mill's condemnation as 'obnoxious'? This is similar to the charges which Joseph Carrig and others level against Locke – that his theory of liberal education leads to an indoctrination of liberal values which most students (and adult graduates of such an education) would then lack the skills to criticise.

Part of the answer lies in the claim (common to Mill and Locke, but opposed by Plato and, to a lesser extent by Rousseau) that one of the most important things to teach children is how to think critically. The values of critical thinking, or more fully, thinking analytically which should involve thinking creatively and, as Mill says, imaginatively, are what lies at the core of democracy and of a democratic education.

In itself this response is not sufficient because a method of critical analysis can, if used improperly, be a means of negatively undermining one's opponents without offering a viable alternative. As I argued in Chapter 2, Plato levelled this criticism at the Sophists, and it is a charge which populists sometimes make of what they see as the relentlessly negative criticism engendered by liberal education practice. I also argued that when discussing the Socratic Method with the benefit of having read the *Republic*, Socrates' own practice might be seen as a process of debunking self-styled experts in order to pave the way for the acceptance of the later theory of Forms. This also has echoes, I suggested, in populist attacks (anticipated by Rousseau) on the elite experts in liberal society whose unpatriotic, cosmopolitan education has left them unable to grasp the deeper truths understood by the people at large.

There is, though, a second part of Mill's defence against the charge that he is unwilling to challenge the most basic liberal values, and that he wants to enshrine them in the education system. This is that all knowledge, not least about politics and society, is provisional and subject to revision. It is an idea which he shares with Locke. 'Every step the mind takes in its progress towards knowledge', Locke writes in the 'Epistle to the Reader' at the start of the *Essay*, 'makes some discovery, which is not only new, but the best too, for the time at least' (Locke 1824). The phrase 'the best ... for the time at least' exemplifies what I described in Chapter 3 and in the section on education and critical thinking earlier in this chapter as the essential intellectual modesty of empiricism. This an argument about epistemology but it is also about metaphysics in that it claims this is how the world is. Given this is the case, an education which does not recognise that all knowledge is provisional, and which fails both to convey this to those who are being taught and to provide them with the intellectual skills to live in such a world, is significantly deficient.

This view also implies the need for education to be lifelong, particularly in societies such as that of the early twenty-first century where change is constant. Here Mead's argument about the need for educational provision to adapt to the changing circumstances of society links with liberals such as Locke and Mill. This education may well be partly vocational, enabling people to develop new skills as technologies and working practices change but it should also involve reflection and debate about the political, social and economic implications of those changes.

Mead is right to see a measure of optimism when looking to the past, but it must be tempered by the realisation of the need to actively engage in bringing about the right kind of changes. At the same time that the United States was passing through the Gilded Age, nineteenth century liberals in Britain developed an increasingly positive view of the ability of newly enfranchised working-class men to engage seriously in political life. This was linked in their minds to the need to ensure the high quality of public debate as the franchise was extended, and of the central contribution of a serious press which regularly reported important political speeches verbatim. A telling example of this is in the case of Gladstone, a contemporary of Mill, many of whose values he shared and who he once described as the conscience of liberalism.

In the early stages of his career, Gladstone shared the fears of most of his contemporaries in the British political class that extending the franchise beyond the narrow limits set by the Reform Act of 1832 would endanger the political and economic fabric of society. Yet over time he came to believe that the political education of the adult population, partly in the form of political oratory extensively reported in the newspapers but also through a much expanded and improved education system, would, in the words of the editor of his diaries and biographer Matthew, greatly ease 'the legitimation of the Victorian State' (Matthew 1995: 94) as voters were able to follow the great debates of the day.[14]

Gladstone's frequent pamphleteering on issues such as the Bulgarian atrocities, over which he appealed to the public in a manner that was critical of the Tory government of Disraeli, which he saw as elitist and corrupt, and the whole tenor of the Midlothian Campaign would seem to bear this out. It is important to emphasise, as Matthew does frequently, that it was because the voting population were so well-informed and willing to take political and moral issues seriously that this worked. Mill provides a powerful intellectual justification for these views in *Considerations on Representative Government*, where he stresses both the need for formal schooling and for the informal education that came through following debates that were widely published in newspapers as well as through active participation in local politics.

The response of the British Liberal Party, and of the Progressive politicians in the United States at the end of the nineteenth and beginning of the twentieth centuries demonstrated not a mixture of fear and disdain but a respect for those outside the traditional elite that is not always so obvious today. Of course there were problems – such as the racist attitudes of otherwise liberal politicians such as President Woodrow Wilson and the widespread belief in the 'cleansing power' of eugenics[15] – but there were also very significant moves towards encouraging greater participation. The 'Progressive Amendments' to the American Constitution, particularly the Seventeenth which allowed for direct election of Senators and the Nineteenth which protected women's right to vote, showed considerably more trust in the political thinking and action of the non-elite than the Founders had displayed.

In works like *The Subjection of Women* (CW, XXI: 259–340) which provided the intellectual groundwork for such changes, Mill argues that a far-reaching extension and reform of education is central to ensuring their success. In saying this, he does not think that such an education would reinforce the values of Victorian England and preserve the status quo. His argument is the opposite of Rousseau's at this point. Education should prepare children and adults to question the values which have hitherto been accepted, values which Mill believes reflect the interests of such reactionary groups as, to use the examples with Matthew attributes to Gladstone, the army, the established clergy and the agricultural interest (that is, the landed aristocracy). Education should be the driver of the necessary changes and disruption which Mill believes are essential to bring about the needed improvement in society.

From Mill's perspective, populist criticisms offer important insights into what is problematic about contemporary education and society. An elitist education which excludes the many and reinforces in the few a belief both in their own superiority and global citizenship over citizenship of one's own country is divisive and unjust. Moreover, by restricting the provision of high-quality education so that men and women from non-elite backgrounds are excluded, it deprives the country of many potentially dynamic and resourceful leaders. It is not surprising that many people feel disillusioned and angry.

But a liberal such as Mill would also argue that the solutions which populists offer are inadequate. At a political level, populists offer an alternative that is too narrow and unimaginative – the return to a nationalism that is closed and unable to interact creatively and confidently with a rapidly changing world. In education this is reinforced by an emphasis on national identity and values that must necessarily be defensive and fearful both of external cultural influences and of the critical thinking that is necessary for a society to learn from its mistakes and develop new plans for the future. At times of crisis populism lacks the resources to embrace the radical changes that are necessary.

The fundamental reason for the current crisis of democracy, though, from Mill's perspective, is not the rise of populism, which is only a symptom. The real problem is the failure of liberalism and, particularly from our perspective, the failings of liberal education. At the heart of Mill's argument, and of Locke's too, is a belief that education provides an essential basis for commitment to, and participation in, society. When education fails to achieve this, as it appears to be doing for large numbers of people in contemporary Europe and North America, the sense of identity and belonging which Mill thought essential to a free society begin to disappear. So too does the civility which Locke thought indispensable, as does the will and commitment to seize the opportunity to bring about innovative change. The crisis of democracy in liberal societies is to a considerable extent a crisis of an education which is itself in urgent need of renewal.

Notes

1 Bourdieu also argues that children from non-privileged backgrounds are handicapped when competing to study at more prestigious schools and universities because they lack the social capital which gives children of wealthy and well-educated parents a distinct advantage. This is also a criticism made by some populists.
2 For Mazzini's life and thought see Denis Mack Smith's *Mazzini* (1994) and for a discussion of his cosmopolitan view of a Europe of Nations, and his belief in the need for universal education, see C. A. Bayly and E. F. Giuseppe Biagini (2008).
3 Mill wrote to Mazzini (21st February 1858) to say that he regarded him as someone with whom he had many thoughts and feelings in common, and, most unusually, that he and his wife would welcome Mazzini as a guest (CW, XV: 548).
4 Huntington devotes a long chapter of *Who Are We: The Challenges to America's National Identity* to his claims about the danger that Mexican/Hispanic migration presents to the future of the United States (Huntington 2004: Chapter 9). He argues that one of the major problems is the lack of educational assimilation of Mexican-Americans (Huntington 2004: 232–4).
5 Even if the knowledge is true this should not require unquestioning obedience as long as the people have the opportunity to challenge both the knowledge and its application. This in turn requires that the elite holders of knowledge be willing to be as open as possible about the knowledge and its application, and to be willing to enter into a genuinely educative dialogue with the people at large. This genuinely educative dialogue is a lot harder to achieve than might first appear. One reason is the psychological difficulty some experts have in sharing their knowledge based perhaps on arrogance and a confusion between the relatively poor education many from non-elite backgrounds have experienced and their potential ability when provided with the appropriate information and skills. Another, sometimes linked to the first, is that the populist criticism of elites as wishing to maximise their own power for political or financial reasons is sometimes justified. A third reason is that some experts are ill-equipped to present their detailed knowledge clearly to non-specialists. While this might be understandable in some areas of theoretical physics it is much less clear why this should be the case in political science or social policy.
6 Huntington agrees with this argument from his vantage point at Harvard University (Huntington 2004: 270).
7 In the myth of the metals Plato even suggests that those who become philosopher rulers after the republic is established will share in the common belief of the myth

148 *Education in democratic societies*

(*Republic* 415a–c). While this raises problems about how philosophers trained to the exceptional heights that Plato proposes would be unable to see through the myth, it does underline that the rulers ought to be deeply integrated into society (which is the point he wants to make here).

8   Rousseau is uneasy about the claim that the Lawgiver for Poland should be a non-Pole, which was precisely the position in which he found himself (Rousseau 2019b: 181). Unlike the situation of people who have just left the state of nature, Poles already have a culture which the Lawgiver needs to understand and, where possible, build upon.

9   Compare also his discussion of Emile's acceptance of the values inculcated by his education (Riley 2001: 133).

10 Mazzini, to take a historical example, thought that the Papacy formed one of the gravest challenges to democracy in a unified Italy (Smith 1994: 193).

11 Coincidentally, Mead is a Professor of Foreign Affairs and Humanities at Bard College in New York, the American institution to which the CEU is affiliated.

12 For an illuminating discussion of this period see Richard White *The Republic for Which it Stands: The United States during Reconstruction and the Gilded Age, 1865–1896* (2018).

13 I am not suggesting that Mead would deny this. His books such as *Special Providence: American Foreign Policy and How it Changed the World* (2001), and *God and Gold: Britain, America and the Making of the Modern World* (2007) are models of the kind of works on politics and history which should form the backbone of a humanistic education. The point I wish to make is that by emphasising the need to provide a more appropriate education, often focusing, as in recent government initiatives in the United Kingdom on STEM, there is the danger of less importance been given (and less funding being made available) for humanities and liberal arts subjects.

14 Gladstone in turn came to have a great deal of respect for the views of the less sophisticated members of society because he believed that, in Matthew's words, 'large and influential groups within society – the army, the established clergy, the agricultural interest – were ready to assert a class interest in politics…' (1995: 95).

15 For a criticism of the Progressive era which emphasises these and other defects see Thomas C. Leonard, *Illiberal Reformers: Race, Eugenics and American Economics in the Progressive Era* (2016).

Bibliography

Albright, Madeline (2018) *Fascism: A Warning*, New York: Collins
Anderson, Benedict (1983) *Imagined Communities*, London: Verso
Annas, Julia (1981) *An Introduction to Plato's Republic*, Oxford: Oxford University Press
Annas, Julia (1995) 'Introduction' in *Plato Statesman* eds. Julia Annas and Robin Waterfield, trans. Robin Waterfield, Cambridge: Cambridge University Press
Arblaster, Anthony (2002) *Democracy* (3rd edition), Milton Keynes: Open University Press
Ashton, Rosemary (2012) *Victorian Bloomsbury*, London: Yale University Press
Atack, Carol (2017) 'The History of Athenian Democracy, Now', *History of Political Thought* Vol. 38, No. 3: 576–88
Bayly, C. A. and Biagini, E. F. Giuseppe (2008) eds. *Mazzini and the Globalization of Democratic Nationalism, 1830–1920*, Oxford, Oxford University Press
Bejan, Teresa M. (2016) 'Locke on Toleration, (In)Civility and the Quest for Concord', *History of Political Thought*, Vol. 37, No. 3: 556–87
Bejan, Teresa M. (2017) *Mere Civility*, Cambridge: Harvard University Press
Berlin, Isaiah (1969a) 'Two Concepts of Liberty' in *Four Essays on Liberty*, Oxford: Oxford University Press
Berlin, Isaiah (1969b) 'John Stuart Mill and the Ends of Life' in *Four Essays on Liberty*, Oxford: Oxford University Press
Berlin, Isaiah (1979) *Nationalism: Past Neglect and Current Power Against the Current* ed. Henry Hardy, intro. Roger Hausheer, Oxford: Clarendon Press
Berlin, Isaiah (1990a) 'The Bent Twig: On the Rise of Nationalism' in *The Crooked Timber of Humanity* ed. Henry Hardy, London: Fontana Press
Berlin, Isaiah (1990b) 'The Pursuit of the Ideal' in *The Crooked Timber of Humanity* ed. Henry Hardy, London: Fontana Press
Berlin, Isaiah (2002) 'Two Concepts of Liberty' in *Liberty* ed. Henry Hardy, Oxford: Oxford University Press
Bertram, Christopher (2004) *Rousseau and The Social Contract*, London: Routledge
Blackburn, Simon (2006) *Plato's Republic: A Biography*, London: Atlantic Books
Blanning, Timothy (2015) *Frederick the Great: King of Prussia*, Harmondsworth: Penguin
Bourdieu, Pierre (1998) *The State Nobility: Elite Schools in the Field of Power*, London, Polity Press
Bourdieu, Pierre and Passeron, Jean (1990) *Reproduction in Education, Society and Culture*, London: Sage
Brown, Stephen (2012) *The Radical Pedagogies of Socrates and Freire*, London: Taylor & Francis

Bibliography

Burke, Edmund (1993) *Reflections on the Revolution in France* ed. L. G. Mitchell, Oxford: Oxford University Press

Calvin, John (1960) *The Institutes of the Christian Religion* ed. John T. McNeill, trans. Ford Lewis Battles, Philadelphia: Westminster Press

Capaldi, Nicholas (2004) *John Stuart Mill: A Biography*, Cambridge: Cambridge University Press

Carrig, Joseph (2001) 'Liberal Impediments to Liberal Education: The Assent to Locke', *The Review of Politics*, Vol. 63, No. 1, Winter: 41–76

Cartledge, Paul (2016) *Democracy: A Life*, Oxford: Oxford University Press

Collini, Stefan (1984) 'Introduction' in *The Collected Works of John Stuart Mill, Volume XXI – Essays on Equality, Law, and Education* John Stuart Mill, ed. John M. Robson, intro. Stefan Collini, Toronto: University of Toronto Press, London: Routledge and Kegan Paul

Cranston, Maurice (1957) *John Locke: A Biography*, Oxford, Oxford University Press

Cranston, Maurice (1982) *Jean-Jacques: The Life and Works of Jean Jacques Rousseau 1712–1754*, London: University of Chicago Press

Dahl, Robert A. (2006) *A Preface to Democratic Theory* (expanded edition), Chicago: University of Chicago Press

d'Alembert, Jean-Baptiste le Rond (2003) 'Geneva' in *The Encyclopedia of Diderot & d'Alembert Collaborative Translation Project* trans. Nelly S. Hoyt and Thomas Cassirer, Ann Arbor: Michigan Publishing

Davies, John (2006) *A History of Wales* (revised edition), Harmondsworth: Penguin

Dewey, John (1916) *Democracy and Education*, London: Macmillan

Dewey, John (1936) *Experience and Education*, New York: Free Press

Diderot, Denis (2009) 'Natural Rights' in *The Encyclopedia of Diderot & d'Alembert Collaborative Translation Project* trans. Stephen J. Gendzier, Ann Arbor: Michigan Publishing

Dunn, John (1984) *Locke*, Oxford: Oxford University Press

Eatwell, Roger and Godwin, Matthew (2018) *National Populism: The Revolt against Liberal Democracy*, Harmondsworth: Penguin

Farr, James and Williams, David Lay (2015) eds. *The General Will: The Evolution of a Concept*, Cambridge: Cambridge University Press

Finchelstein, Federico (2017) *From Fascism to Populism in History*, Oakland: University of California Press

Foer, Franklin (2019) 'Liberalism's Last Stand', *The Atlantic*, June

Freire, Paulo (1993) *The Pedagogy of the Oppressed* (revised edition), Harmondsworth: Penguin

Fronterotta, Francesco (2010) 'Plato's *Republic* in the Recent Debate', *Journal of the History of Philosophy*, Vol. 48, No. 2: 125–51

Fukuyama, Francis (1989) 'The End of History?', *The National Interest*, Summer

Fukuyama, Francis (1992) *The End of History and the Last Man*, New York: Free Press

Fukuyama, Francis (2014) *Political Order and Political Decay: From the Industrial Revolution to the Globalization of Democracy*, London: Profile Books

Fukuyama, Francis (2018a) 'Why National Identity Matters', *Journal of Democracy* Vol. 29, No. 4: 5–15

Fukuyama, Francis (2018b) *Identity: Contemporary Identity Politics and the Struggle for Recognition*, London: Profile Books

Gerson, Michael (2017) 'Trump's Funeral Oration at the Death of Reaganism', *Washington Post*, 21st January

Gilman, Nils (2018) 'Revisiting Hofstadter's Populism', *The American Interest* Vol. 14, No. 1, September/October: 39–41

Ginsborg, Paul (2008) *Democracy: Crisis and Renewal*, London: Profile Books

Goodwyn, Lawrence (1978) *The Populist Moment*, New York: Oxford University Press
Held, David (2004) *Global Covenant*, Cambridge: Polity Press
Held, David (2006) *Models of Democracy*, Cambridge: Polity Press
Hobbes, Thomas (1996) *Leviathan*, Oxford: Oxford University Press
Hofstadter, Richard (1955) *The Age of Reform: From Bryan to F.D.R.*, New York: Random House
Huntington, Samuel (1993) 'The Clash of Civilizations?', *Foreign Affairs* Vol. 72, No. 3, Summer: 22–49
Huntington, Samuel (1996) *The Clash of Civilizations and the Remaking of World Order*, New York: Simon and Schuster
Huntington, Samuel (2004) *Who Are We: The Challenges to America's National Identity*, New York: The Free Press
Ignatieff, Michael (1998) *Isaiah Berlin*, London: Vintage
Irwin, Jones (2012) *Paulo Freire's Philosophy of Education: Origins, Developments, Impacts and Legacies*, London: Bloomsbury
Jarvis, Peter (2010) *Adult Education and Lifelong Learning: Theory and Practice* (4th edition), London: Routledge
Jefferson, Thomas (1801) 'First Inaugural Address' in *The Papers of Thomas Jefferson, vol. 33, 17 February–30 April 1801* ed. Barbara B. Oberg, Princeton: Princeton University Press: 148–52
Jefferson, Thomas (1802) 'Letter to the Danbury Baptists', Library of Congress www.loc.gov/loc/lcib/9806/danpre.html (Accessed 31st October 2018)
Jenkyns, R. (1984) *The Victorians and Ancient Greece*, London: Harvard University Press
Jolley, Nicholas (2016) *Toleration and Understanding in Locke*, Oxford: Oxford University Press
Judis, John B. (2016) *The Populist Explosion: How the Great Recession Transformed American and European Politics*, New York: Colombia Global Reports
Judis, John B. (2018) *The Nationalist Revival: Trade, Immigration, and the Revolt Against Globalization*, New York: Colombia Global Reports
Kant, Immanuel (1991) *Political Writings* (2nd edition) trans. H. B. Nisbet, ed. Hans Reiss, Cambridge: Cambridge University Press
Kazin, Michael (2017) *The Populist Persuasion* (revised edition), London: Cornell University Press
Kelly, Paul (2007) *Locke's Second Treatise on Government*, London: Routledge
Kloppenberg, James T. (2012) *Reading Obama: Dreams, Hope, and the American Political Tradition*, Princeton: Princeton University Press
Kloppenberg, James T. (2014) 'Barack Obama and Progressive Democracy' in *Making the American Century: Essays on the Political Culture of Twentieth Century America* ed. Bruce J. Schulman, New York: Oxford University Press
Kloppenberg, James T. (2016a) *Toward Democracy*, Oxford: Oxford University Press
Kloppenberg, James T. (2016b) 'How Obama Sees America: The Intellectual Legacy of our 44th President', *The Chronicle of Higher Education Special Report: The Obama Issue*, 30th September
Kloppenberg, James T. (2017) 'Trump's Inaugural Address was a Radical Break with American Tradition', *Washington Post*, 20th January
Koganzon, Rita (2016) '"Contesting the Empire of Habit": Habituation and Liberty in Lockean Education', *American Political Science Review* Vol. 110, No. 3: 547–58
Krekó, Péter and Enyedi, Zsolt (2018) 'Orban's Laboratory of Illiberalism', *Journal of Democracy* Vol. 29, No. 3: 39–51
Kuhn, Thomas S. (1970) *The Structure of Scientific Revolutions* (2nd edition), Chicago: University of Chicago Press

152   Bibliography

Kymlicka, Will (1995a) *Multicultural Citizenship: A Liberal Theory of Minority Rights*, Oxford: Clarendon Press

Kymlicka, Will (1995b) ed. *The Rights of Minority Cultures*, Oxford: Oxford University Press

Laclau, Ernesto (2005) *On Populist Reason*, London: Verso

Laclau, Ernesto (2006) 'Why Constructing a People is the Main Task of Radical Politics', *Critical Inquiry* Vol. 32, No. 4: 646–80

Laks, André (1990) 'Legislation and Demiurgy: On the Relationship between Plato's "Republic" and "Laws"', *Classical Antiquity* Vol. 9, No. 2: 209–29

Lendvai, Paul (2017) *Orbán: Europe's New Strongman*, London: Oxford University Press

Leonard, Thomas C. (2016) *Illiberal Reformers: Race, Eugenics, and American Economics in the Progressive Era*, New Jersey: Princeton University Press

Liu, Jian (2012) 'Examining Massification Policies and their Consequences for Equality in Chinese Higher Education: A Cultural Perspective', *Higher Education* Vol. 64: 647–60

Locke, John (1824) *The Works of John Locke in Nine Volumes* (12th edition), London: Rivington

Locke, John (1968) 'Some Thoughts Concerning Education' in *The Educational Writings of John Locke* ed. James L. Axtell, Cambridge: Cambridge University Press

Locke, John (1975) *An Essay Concerning Human Understanding* ed. Peter Nidditch, Oxford: Clarendon Press

Locke, John (1988) *Two Treatises of Civil Government* ed. Peter Laslett, Cambridge: Cambridge University Press

Locke, John (1989) *Some Thoughts Concerning Education* ed. and intro. John W. Yolton and Jean S. Yolton, Oxford: Clarendon Press

Locke, John (1993) *A Letter Concerning Toleration* in *Political Writings* ed. David Wootton, Harmondsworth: Penguin: 390–435

Locke, John (1996) *Some Thoughts Concerning Education & of the Conduct of the Understanding* eds. Ruth W. Grant and Nathan Tarcov, London: Hackett

Madison, James (1999) *Writings*, New York: Library of America

Madison, James, Hamilton, Alexander and Jay, John (1987) *The Federalist Papers*, Harmondsworth: Penguin

Matthew, H. C. G. (1995) *Gladstone, 1875–1898*, Oxford: Oxford University Press

Mazzini, G (1907) *The Duties of Man and Other Writings* (Introduction by Thomas Jones), London: Dent

McPherson, C. B. (1962) *Political Theory of Possessive Individualism: Hobbes to Locke*, Oxford: Oxford University Press

Mead, Walter Russell (2001) *Special Providence: American Foreign Policy and How it Changed the World*, New York: Alfred A. Knopf

Mead, Walter Russell (2007) *God and Gold: Britain, America and the Making of the Modern World*, New York: Alfred A. Knopf

Mead, Walter Russell (2018) 'The Big Shift: How American Democracy Fails its Way to Success', *Foreign Affairs* Vol. 97, No. 3: 10–19

Mezirow, Jack (1991) *The Transformative Dimensions of Adult Education*, San Francisco: Wiley/Josse-Bass

Mezirow, Jack (2000) ed. *Learning as Transformation*, San Francisco: Wiley/Josse-Bass

Mill, John Stuart (1865) *Considerations on Representative Government* (People's Edition), London: Longman, Green, Longman, Roberts and Green

Mill, John Stuart (1873) *Autobiography*, London: Longmans, Green, Reader and Dyer

Mill, John Stuart (1963–1991) *Collected Works of John Stuart Mill* ed. John M. Robson, Toronto: University of Toronto Press, London: Routledge and Kegan Paul

Mill, John Stuart (1972) *Collected Works of John Stuart Mill, Volume XV - The Later Letters of John Stuart Mill 1849–1873 Part II* ed. Francis E. Mineka and Dwight N. Lindley, Toronto: University of Toronto Press, London: Routledge and Kegan Paul

Mill, John Stuart (1977a) *The Collected Works of John Stuart Mill, Volume XVIII – Essays on Politics and Society Part I* ed. John M. Robson, intro. Alexander Brady, Toronto: University of Toronto Press, London: Routledge and Kegan Paul

Mill, John Stuart (1977b) *The Collected Works of John Stuart Mill, Volume XIX – Essays on Politics and Society Part II* ed. John M. Robson, intro. Alexander Brady, Toronto: University of Toronto Press, London: Routledge and Kegan Paul

Mill, John Stuart (1978) *The Collected Works of John Stuart Mill, Volume XI – Essays on Philosophy and the Classics* ed. John M. Robson, intro. F. E. Sparshott, Toronto: University of Toronto Press, London: Routledge and Kegan Paul

Mill, John Stuart (1981) *The Collected Works of John Stuart Mill, Volume I – Autobiography and Literary Essays* eds. John M. Robson and Jack Stillinger, intro. Lord Robbins, Toronto: University of Toronto Press, London: Routledge and Kegan Paul

Mill, John Stuart (1984) *The Collected Works of John Stuart Mill, Volume XXI – Essays on Equality, Law, and Education* ed. John M. Robson, intro. Stefan Collini, Toronto: University of Toronto Press, London: Routledge and Kegan Paul

Mill, John Stuart (1985) *The Collected Works of John Stuart Mill, Volume X – Essays on Ethics, Religion, and Society* ed. John M. Robson, intro. F. E. L. Priestley, Toronto: University of Toronto Press, London: Routledge and Kegan Paul

Mill, John Stuart (1988) *The Collected Works of John Stuart Mill, Volume XXVIII – Public and Parliamentary Speeches Part I November 1850 – November 1868* eds. John M. Robson and Bruce L. Kinzer, Toronto: University of Toronto Press, London: Routledge and Kegan Paul

Mill, John Stuart (2015) *On Liberty, Utilitarianism and Other Writings* eds. Mark Philp and Frederick Rosen, Oxford: Oxford University Press

Mishra, Pankaj (2016) 'The Anti-Élite, Post-Fact Worlds of Trump and Rousseau', *The New Yorker*, November

Mitchell, Thomas (2015) *Democracy's Beginnings: The Athenian Story*, New Haven: Yale University Press

Mouffe, Chantal and Errejon, Inigo (2016) *Podemos: In the Name of the People*, London: Lawrence and Wishart

Moyn, Samuel (2010) *The Last Utopia: Human Rights in History*, Cambridge, Massachusetts: Harvard University Press

Moyn, Samuel (2014) *Human Rights and the Uses of History*, London: Verso

Mudde, Cass (2004) 'The Populist Zeitgeist', *Government and Opposition*, Vol. 39, Iss. 4: 541–63

Mudde, Cass and Kaltwasser, Cristóbal Rovira (2013) 'Populism' in *The Oxford Handbook of Political Ideologies* eds. Michael Freeden, Lyman Tower Sargent and Marc Stears, Oxford: Oxford University Press

Mudde, Cass and Kaltwasser, Cristóbal Rovira (2017) *Populism*, Oxford: Oxford University Press

Müller, Jan-Werner (2016) *What is Populism?*, Philadelphia: University of Pennsylvania Press

Nodia, Ghia (2017) 'The End of the Postnational Illusion', *Journal of Democracy* Vol. 28, No. 2: 5–19

O'Sullivan, John and Pócza, Kálmán (2015) *The Second Term of Viktor Orbán: Beyond Prejudice and Enthusiasm*, London: Social Affairs Unit

Pagden, Anthony (2013) *The Enlightenment and Why it Still Matters*, Oxford: Oxford University Press

Pappas, Nikolas (1995) *Plato and the Republic*, London: Routledge and Kegan Paul

Bibliography

Parekh, Bhikhu (1994) 'Decolonising Liberalism' in *The End of 'Isms'? Reflections on the Fate of Ideological Politics after Communism's Collapse*, Oxford: Blackwell: 85–103

Parry, Geriant (2001) 'Emile: Learning to Be Men, Women, and Citizens' in *Cambridge Companion to Rousseau* ed. Patrick Riley, Cambridge: Cambridge University Press: 247–71

Peters, Michael A. (2015) 'Socrates and Confucius: The Cultural Foundations and Ethics of Learning', *Educational Philosophy and Theory* Vol. 47, No. 5: 423–7

Plato (1875) *The Dialogues of Plato* trans. Benjamin Jowett, Oxford: Clarendon Press

Plato (1997) *Complete Works* ed. John M. Cooper, London: Hackett

Plato (2000) *Republic* ed. G. R. F. Ferrari, trans. Tom Griffith, Cambridge: Cambridge University Press

Polansky, David (2018) 'Who are the People?', www.the-american-interest.com/2018/04/12/who-are-the-people

Popper, Karl (1945) *The Open Society and Its Enemies* (Volume I), London: Routledge and Kegan Paul

Postel, Charles (2007) *The Populist Vision*, Oxford: Oxford University Press

Reeves, Richard (2007) *John Stuart Mill: Victorian Firebrand*, London: Atlantic Books

Riley, Patrick (1986) *The General Will before Rousseau: The Transformation of the Divine into the Civic*, New Jersey: Princeton University Press

Riley, Patrick (2001) 'Rousseau's General Will' in *The Cambridge Companion to Rousseau* ed. Patrick Riley, Cambridge: Cambridge University Press: 124–53

Riley, Patrick (2008) 'Jean-Jacques Rousseau' in *Blackwell Companion to Early Modern Philosophy* ed. Stephen N. Nadler, Oxford: Blackwell

Roch, Stefan (2018) 'Educating Skeptical but Passionate Citizens: The Open Society Ideal as a University Mission', in *Rethinking Open Society* eds. Michael Ignatieff and Stefan Roch, Budapest: Central European University Press

Rosen, Jeffrey (2018) *William Howard Taft*, New York: Times Books

Rousseau, Jean-Jacques (1960) *Politics and the Arts: A Letter to M. d'Alembert on the Theatre* trans. and intro. Alan Bloom, Ithaca: Cornell University Press

Rousseau, Jean-Jacques (1979) *Emile* trans. and intro. Alan Bloom, New York: Basic Books

Rousseau, Jean-Jacques (1991) 'Abstract and Judgement of Saint-Pierre's Project for Perpetual Peace' in *Rousseau on International Relations* eds. Stanley Hoffman and David P. Fidler, Oxford: Clarendon Press

Rousseau, Jean-Jacques (1992) *Discourse on the Sciences and Arts (First Discourse) and Polemics (Collected Writings of Jean-Jacques Rousseau Volume II)* eds. Roger D. Masters and Christopher Kelly, trans. Judith R. Bush, Roger D. Masters and Christopher Kelly, Hanover, N. H.: University of New England Press

Rousseau, Jean-Jacques (1995) *The Confessions and Correspondence, Including the Letters to Malesherbes (The Collected Writings of Jean-Jacques Rousseau Volume V)* eds. Christopher Kelly, Roger D. Masters and Peter G. Stillman, trans. Christopher Kelly, Hanover N. H.: University of New England Press

Rousseau, Jean-Jacques (1997) *Julie, or the New Heloise (Collected Writings of Jean-Jacques Rousseau Volume VI)* trans. and annotated Philip Stewart and Jean Vaché, Hanover N. H.: University of New England Press

Rousseau, Jean-Jacques (2011) *Reveries of a Solitary Walker* trans. and intro. Russell Goulbourne, Oxford: Oxford University Press

Rousseau, Jean-Jacques (2012) *Of The Social Contract and Other Political Writings* trans. Quintan Hoare, ed. Christopher Bertram, Harmondsworth: Penguin

Rousseau, Jean-Jacques (2019a) *The Discourses and Other Early Political Writings* (2nd edition) ed. and trans. Victor Gourevitch, Cambridge: Cambridge University Press

Rousseau, Jean-Jacques (2019b) *The Social Contract and Other Later Political Writings* (2nd edition) ed. and trans. Victor Gourevitch, Cambridge: Cambridge University Press

Rowe, Christopher J. (1999) 'Introduction' in *Statesman* Plato, Indianapolis: Hackett

Runciman, David (2013) *The Confidence Trap: A History of Democracy in Crisis from World War I to the Present*, Philadelphia: Princeton University Press

Ryan, Alan (2012) *On Politics*, London: Allen Lane

Scheuerman, William E. (2009) *Morgenthau*, Cambridge: Polity Press

Schofield, Malcolm (2016) 'Introduction' in *The Laws* Plato, Cambridge: Cambridge University Press

Scurr, Ruth (2006) *Fatal Purity: Robespierre and the French Revolution*, London: Chatto & Windus

Shklar, Judith N. (1985) *Men and Citizens: A Study of Rousseau's Social Theory* (2nd edition), Cambridge: Cambridge University Press

Smith, Denis Mack (1994) *Mazzini*, London: Yale University Press

Stanley, Jason (2018) *How Fascism Works*, New York: Random House

Stone, Norman (2019) *Hungary: A Short History*, London: Profile Books

Sullivan, Andrew (2016) 'Democracies End when They are Too Democratic', *New York Magazine*, May

Tamir, Yael (2019) *Why Nationalism*, New Jersey: Princeton University Press

Tarcov, Nathan (1984) *Locke's Essay for Liberty*, Chicago: University of Chicago Press

Taylor, Charles (1991) *The Ethics of Authenticity*, Cambridge, Mass: Harvard University Press

Taylor, Charles (2007) *A Secular Age*, London: Bellknap Press of Harvard University Press

Thomas, Keith (2018) *In Pursuit of Civility: Manners and Civilization in Early Modern England*, London: Yale University Press

Varouxakis, Georgios (2002) *Mill on Nationality*, London: Routledge

Voltaire (1980) *Letters on England* trans. Leonard Tancock, Harmondsworth: Penguin

Walzer, Michael (1977/2015) *Just and Unjust Wars: A Moral Argument with Historical Illustrations* (5th Edition), London: Basic Books

Waterfield, Robin (2009) *Why Socrates Died*, London: W.W. Norton

Watson, John (1970) *Behaviourism*, New York: W.W. Norton

White, Richard (2018) *The Republic for Which it Stands: The United States During Reconstruction and the Gilded Age, 1865–1896*, Oxford: Oxford University Press

Whitehead, A. N. (1941) 'Autobiographical Notes' in *The Philosophy of Alfred North Whitehead* ed. Paul Arthur Schlipp, Evanston and Chicago: Northwestern University Press

Williams, David Lay (2007) *Rousseau's Platonic Enlightenment*, Philadelphia: University of Pennsylvania Press

Williams, David Lay (2014) *Rousseau's Social Contract: An Introduction*, Cambridge: Cambridge University Press

Williams, David Lay (2017) 'Would Jean-Jacques Rousseau Actually Approve of Trump? Not Exactly', *Washington Post*, 28th January

Witte, Griff (2018) 'Soros-founded University Says it has been Kicked out of Hungary as Autocrat Tightens his Grip', *Washington Post*, 3rd December

Wokler, Robert (1993) *Rousseau*, Oxford: Oxford University Press

Wolff, Michael (2018) *Fire and Fury: Inside the Trump White House*, London: Little, Brown

Woodward, C. Vann (1960) *The Burden of Southern History*, Baton Rouge: University of Louisiana Press

Woolhouse, John (2007) *John Locke: A Biography*, Cambridge: Cambridge University Press
Yang, Rui (2010) 'Soft Power and Higher Education: An Examination of China's Confucius Institutes', *Globalisation, Societies and Education* Vol. 8, Iss. 2: 35–45
Zakaria, Fareed (2007) *The Future of Freedom: Illiberal Democracy at Home and Abroad*, New York: W.W. Norton
Zakaria, Fareed (2016) 'Populism on the March: Why the West is in Trouble', *Foreign Affairs*, November/December: 9–15

Index

absolutism 12, 81
abuse 56, 114, 125, 128
active citizens 23, 55, 66, 109, 119, 142
adults 64–5, 104, 113, 118, 136, 144, 146; equal 137; independently-minded 94; responsible 136; young 5, 125
affirmative action 3
'age of reason' 99
Albright, Madeline 8, 21
Alcibiades (Athenian statesman) 38
Apology (Plato) 39, 60, 84
apprentices 129–30
arguments 4–5, 13–14, 18–20, 28–9, 33–4, 46–9, 53–60, 63–4, 66–7, 81–2, 97–8, 111–12, 118–19, 123–30, 133–6; abstract 37; authoritarian 94; East Central European and Russian Orthodox populist 60; liberal 51, 125; of Paul-Michel Foucault concerning 'internalized social discipline' 64; populist 32, 41, 56, 59–60, 80, 120, 127, 129, 131, 142; reasoned 87, 115
Athenian democracy 33–5, 38, 41; opposed by Socrates 38; Plato's criticisms of 34; and the role of the state in education 34; and society 33–4, 39, 140
Athenians 33–4, 84, 109, 119
Athens 33–4, 40, 84, 87
authoritarian 8–10, 38, 82, 93–4, 107, 116, 118, 120, 139; arguments 94; education 94; government 116, 118, 120; society 82, 94
authoritarianism 8–9, 82, 93
Autobiography (Mill) 103–6, 108, 113, 115, 117, 143
autonomy 6–7, 13, 27, 37, 60, 64, 74, 81, 84, 113, 131, 135–7; and critical thinking 64, 81; in education and politics 6, 135; moral 44; national 136; personal 14, 18, 31, 57, 60, 106, 123, 136, 139; promotion of 4, 26
auxiliaries 34–7; *see also* soldiers

beliefs 5–6, 9–10, 12–14, 20–2, 37–9, 51, 57, 59, 64, 70–1, 115–18, 129–31, 133–5, 143–4, 146–7; commonplace 115; false 61; fundamental 128; ideological 4, 123; and John Stuart Mill's insistence on importance of challenging commonly held 115; philosophical 52; theistic 116
Berlin, Isiah 13–14
boarding schools 65, 67
Bourdieu, Pierre 125
Brexit campaign 133
Britain 11, 111, 125, 133, 143, 145; and membership of the European Union 18; political classes 145
British Liberal Party 51, 107, 146
British referendum 2016 18, 131

Cambridge Platonists 48, 52
Carrig, Joseph 64–5, 144
Central European University 1–2, 6, 9, 21, 23–4, 26–8, 59, 64, 80, 84, 110, 113, 118, 126, 143; claims that educational institutions should be internationalist in outlook 27; and the objections of the Orbán government 90; and the position of liberals such as John Stuart Mill 27
CEU *see* Central European University
children 14–15, 34–6, 46–9, 54–6, 61–2, 64–7, 71–8, 80, 82, 85–6, 92–5, 98, 103–5, 136, 138; 'allegedly corrupted by promoting liberal ideas 76; developing minds of 48; educating of 96; indoctrinating of 125; and Locke's view on the father's authority 136; teaching of 6, 46, 144; and the working environment of the industrial age 142
Christian 9, 50, 96–7, 116; beliefs and practices 62; civilisation 9; identity 25; society 76; values 63, 76
Christian Democrat Party, Hungary 24
Christianity 59, 76, 96–7

158 Index

church and state, separation of 57–8, 97
Church of England 58; *see also* Christianity
citizens 12–13, 15, 18–20, 33, 55–7, 72, 77–9, 83, 88–92, 95, 97, 113, 115–17, 127–8, 136–9; active 23, 55, 66, 109, 119, 142; adult 51, 71; educated 55, 108, 137, 141; good 45, 53, 61, 89, 97, 138; patriotically-minded 5, 127; responsible 6, 45, 61, 71, 136, 143; virtuous 98; well-educated 55
citizenship 15, 79, 84, 91, 95, 124, 146; cosmopolitan 84; French 111; global 15, 84, 146
civility 5–6, 18, 41, 59–63, 66, 94, 109, 116, 123–6, 128, 147; cosmopolitan 126; inner 63; liberal 143; Locke's defence of 62; political 126; sense of 109, 116; teaching of 5, 62, 125, 131
classes 23, 34, 37, 51, 126; leisured 50; middle 119; political 145
Cold War 1, 8–9
communism 8–9, 20, 24, 26, 59, 107, 139
community 5–6, 19–20, 25, 28, 40–1, 55–6, 60, 78–9, 81–4, 86, 88–91, 109, 126–7, 131–3, 135–6; academic 1, 9, 130; global 15; harmonious 78; national 6, 126–7, 143; political 124; stable 59
consensus 2, 4, 117, 123, 127; measure of stability and 4, 123; social 126
contemporary populism 5, 17–18, 28, 84, 126–7; and Jean-Jacques Rousseau 5; and nationalism 5, 125–6
contemporary society 60, 76, 84, 90
Copernicanism 74, 76
corporal punishment 46, 66
corruption 25, 39, 71–3, 76, 79–81, 84, 94–5, 116, 133, 135, 138, 140; alleged 40; political 66; and the rejection by Plato of its presence in his society 135; in society 72, 74, 76–7, 80, 86, 94–5, 135
Corsican societies 80–1, 89–90
cosmopolitanism 14, 54, 70, 83, 126–7, 140, 143
crisis 8, 17, 35, 140, 142–3, 147; of democracy 8, 17, 123, 140–1, 147; financial 19, 24, 42
critical thinking 2, 4, 6, 12, 14, 26–7, 36–7, 41, 51–2, 56–7, 60–1, 105–7, 131–2, 134–5, 143–5; and autonomy 64, 81; and expertise 52; independent 90
curriculum, state-regulated 28

Dahl, Robert 10, 18
dangers 3, 5–6, 11–12, 14–15, 20, 39, 54, 64–5, 106, 108, 116, 118, 120, 128, 141; constant 86; greatest 96; real 10

de Tocqueville, Alexis 105, 140
debates 2, 55–6, 116
democracy *see also* liberal democracy 7–10, 16–22, 28, 31–5, 38–42, 87, 89, 105, 107, 117–18, 123–4, 131, 133–4, 139–41, 147; Athenian 33–5, 38, 41; crisis of 8, 17, 123, 140–1, 147; ideas of liberalism and liberal 108, 141; ill-regulated 140; populist 22, 34, 123, 137
democratic governments 2, 24, 117–18, 124
democratic institutions 23
democratic societies 1–2, 20, 23, 26–7, 39–40, 94, 105–6, 123–4, 134, 139, 143; contemporary 124; education in 123–47; healthy 10; liberal 1, 4, 8–9, 26, 31, 41, 67, 123, 134, 137
DeVos, Betsy 3, 21
Dewey, John 11, 35–6, 75, 86–7
dialectic, study and training in 37–40
dialogues, Platonic 32, 38–40, 76, 87, 90, 103, 134; early 38–9; middle 37; Mill's early reading of 103
Diderot, Denis 44, 83
Discourse on the Sciences and Arts (Rousseau) 70–2, 74, 77, 83, 85, 98
dissent 23, 92–4, 118, 138
Divine Right of Kings (theory) 64, 129, 139
Dunn, John 50

Eastern Europe 9, 26–7, 107
economic policies 25, 144; national 25; neo-liberal 25
education 1–15, 18–21, 23–8, 31–9, 41, 44–67, 70–99, 103–9, 112–20, 123–47; adult 118–19; contemporary 71, 138, 142, 146; cosmopolitan 144; democratic 144; elite 36, 70; equipping citizens to actively participate as free-thinking individuals 113; formal 36, 51, 96, 127, 133; general 55–6; in Hungary 59, 76; illiberal 41; informal 36, 119, 127, 133, 146; and institutions 3, 8, 27–8, 56, 71, 106, 110, 130; liberal 9–29, 52, 57, 64, 125, 144, 147; and liberty 103; mass 21; moral 62; multi-culturalist 130; in Poland 79, 82, 93, 95, 104, 137; policies 1, 13, 73; provisions 28, 72, 120; public 86, 95, 130; sophisticated 125; sound 61, 63–4, 72, 118, 138; systems 4–5, 18–19, 56, 59, 65, 89–90, 92–4, 99, 111–12, 120, 128, 132–3, 137, 139, 142–3; universal 6, 12, 117–18
elites 18–19, 53, 60–1, 67, 70, 75, 125, 130, 138, 140–1; corrupt 20;

cosmopolitan 21, 128; educated 6, 34, 59, 67, 89, 120; global 90, 140; intellectual 70; international 84; liberal 5, 64; members of 19; small 72, 130; unresponsive internal 7, 135; wealthy 51
Emile (Rousseau) 4, 28, 36, 45, 67, 70, 72–81, 84–7, 90–1, 93–6, 98, 103–5, 135, 138–9
empirical knowledge 44, 88
Enlightenment 44–5, 54, 83, 99, 132, 139; eighteenth century 14; *philosophes* 50; thinkers 44, 83, 129
Enlightenment thinkers 44, 83, 129
equality 13–14, 80, 128; economic 88; political 33
Essay Concerning Human Understanding (Locke) 45–7, 52, 56, 67, 138, 145
European societies 72–4, 84–5, 124
European Union 7–9, 15, 18, 21, 24, 59, 70, 80, 96, 100, 126, 131, 135; and Abbé St Pierre 70, 96; emphasis on education exchanges and partnerships between individuals and institutions 21; governance of the 42; and the United Kingdom referendum 18
expertise 4–5, 23, 26–7, 34, 40, 52, 54–7, 61, 118, 128–31; claims to 39–40, 130, 135; and critical thinking 52; in education and politics 5, 128; skill-based 55; specialist 23, 56; true 39–40
experts 3, 13, 23, 27, 31, 35, 37–40, 42, 54–7, 60, 117–18, 128–9, 131–2, 134; distrust of 23; elite 37, 144; Kant's discussion of 132; opinions of 42, 54–6; skilled 31, 88, 117; Socrates' criticism of 39

faith 29, 50–1, 58–9, 74, 97, 116–17
Farr, James 82
fathers 65–6, 103–5, 125, 136–7
fears 4, 8, 10–11, 14, 64–6, 100, 105, 107, 110, 112, 116, 123, 127, 141, 145–6
feelings 36, 44, 53–4, 73–4, 85, 87–8, 96–7, 134; audience's 96; innate 87; natural human 88, 136
Foer, Franklin 1
Foucault, Paul-Michel 64
foundations 37, 42, 50, 52, 58–9, 67, 81, 138; intellectual 3; metaphysical 114; philosophical 9; political 56; religious 116
France 51, 57, 59, 81, 85, 95, 104, 143
franchise 51, 105, 107, 117–18, 120, 145
Freire, Paulo 38, 49–50
Fukuyama, Francis 17, 22, 112, 124

generations 2, 72, 80–1, 88, 93, 98–9, 106, 108, 120, 124, 138, 140–1, 144
Geneva 73, 80, 82, 91, 96–8, 127

Geneva Manuscript (Rousseau) 83
Gerson, Michael 2
Gilman, Nils 15
Ginsborg, Paul 8, 17
Gladstone, William 51, 106, 145–6
global elites 90, 140
God 12–13, 48, 58–60, 82, 84, 96, 116, 128
Goodwyn, Lawrence 16
government 1–2, 7–9, 11–12, 35, 44–5, 57–8, 70, 86, 89, 92–5, 106, 110, 112–13, 129, 143–4; authoritarian 116, 118, 120; control 86, 99, 133; democratic 2, 24, 117–18, 124; of France 51; of Hungary 1–2, 6, 20, 23–4, 26, 59, 107, 112, 126, 143; liberal 57; local 106, 119, 130; mixed 81; oppressive 50; of Poland 20, 28, 59, 70, 72, 106, 109; populist 23, 37, 56–7, 107, 128, 141; powers 12, 106; representative 5, 16, 22, 41, 67, 106, 110, 112, 118, 120, 128, 138–9, 146
Grote, George 32, 114

Havel, Vaclev 24
HEEA *see* Higher European Education Area
Held, David 15
higher education 1, 6, 9, 35–7, 91, 119
Higher European Education Area 91
Hobbes, Thomas 10, 81–3, 85
Hofstadter, Richard 15–16
human mind *see* minds
Hungarian government of Viktor Orbán 1–2, 6, 23–4, 26, 107, 112, 126, 143; criticism of the CEU 1–2, 6, 21; populist 1, 23
Hungarian society 25, 58–9
Hungary 1, 6, 8–9, 18, 20, 23–4, 26, 37, 59, 73, 80, 128, 134, 141, 143; and the Christian Democrats 24; education system 59, 76; Fidesz government in 18; government of 1–2, 6, 23–4, 26, 107, 112, 126, 143; and the policies of Orbán 72; Soviet rule in 24
Huntington, Samuel 17, 84, 124, 128, 130

ideological beliefs 4, 123
Ignatieff, Michael 1
illiberal 5, 8, 14, 17, 38, 80, 111–12, 128, 138; education 41; governments 2, 141; rulers 6; societies 1, 24, 64; states 8, 26
indifference 52–3, 55; attitude of 52, 54; epistemological 53; political 53
individual liberty 12, 28, 70, 77, 105

Index

individuals 6, 12, 16, 21, 25, 52, 63–4, 71, 83, 85–6, 90, 92, 109, 132–3; adult 115; autonomous 74, 118; critically-minded 59; free-thinking 113; self-centred 62, 106; well-rounded 54
inequality 19, 77, 85
innate ideas 45, 47–8
institutions 9, 16, 21, 23, 25, 53, 59, 91, 119–20, 140, 142; democratic 23; educational 3, 8, 27–8, 56, 71, 106, 110, 130; higher education 91; intermediate 106; liberal 64; liberal democratic 1, 4, 8–9, 23, 26, 31, 41, 67, 123, 134, 137; political 34, 124; social 60, 78, 95; stable 140
interests 2–3, 23, 28, 53, 56, 84, 86, 89, 91–2, 96–7, 106, 108, 111, 131–2, 138; agricultural 146; informed 106; particular 53, 75; personal 78; of society 27, 120; true 71–2, 97–8, 132

Jackson, Andrew 22
Jefferson, Thomas 11, 50, 58, 97, 129
Jolley, Nicholas 45, 58
Jowett, Benjamin 32, 36
Judis, John B. 17, 22, 112

Kaltwasser, Cristóbal Rovira 17
Kant, Immanuel 12, 14, 98–9, 132
Kloppenberg, James 3, 10–11, 133
knowledge 34, 37, 39, 44, 46–8, 50, 52, 54–6, 89, 129–30, 132, 134–5, 137, 142, 145; detailed 54, 61, 81; empirical 44, 88; materials of 49, 65; specialist 44, 54, 56, 130
Koganzon, Rita 46, 64

law 12, 32–4, 58–9, 67, 78, 80, 82–3, 86, 88–9, 91–3, 106, 133; basic 78; justified criticism of 89; moral 13, 99; natural 89, 137; rule of 12, 16, 138
lawgivers 77–8, 80, 99, 133
The Laws (Plato) 32
learning 2, 62, 66, 71, 74–5, 77–8, 80, 85, 104, 131–2; of children 95; maturity 2; styles 38
legislative powers 58
Letter to M. d'Alembert on the Theatre (Rousseau) 79, 83, 96–7, 127
liberal democracy 8–9, 17, 20, 22, 27, 41, 94, 107–8, 112, 115, 119, 123, 137, 139–41, 144; institutions 1, 4, 8–9, 23, 26, 31, 41, 67, 123, 134, 137; modern 31, 33; and populism 7, 10, 22–3, 31, 123; representatives of 139
liberal education 9–29, 52, 57, 64, 125, 144, 147

liberal nationalism 22, 110, 127
Liberal Party *see* British Liberal Party
liberal society 4, 13–14, 45, 52, 57–9, 61–2, 64–6, 111, 114–16, 123, 125, 136–7, 144, 147
liberal thinkers 3, 41, 47, 114, 127
liberal values 1, 5, 13, 20, 25, 27, 34, 52, 63–4, 105, 108, 116, 127, 144–5
liberalism 1, 6, 10–13, 19, 22, 44–5, 49–51, 59, 63–4, 103, 106–8, 110, 141, 145, 147
liberals 5–7, 10, 13, 19, 23, 27, 51, 56, 64, 99–100, 105, 126–7, 129, 131, 135–6; cosmopolitan 110; left-wing Western 25; and populists 4–5, 14, 20, 23, 26, 29; seeking limits on the power of the state 12; stressing the freedom of the individual 12, 51; and the visions of nineteenth and twentieth century 67, 145
liberty 4, 6–7, 14, 25, 27, 51, 103, 105, 108–9, 113, 115, 118, 128, 139, 144; and education 103; individual 12, 28, 70, 77, 105; principle of 13, 27, 33, 144
Locke, John 4–7, 10–13, 27–8, 44–67, 81–2, 89–90, 94, 103–4, 108–9, 116, 123–5, 130–1, 135–41, 143–5, 147; argues that education should be general to enable a gentleman to take his place in society 131; belief in the importance of education taking place within the family 60, 65; belief that the teaching of critical thinking is an important part of education 60; and the concept of toleration 45; criticises the theory of innate ideas 47; epistemology 47, 49; and his argument concerning the basis of knowledge 47; and his belief that rights are given by God 12; and his theory of knowledge 52; publications had a profound effect on the Enlightenment thinkers of the eighteenth century 44

Madison, James 11, 16, 44, 50, 97, 120, 129
Marx, Karl 22, 50
Masters, R.D. 98
mathematics 37, 47–8, 54, 76
Mead, Walter Russell 142, 145
middle classes 119
Mill, James (father of John Stuart Mill) 103–5, 119
Mill, John Stuart 4–7, 10–14, 22, 27–9, 31–4, 36, 40–1, 67, 86–7, 99–100, 103–20, 127–8, 130–1, 134–9, 141–7; accused of claiming that small and less advanced nations may be absorbed into

larger ones 111; argues that the principle of liberty is a universal principle 13, 112–13, 117; and the *Autobiography* 103–6, 108, 113, 115, 117, 143; discussion of nationality 22, 117, 128, 143; dismisses the metaphysical foundations of the theory of Forms 114; insistence on the importance of challenging commonly held beliefs 115; interpretation of the Socratic Method 109

minds 8, 47–9, 51–4, 56, 60–1, 64–6, 71, 74–5, 78, 100, 108, 112, 114, 137, 145; enquiring 104; individual 48; internal civility of the 61; young 49

Mitchell, Thomas 33–4, 38

Monet, Jean 21

moral law 13, 99

moral truths 13, 84

moral values 14, 107

Mudde, Cas 17

Müller, Jan-Werner 17, 20

national community 6, 126–7, 143

national education 84, 126

national identity 5, 21–2, 96, 110–12, 126–7, 142–3, 146

national values 21, 26, 140, 142–3

nationalism 5, 15, 18, 21–2, 41, 110, 112, 126–8, 139, 146; aggressive 112; anti-liberal 110; and contemporary populism 5, 125–6; language of 21, 110; populist 22; pragmatic 143

nationality 5, 22, 110–12, 117, 128, 143; discussions of 109, 143; Mill's defence of in *Considerations on Representative Government* 32, 128; and national education 126–8

nations 18, 21, 25–7, 41, 57, 90, 111, 127, 143

natural law 89, 137

newspapers 112, 145–6

non-democratic states 9, 25

Obama, Barack 25

obligations 12, 15, 53, 124

Orbán, Viktor 2, 15, 18, 21, 24–5, 27–8, 56, 58–9, 84, 107, 112, 136; argues that the Hungarian nation must be organised and reinforced 25; government of 90, 100, 118, 133; and the Hungarian government 24

O'Sullivan, John 25

personal autonomy 14, 18, 31, 57, 60, 106, 123, 136, 139

philosopher rulers 34–6, 39, 41, 87, 126, 131, 138

philosophers 3–4, 28, 32, 37, 39–40, 44, 46–7, 70, 87, 97, 103, 123; and historians of ideas 82; liberal 14, 33; potential 37; pre-Socratic 114; seventeenth century 52

philosophical beliefs 52

philosophy 2, 4, 6, 31, 37, 40, 75, 97, 104; educational 44, 79; moral 71; political 63; speculative 114

Pierre, Abbé St 70, 96

Plato 3–5, 27, 31–42, 44, 57, 80, 86–8, 113–15, 117, 119, 123, 125–6, 130–1, 133–5, 137–40; argues that current society cannot be reformed but must be recreated 31, 42; argument of the need for wise rulers to guide the unenlightened majority 31; attributes of 39; criticises Athenian democracy 34; criticisms of 37; fears of democratic societies to be driven by irrational, confused and self-centred individuals 106; and his influence on Jean-Jacques Rousseau 20, 42, 67, 88, 135, 138; Karl Popper's criticisms of 37; and *The Laws* 32; misgivings about democracy 41; and the philosopher rulers 34–6, 39, 41, 87, 126, 131, 138; rejection of empiricism 52, 135; rejection of the corruption of his society 135; and the *Republic* 42, 84, 138; and the soldiers 34, 131; and *The Statesman* 32; stresses that those who are to become rulers need to be educated to develop the skill of ruling 35; stresses that those who are to become rulers need to become experts in government 35, 37; theory of education 52, 80, 87; and the workers 15, 34, 49, 106

Polansky, David 19

policies 2, 9, 20, 27, 42, 53–4, 70, 89, 107, 113, 117–18, 120, 133; economic 25, 144; education 1, 13, 73; educational 2, 23, 54, 56, 83, 107; liberal 3, 24; New Deal 11; populist education 72, 112; social 67; transnational 80

political community 124

political equality 33

political philosophy 63

political powers 5

political societies 2, 12, 31, 41, 45, 110

political systems 9, 23, 120

politicians 2–3, 7, 9, 24, 40, 54, 124, 127, 130, 135, 137, 140–2; elite 133; European 15; liberal 133, 146; populist 3, 21, 110, 133; professional 19; progressive 146

Popper, Karl 14, 35, 37

populism 7–29, 31, 40, 42, 45, 53, 56, 60, 67, 70, 72, 82–3, 106, 110, 112–13; growth of 8–9, 110, 140; Hofstadter's perception of 15; and Jean-Jacques Rousseau 5; left-wing 18; and liberal democracy 7, 10, 22–3, 31, 123; modern 93, 96; and nationalism 5, 125–6; right-wing 1, 17–18; twenty-first century 3, 22, 142
populist arguments 32, 41, 56, 59–60, 80, 120, 127, 129, 131, 142
populist criticisms 61–2, 146
populist education policies 72, 112
populist governments 23, 37, 56–7, 107, 128, 141
populist nationalism 22
populists 3–7, 10, 13–14, 16–20, 22–3, 26–7, 31–3, 41, 57–9, 64, 125–8, 130, 132–3, 135–6, 146; contemporary 5, 42, 59, 126, 130; European 96; left-wing 18; right-wing 94
Postel, Charles 16
powers 12, 19–20, 24, 51, 56, 61, 92, 97, 106–7, 110, 118–19, 125, 129, 137, 140; exercising of 35; of government 12, 106; legislative 58; political 5
Protestant Dissenters 59
public education 86, 95, 130
punishment, corporal 46, 66
Putin, Vladimir 94

Rawls, John 12
reasoning 85, 88, 93–4, 113, 125; abstract 44, 90; with children 94; good 116; negative 115
referendums 16, 18; *see also* British referendum
religion 10, 51, 57–8, 62, 73, 76, 96–7, 110, 135
religious beliefs 57–8, 60, 63, 116
Republic (Plato) 4–5, 31–41, 52, 78, 80–1, 86, 94, 96, 99, 117, 126, 130–3, 139, 144
Riley, Patrick 82, 98–9, 137
Roch, Stefan 26–7
Roman Catholicism 51, 57–8
Roman Catholics 20, 59, 63, 73, 107–8, 118; British 59; conservative values of 76, 80; orthodox 73, 96
Roosevelt, Franklin D. 11, 16
Roosevelt, Theodore 11, 16
Rousseau, Jean-Jacques 2–6, 17–18, 27–9, 31–4, 39, 41–2, 45, 61, 66–7, 70–100, 103–6, 125–7, 132, 134–40, 143–4; ambiguous relationship to the Enlightenment and liberalism 44; argues that a school, or a university teaching students from a liberal cosmopolitan perspective, is bound to act contrary to the interests of the community 91; argues that not all states are suitable for the form of self-government 80; arguments about social institutions and citizenship at the beginning of *Emile* 95; claims in *The Social Contract* that the English are only free when they vote in parliamentary elections 76, 89; claims that in a just society sovereignty must always remain with the people 89; and contemporary populism 5; contends that duties to the community take precedence over individual freedom 6, 71; contrasts with the liberal idea of a universal will which reflects the good of humanity 83; and his difference from Locke on the issue of knowledge of the national law 89; and Plato 20, 67, 88, 135, 138; and *The Platonic Enlightenment* 87; rejection of the idea of a theatre in Geneva 91; and *The Social Contract* 12, 72, 76–7, 79–83, 89–90, 92, 96, 98–9, 127, 133, 135, 137
rulers 5, 33, 35, 37, 40–1, 53, 59, 86, 128–31, 133, 135; educated 41, 143; illiberal 6; philosopher 34–6, 39, 41, 87, 126, 131, 138; potential 129
Runciman, David 9, 17
Russell, Algernon Sydney Lord William 50
Russia 9, 24–5

Sanders, Bernie 15, 18
schools 57, 65, 67, 76, 88, 91, 93, 111, 127, 130; boarding 65, 67; Polish 133; primary 134; publicly-funded 3, 57; secular 76; Welsh 111; Western 83
Second Reform Act 51
self-development 108–9, 113
self-love 85, 87–8
sentiments 106, 110; current 114; national 110, 112; nationalist 21, 112
separation of church and state 57–8, 97
skilled experts 31, 88, 117
skills 19, 27, 35, 40, 49, 55, 86, 88–9, 106, 113, 124–5, 128, 130–1, 135, 144
The Social Contract (Rousseau) 12, 72, 76–7, 79–83, 89–90, 92, 96, 98–9, 127, 133, 135, 137
social order 49–50, 57, 105
society 4–6, 12–15, 17–23, 26–8, 31–2, 34–5, 37–41, 55–67, 70–4, 76–8, 80–100, 123–8, 130–1, 133–40, 144–7; adversarial 5; Christian 76; civil 61–2; cohesive 14, 81, 113; contemporary 60, 76, 84, 90; Corsican 80–1, 89–90; free 6, 85, 99, 113, 147; good 81, 87;

hierarchical 34, 44, 49; host 128, 130; Hungarian 25, 58–9; ideal 72, 95, 137–8; and Jean-Jacques Rousseau 72; Mill's conception of 119; modern 1, 66, 77; Plato's understanding of 131; and Poland 78, 82, 88; purification of 18, 20–1; stable 4, 18, 26–7, 31, 59, 123, 127

Socrates 32, 34, 38–40, 60, 76, 84, 103, 109, 114–17, 134, 144; and the *Apology* 39, 60, 84; constant questioning of the so-called experts 39, 60; criticises the acceptance of traditional opinions and current sentiment 114; criticism of experts in the *Apology* 39; opposes Athenian democracy 38; relentless negative questioning 60; support for democracy 38

Socratic Method 32, 37–8, 40–2, 60, 107, 109, 113–15, 117, 134–5, 138, 144

soldiers 34, 131

Some Thoughts Concerning Education (Locke) 4, 45–6, 48, 54, 60–6, 103, 108–9, 136, 138

Soros, George 24, 27

sovereign 72, 82–3, 86, 88–92, 136–7; absolute 10, 83; citizen body 72, 89

specialists 47, 54, 56, 67, 139

St Pierre, Abbe 70, 126

Stanley, Jason 8, 21, 115–16

state education systems 56, 118

state-regulated curriculum 28

states 9, 11–12, 19–21, 24–5, 33–7, 56–9, 63, 72–3, 76–7, 80, 85–6, 88–92, 97, 112–13, 127–8; illiberal 8, 26; liberal 51, 56–7, 67, 110; non-democratic 9, 25; non-liberal 26

The Statesman (Plato) 32

students 3, 13–14, 26–7, 46, 58, 74–5, 90–1, 104, 113, 118, 129, 132, 142, 144

The Subjection of Women (Mill) 146

subjects 17, 24, 52, 55, 61–2, 92, 107–8, 117, 134, 136–7, 141, 145; abstract 104; religious 73; social 125; teaching of 76

Sullivan, Andrew 3, 31

systems 12, 19, 22, 25, 38, 40, 60, 92–3, 106, 112, 118, 120; authoritarian 120; democratic 120; education 4–5, 18–19, 56, 59, 65, 89–90, 92–4, 99, 111–12, 120, 128, 132–3, 137, 139, 142–3; egalitarian education 36; enlarged formal education 119; funded education 12; hierarchical education 19; nationalistic education 26; patriotic education 72; state education 56, 118; unifying education 128

Tarcov, Nathan 47, 50, 57

Taylor, Charles 116–17

Taylor, Harriet 105–6

teaching 1, 6, 24, 26, 38, 41, 57–8, 60, 62–3, 75, 97, 103–4, 129, 131, 135; of children 6, 46, 144; of civility 5, 62, 125, 131; esoteric 98; ideas 126; moral 57, 108, 118

tensions 27, 113, 131, 134, 136, 139–40

terms 3, 6–7, 9–13, 15–19, 22, 33–4, 37, 41, 82–3, 85, 106–7, 110, 112, 135, 138; abstract 114; democratic 110; equal 111; metaphysical 60; unintelligible 56

theatre 36, 71, 79, 91, 96–8, 127

theology 48, 51, 58; Calvinist 82; and innate ideas 47

theory 11, 32, 38–40, 44, 47–8, 52, 63–4, 73, 77, 82, 114, 120, 134, 139, 144; contemporary populist 23; educational 39, 86; empiricist 52; of Freire 49; liberal 12–13, 27, 49, 58, 134; pedagogic 104; social contract 12

thinking 11, 33, 42, 45, 47–50, 52–3, 56, 58, 64–5, 76, 90, 94, 99, 127, 144; abstract 37, 70; critical 2, 4, 6, 12, 14, 26–7, 36–7, 41, 51–2, 56–7, 60–1, 105–7, 131–2, 134–5, 143–5; passive 65; political 146; populist 10; progressive 45

Thirty Years War 10

Thomas, Keith 124

Trump, Donald 2–3, 8: liberal critics of 3; and the policy on migrants 20; and the rallies 125; slogan Make America Great 18; and the United States 2, 8, 15–16, 18, 21–2, 133

truth 20, 40–1, 48, 51, 53, 60, 87–8, 109, 115, 134–5, 139, 144; absolute 44; eternal 87; moral 13, 84; timeless 52, 87; universal 32

tutors 46, 73, 75–6, 93, 95, 104

United Nations 7, 15, 135

United States 1–3, 8, 10–11, 15–17, 19, 73, 124–5, 128–30, 133, 145–6

United States Supreme Court 16

values 5–6, 18–22, 26–8, 41–2, 44, 55–61, 80–4, 87–91, 93–100, 107–8, 120, 126–8, 130–4, 141–2, 144–6; Christian 63, 76; educational 40, 130; fundamental 23, 27, 57, 64, 82, 116, 139; Hungarian 118; liberal 1, 5, 13, 20, 25, 27, 34, 52, 63–4, 105, 108, 116, 127, 144–5; moral 14, 107; national 21, 26, 140, 143; Polish 80, 88, 90; religious 57, 60; shared 63, 78, 126; traditional 14; universal 34, 87

Waterfield, Robin 38
Watson, John 47, 62
Western schools 83
Western society 9, 31, 110, 140, 142
Whitehead, Alfred North 13
Williams, David Lay 87, 141
women 13, 20, 33, 35–6, 67, 70, 100, 107–8, 120, 124, 146; and protecting their right to vote 146; standing for parliament 108
workers 15, 34, 49, 106

Yolton, Jean 45, 48, 61–2
Yolton, John 45, 48

Zakaria, Fareed 17

Printed in the United States
By Bookmasters